African Americans and the **Culture of Pain**

Cᴜʟᴛᴜʀᴀʟ Fʀᴀᴍᴇs, Fʀᴀᴍɪɴɢ Cᴜʟᴛᴜʀᴇ
Robert Newman, *Editor*

African Americans

and the
Culture of Pain

Debra Walker King

University of Virginia Press   *Charlottesville and London*

University of Virginia Press
© 2008 by the Rector and Visitors of the University of Virginia
Printed in the United States of America on acid-free paper

First published 2008

9 8 7 6 5 4 3 2 1

LIBRARY OF CONGRESS CATALOGING-IN-PUBLICATION DATA

King, Debra Walker, 1959–
    African Americans and the culture of pain / Debra Walker King.
        p.   cm. — (Cultural frames, framing culture)
    Includes bibliographical references and index.
    Filmography and discography: p.
    ISBN 978-0-8139-2680-3 (cloth : alk. paper) — ISBN 978-0-8139-2681-0 (pbk. : alk.
paper) — ISBN 978-0-8139-2690-2 (e-book)
    1. African Americans—Race identity. 2. African Americans—Social conditions. 3. African
Americans—Politics and government. 4. Body, Human—Social aspects—United States.
5. Pain—Social aspects—United States. 6. United States—Race relations. 7. Racism—United
States. 8. African Americans in popular culture. 9. Rhetoric—Social aspects—United States.
10. Rhetoric—Political aspects—United States. I. Title.
    E185.625.K56 2008
    305.896'073—dc22

                                                                                    2007022920

For my son, Christopher

May God's hand be with you always, protecting you from racial hurt and soul-wounding pain

Contents

Preface

I first considered writing this book in 1994, when David B. Morris, author of *The Culture of Pain* (1991), visited the University of Florida and presented a lecture on the psychosocial construction of pain in history and culture. For months after his visit, I contemplated questions and options for beginning a project focused on black bodies in pain. I asked myself, where does lynching fit into Morris's culture of pain? How does black pain function as cultural property? What is its value as symbolic capital? Why did the black author Carlene Hatcher Polite title her 1967 novel *The Flagellants*? What is the relationship of pleasure, leisure, and entertainment to black pain? How deeply do we understand the painful implications of Fanny Lou Hammer's declaration "I'm sick and tired of being sick and tired"? Who defines . . . well, as you can see, my list of concerns proliferated, became personal and abstract, exciting and essential—so much so that I could never forget the avenues of inquiry that presented themselves or the opportunities for reflection the subject invited.

I moved from opportunity to research, analysis, writing, and production after completing *Deep Talk: Reading African-American Literary Names* (1998). Still, I have left much of the "meat and bones" of my original contemplations about black bodies and pain out of this book. Some were too impassioned to offer as *scholarship;* others were too big to explore together in one volume; while yet others, I was warned, were too *perverse* (an assessment I never understood fully). At any rate, I hope I have found the right balance. With this text, I honor both the pain and its release, the fury and the purging. What is included here, then, is the heart of the "beast" presented with my best intentions and professional grace.

When I began my research for this book, several scholars of black cultural and literary studies were working on projects about death, dying, woundedness, trauma, and survival. Many published their work long before I began writing. As each publication appeared, I found inspiration for moving forward, asking harder questions, saying what was difficult, and peeling away the layers of black pain's story until my soul's stirring for deeper exploration calmed. I found myself enthralled by Orlando Patterson's *Rituals of Blood: Consequences of Slavery in Two American Centuries* (1998), Trudier Harris's *Saints, Sinners, Saviors: Strong Black Women in African American Literature* (2002), Karla Holloway's *Passed On: African American Mourning Stories* (2002), Anne P. Rice's edited volume *Witnessing Lynching: American Writers Respond* (2003), and Harriet A. Washington's *Medical Apartheid: The Dark History of Medical Experimentation on Black Americans from Colonial Times to the Present* (2006), among others. Considering the effect publications like these had on my determination to learn more about the relationship of race, racial marking, and pain, I offer my gratitude to the authors of them all. I am especially grateful for the wonderful scholars who keep the study of African American literature and culture invigorated during professional meetings like the College Language Association Conferences and the Modern Language Association, and who bring to it new inflections and intellectual challenges every day in their classrooms and scholarship. I thank you for your dedication, truthfulness, courage, and constant inspiration.

I have many to thank by name for assistance in bringing this project to fruition. I would not have accomplished anything had it not been for the time that fellowships and academic leaves provided. I am appreciative, therefore, of the University of Florida for allowing sufficient research leave. I am particularly indebted to Janie Fouke, University Provost and Senior Vice President of Academic Affairs, for providing production support and encouragement. I would be remiss if I did not also thank her for lighting new paths in my professional journey. I also thank another light, David Colburn, immediate past Provost and Senior Vice President for Academic Affairs, for his faith in my work and me.

It is my honor to also acknowledge the fellowship support provided by the National Research Council and the Ford Foundation, the Schomburg Center for Research in Black Culture, and the Aaron Diamond Foundation. Because of the funding each provided, I was able to "fast start" this project and develop its foundational concepts. I extend special thanks to Diana Lachatanere, who is the Schomburg Scholars-in-Residence Program Manager; Zita Nunes, Assistant Director; the Schomburg curators and other Center staff. I must not forget my program colleagues—Carolyn Anderson Brown, Leslie Harris, Martha Elizabeth Hodes, Jeffrey Conrad Stewart, Craig Steven Wilder, and Margaret Rose Vendryes—for their enthusiasm, interdisciplinary input, and advice. Karla Holloway, who was researching *Passed On* as I began my work, allowed me space in the African and African American Studies Program office during my research stay at Duke University. Thank you.

I follow these acknowledgements with thanks and praise for the graduate students, friends, and colleagues who assisted in various ways to move this project forward. For counsel, frank appraisals, and for reading segments of this text, I thank my colleagues David Leverenz, Stephanie Smith, Joe Feagin, Hernan Vera, and Tace Hedrick. I also thank Anne Butler of Kentucky State University and Kaye Jeter of Central State University, the 2004 Bryn Mawr Summer Institute participants who read portions of the manuscript and asked challenging questions about its claims, purpose, and interpretive gestures. For editing and proofreading assistance, I thank the following students: Sarah Brusky, Marlo David, Brenda Rueichi Lee, Alexandra Marie Mass, Sabdy Liesl Pacheco.

Of course, I owe Cathie Brettschneider, Humanities Editor, University of Virginia Press, many thanks for her willingness to take on this project as well as propose its inclusion in the Cultural Frames, Framing Culture series. I thank the series editor, Robert D. Newman of the University of Utah, for including this book in the series. Angie Hogan, Acquisitions Assistant, earned my respect with her notes of encouragement and direction. Thanks to the freelance copyeditor Beth Ina and the press's peer reviewers for reading the entire manuscript and offering helpful suggestions.

I warmly acknowledge the Indiana University Press for allowing me to publish in this volume a slightly revised version of my essay "Writing in Red Ink" (the essay was originally published in *Body Politics and the Fictional Double*, ed. Debra Walker King, 2000, pp. 56–70). I thank the Manuscripts, Archives and Rare Books Division of the Schomburg Center for Research in Black Culture and the New York Public Library, Astor, Lenox, and Tilden Foundations, for permission to include transcriptions of four jokes written down by Alex Rogers and included in the "Bert Williams Joke Books."

My son, Christopher, to whom this book is dedicated, was born the year I began my research. Lying in a comfortable pouch attached to my shoulders and pressed against my chest, he ventured with me to Duke University, the Schomburg Center in New York, and many other libraries and sites where I conducted my research. He is my "sweet boy" and a very precious gift; I thank God for him. I thank my mother, Mollie Taylor, for her maternal care while Christopher and I visited Duke University, especially when going to the library was not exactly what Christopher had in mind for a day's outing. I thank my father, Peter Taylor, for his quiet strength and faith; and, as always, I thank my husband for his unwavering dedication and encouragement. Thank you, Mike, for all you do to keep us strong every day. May God bless you indeed!

Introduction

> [Sheriff] Rowles thought of the excruciatingly painful words he was not about
> to say—that forty-nine-year-old James Byrd, Jr., . . . son, . . . brother, . . .
> loved one was out in the middle of the road like so many scattered pieces
> of a puzzle, dragged to death like an animal. He could not say that.
> —Joyce King, *Hate Crime*

Not long after I finished the first draft of this book I witnessed a series of images so horrible they drove me from the family room of my home in tears. I was watching a Showtime Original Movie titled *Jasper, Texas* (2003). The movie, directed by Jeff Byrd and written by Jonathan Estrin, tells the story of the June 14, 1998, beating, dragging, and decapitation of James Byrd Jr., a father of three and a distant relative of the film's director.[1] As I watched the movie, years of research and discovery too painful to contain erupted within me. A sensation surfaced that at once angered, frightened, and sickened me. It was clear that, even after writing about black bodies in pain, I was not prepared to witness a black man reduced to broken and mutilated body parts.

I was even less prepared for the way that body was presented on film. Flashes of a torso scarred with flesh scraped to the bone, ankles shredded by a chain, internal organs exposed and mangled, and a head attached to a jagged-edged neck (indicating that the severed part was not made so by a guillotine or anything else so carefully designed) dominated the first half of the movie. But these moments were not what terrified me. My cries resulted from seeing, unexpectedly and without preface, the image of a black man shrieking in agony as three white men dragged him chained behind a truck. I was horrified by the anticipation of what was about to happen. I ran from fear that the film would show more pain and, thereby, demand more of my emotions and intellect than I could give.

The next night I was reminded of another murder as I watched "Speaking for Laci," a *Dateline* interview with Laci Peterson's family and friends. Peterson disappeared in 2002 on Christmas Eve. Her body and that of her son, Conner, were found a few days apart on the shore of the San Francisco Bay fourteen weeks later. The horror of her murder and the scientifically explained spontaneous birth of her son after the mother's death offered perfect material for a sensationalized account of the tragedy, yet *Dateline* took a more sensitive and caring approach to telling her story.

Faced with a disquieting juxtaposition of two horrible murders, I could not help but compare their popular culture representations. Everything about them, even their titles, reveals contrasting foci and traditions of cultural expectation, curiosity, and anticipation. Although *Jasper, Texas* gives the black mayor of Jasper, R. C. Horn, a voice, a past, and a heroic role in the town's unfolding drama (something many accounts of Byrd's murder fail to accomplish), it denies Byrd the same respect. It certainly denies him the respectful compassion Peterson receives in the *Dateline* special. Instead, the film leaves Byrd a victim: a symbolic scapegoat for interracial healing, a haunting image of racially motivated hate, and an icon for activism's call. In other words, he is not a man but a discourse expressing the need and hope for racial equality.[2]

While Byrd's image is overcome by bodily wounding so that any semblance of his humanity vanishes, Peterson's wounds fade beneath healing images that embrace her humanity. Instead of a corpse, the *Dateline* special presents a young, beautiful, funny and fun-loving white woman whose hopes and dreams were ravaged by a heartless murderer. There is little mention of the bodies of Peterson and her son beyond the meager facts of their discovery and a rejection of rumors about the baby's autopsy. The television newsmagazine program heightens our sensitivity to, and awareness of, Peterson's life, wholly imagined and normalized—not her death and certainly not her mutilated body.

The body of Laci Peterson recovered from the San Francisco Bay shoreline was decapitated (as was James Byrd's body). The *Dateline* program does not allow its viewers to "believe" in that image, however, and neither does the network movie account of the tragedy, *The Perfect Husband* (2004).[3] In this movie, Peterson's body is retrieved in a manner that masks its decapitation. When we see a representation of her mutilated corpse, we see it from a "safe" distance that does not force us to confront death. We look down on a neatly secured scene. On a gurney, wrapped tightly beneath a coroner's blanket, the body appears small but whole. There is no blood, no suggestion of gore, no haunting image of pain. Instead of witnessing a mutilated or broken white body, viewers of both the television drama and the newsmagazine program are presented with an unblemished picture of Peterson as an American icon. She is *Laci*, an uncompromised American mythology of youth, to be viewed with care and sensitivity. Viewers are encouraged to be outraged by Laci's death because she is one of them or, better, she *is* them. Her death appears to threaten their way of being in the world. This threat cannot, and does not, remain unchallenged, however.

According to the *Dateline* host and narrator Katie Couric, the program's intent is to revise the fragmentation and dehumanization Peterson and her body have acquired during six months of news reports and police investigations. The fragmentation mentioned is nothing close to what Peterson actually suffered, however. "Laci," we are told, "has become a household name." Couric continues: "For months, she's been seen as a face in a photograph. But her family wants us to know the young woman behind the bright eyes and beaming smile, not just as a victim, but as a daughter, sister and friend—someone who seemed to be born on a sunny day" ("Speaking"). Peterson's face and name, not her broken body, have been displayed for public consumption.[4] To achieve a picture of wholeness and wholesomeness, the program employs home videos and family photographs that create an image of Peterson's whole body, not its parts. More specifically, it produces an image easily assumable and, perhaps, even pleasurable to view. It creates *Laci*, America's girl next door, every mother's child.

The *Dateline* program's goal is to humanize this victim of murder and mutilation while normalizing her public image. The program achieves its goal by removing from public memory any remnant of her body's devastation or the threat of trauma we face by witnessing it. Interestingly, the process of normalizing Laci, the girl next door, repeated in virtually all media representations of Peterson's story, also removes her ethnicity. Although she is presented in the media as a white, Anglo-American woman, Peterson was white racially, but of Hispanic ethnicity.[5] The whitening of Laci's public image, then, is a central step in normalizing it as a present and central player in American public (and private) discourses about the tragedy.

Whether imposed, assumed, or adopted, whiteness masks difference. Its

FIG. 1. A choir sings and a huge photo of Laci Peterson smiles upon the congregation during the young woman's memorial service at the First Baptist Church. (*Modesto Bee* photograph [2003] reprinted with permission from Polaris Images Corporation)

symbolic value provides access to meanings that define what is and is not "American." Although *Hispanic* is not a racial category, individuals obviously associated with this ethnic identity find they are similar to Blacks in that they are not easily accepted as "American." If Peterson were presented as Hispanic, media performances intended to normalize her popular culture image as "all American" would have a higher likelihood of failure. This is perhaps why bodies not easily assimilated as "white" do not achieve the same type of public and media attention when victimized by assault.

In May 2002, for instance, another Hispanic woman, Evelyn Hernandez, was in her third trimester of pregnancy with a son when she suffered a fate identical to that of Laci Peterson. Her torso was found in the San Francisco Bay three months after her disappearance. However, her story did not receive the same broad public or investigative attention as Peterson's. Speculations about why the media and law officials did not appear interested in pursuing information about her murder aggressively focused on her ethnicity, economic status, and representation as a "non-American" body. The twenty-four-year-old Hernandez was a legal immigrant from El Salvador who could not easily represent "the all-American girl next door."[6]

If constructing a girl-next-door persona for Peterson is the intent of the *Dateline* program, what is the intent of the Showtime Original Movie presentation of the Byrd tragedy? The audience certainly does not gain an understanding of Byrd's life and accomplishments. The movie reveals nothing about his three children, his relationship with the mother of those children, or his dreams of becoming a musician. Few "tributes" to James Byrd move beyond an image of the man as a victim, a mutilated body, a symbol of hidden racism and a name on a Texas hate-crimes act (the James Byrd Jr. Hate Crimes Act) passed in May 2001.[7] As viewers, we learn more about hate and prejudice than we ever learn about the man whose death provided an opportunity for us to see the horror of racism's continued presence in our lives. Such effects are the result, if not the intent, of the way *Jasper, Texas* presents Byrd's story.

Estrin claims the film seeks "the emotional truth" of the Byrd incident, not the historical facts of a man's lived experiences ("Showtime Offers Portrait"). His efforts as a screenwriter brilliantly document the national shock that followed reports of Byrd's murder. The flashes of horror dispersed throughout the film, often without warning, are meant to shock, jolt, and "shake up" its audience emotionally, and they succeed. Certainly, no one can say with genuine affection, "I liked that movie," or "It was a nice tribute."

Instead, it is a memorial to the pain suffered by the five thousand Black Americans who have been lynched and an alarm signaling the need for an awakening. By mirroring both racism's horror and what Americans make of racism's victims in the haste and confusion of sensational reporting, collective fear, and communal rivalries, it moves viewers outside a position of comfort and subtle disaffection to a place of dynamic awareness and immediacy that is much less "likable."[8] I share my immediate experience with these programs in this introduction (and follow up in the next chapter with analyses) to highlight three of this study's critical hypotheses.

The first of these maintains that the pain-free, white American body exists easily in the cultural imagination and cultural productions of social agents within the United States. Even the most horrific wounding experiences are allowed invisibility, as if this mythological white body is cloaked within a magic circle. As an historical and everyday (or commonplace) sign of suffering, the wounded black body is walled off "legally, socially, and ideologically to benefit those within the magic circle and protect the national body from [pain's] contamination" (Rogin 12). The sheriff and mayor, who are the stars in the Showtime movie, protect their town from injury; they stand guard over contamination. Yet no one protects James Byrd. In fact, the repeated display of his fragmented body diminishes any expectation that it will be protected.

Second, the juxtaposition of these programs exposes popular culture's (as well as our own) denial of and collusion with a value-laden social hierarchy that commodifies the pained black body, rendering it "a representational sign for the democratizing process of U.S. culture itself" (Wiegman, "Black Bodies" 325). The media portrayals of these stories (as well as my experience of them) link leisure time and pleasurable expectations, communal and familial space, pain and race to a naturalizing pedagogy that, once recognized as such, is disquieting. As I watched *Jasper, Texas*, this recognition as well as my rejection of the film's sociocultural contract with a pedagogy of racial bias and exclusion disturbed me. I left the room because I could not "enjoy" the movie from a safe distance. To do so meant accepting racial subordination and exclusion, individual despair, and, subsequently, silent collusion with a naturalizing pedagogy that wounds. In other words, I could never achieve the "safe" distance those who are not Black achieve unless I deny my recognition of the film's naturalizing pedagogy.

Denial, in this case, can be emotionally, spiritually, and even physically wounding. Engaging in denial means accepting the assumptions and personal assaults accompanying the third hypothesis of this study, which contends that the black body is always a memorial to African and African American historical pain. Representations of the black body as torn and shamefully abused, such as that displayed so graphically in *Jasper, Texas*, emphasize that body's use as a metaphorical figure of pain's timeless memory. Through such representations, all black bodies become what Hortense Spillers describes in her famous essay "Mama's Baby, Papa's, Maybe" as "nothing more than a mode of memorial time" (205).

The overwhelming presence of black bodies in pain as memorial time encompasses and structures this study, resulting in a discourse that is circular, self-renewing, and ultimately, self-revising. The organizing logic of this study is not chronological. The primary texts surveyed are not presented as if meaning develops in a progressive or singularly focused and linear fashion. Instead, I organize my discussions in a manner that emphasizes the timeless nature of black pain and its availability as a cultural, social, and political metaphor of woundedness and hurt.

Events that allow black bodies to meet injury and pain orchestrated and defined by white conceptual hegemony determine when and to what extent a text is used. My presentation of examples from selected texts is, therefore, arranged by topics. An image may appear several times, but only as varied topics warrant its discussion. I introduce and reintroduce supporting evidence from texts as that evidence demonstrates additional and diverse aspects of the pained black body's function as memorial time—as metaphor. Accordingly, I weave textual discussions throughout the study in weblike fashion, reframing many and expanding others as I do.

The persistent metaphorical use of the black body in pain in popular culture (particularly film and literature) is a central focus of this study. As Spillers explains, memorial time "enables a writer [and, by extension, a filmmaker, a reporter, or an artist] to perform a variety of conceptual moves at once. Under its hegemony, the human body becomes a defenseless target . . . and the body, in its material and abstract phase, a resource for metaphor" ("Mama" 205). Whether films or novels, the texts surveyed here provide multiple opportunities to demonstrate how black human bodies gain meaning as metaphors perceived out of time. More important, they help illustrate what happens when the subject of pain disappears beneath the weight of an abstract body that is always in motion, always in a state of repetition and revision, and always present during events that shape the lives of those our society labels *ethnic, black,* or both.

Critical Contexts and Motivations

The three hypotheses proposed above outline a spectrum of concepts ignored or perhaps only slightly tapped by some of the most well-known critical discussions concerning how pain functions in our cultural imagination. A gap exists in cultural pain studies that is flanked, but left virtually untouched, by two of its most influential texts. One, David Morris's *The Culture of Pain* (1991), explores how "our biochemistry is inextricably bound up with the personal and cultural meanings that we carve out of pain" (5). The second, *The Body in Pain,* written by Elaine Scarry a decade earlier, explores the ways pain disrupts and, sometimes, destroys the social, cultural, and emotional worlds of individuals and communities tortured or seeking refuge from pain. She also presents evidence of how those so wounded restructure the worlds torn down. Both texts are renowned for their importance in the development of cultural pain studies and both are silent about the relationship of black bodies to cultural constructions of pain and racial marking.

Although *The Body in Pain* considers the operations of pain in war, law, literature, and theology, the relationship of pain to race and racism is never considered. Scarry does not explore the role of terrorism as a function of North American racism, for example. Neither does she discuss how "war" materializes in the everyday lives of black people. Morris, on the other hand, covers almost every imaginable aspect of pain and its relationship to culture. Plato and Socrates are there, as is Mark Zborowski, whose theories are often considered racist (52–56), and Job, who in the Biblical story endures extreme pain as a test of loyalty and faith in God. Vlad the Impaler, "who stands behind modern myths of Count Dracula" (183); The Marquis De Sade, who brought pain irreversibly "into the arena of sexual pleasure" (224); and everyone else, it seems, from Franz Kafka to Frank Oz and "The Little Shop of Horrors" make an appearance, including African Americans and black pain.

Unfortunately, the only bodies Morris mentions in his brief review of black pain are enslaved and Southern. I use the term *bodies* here because Morris never identifies black people as social beings. Instead, he presents the black body as an example of a site where pain's interpretations are often pre-encoded by social and cultural scripts without challenging those codes. It is not difficult to recall his comments. The discussion is so consistent and brief it can be summarized using a single quotation: "Black pain, in the eyes of the white-run Southern culture, had in effect a minimal social existence. White pain, by contrast, cried out for relief" (39). Morris provides a rational explanation for these sentiments—one that moves beyond charges of "ignorant prejudice or uneducated opinion." This he does by explaining the Enlightenment view of "the natural savage," which claims black people, being savages, do not feel pain as do white people (39).

Morris notes that during the nineteenth century this belief resulted in horrendous medical practices, such as the gynecological experiments of some physicians. Dr. James Marion Sims, a gynecological surgeon (noted as the "father of American gynecology"), perfected his procedure to repair vaginal fistulas by experimenting on black women without providing anesthesia. Sims defended his anesthesia-free operations by claiming, "Negresses . . . will bear cutting with nearly, if not quite, as much impunity as dogs and rabbits" (Pernick 56). Sims was supported in his inhumane treatment of black women by leading neurologists and surgeons who also believed black and white people experienced pain differently.[9]

Although black people are presented only as slaves and savages in *The Culture of Pain*, Morris does not advocate an Enlightenment view of black pain.

In his text, however, African Americans are the inheritors of an Enlightenment fallacy who remain not just savages but "natural savages"—with no reprieve and no champion.[10] Indeed, the Enlightenment understanding of "the savage" is the foundation of sentiments that continue to estrange the living presence, being, and humanity of black people from notions of individually experienced pain. Although black people's personal pain is acknowledged, this acknowledgment is not always achieved without bias.

Medical practitioners are still denying black patients pain relief, for instance. A study done in 2000 showed that "black patients with long-bone fractures were less likely to receive analgesics in the [hospital] emergency department than whites" (Talsma 1). Another controlled study completed in 1999 proved that even chest pain is ignored when the patient is Black (Schulman 618). While doing research for *Dying in the City of the Blues: Sickle Cell Anemia and the Politics of Race* (2002), Keith Wailoo discovered white physicians doubted patient claims of pain associated with the disease. Treatment costs and a belief in the stereotypical "drug-addicted" African American outweighed the notions of good faith and trust upon which the patient-doctor relationship is supposed to be built. Wailoo found that without testing or in-depth consultation, patients were denied pain medication. Recent studies such as these reveal various levels and analyses of institutionalized bias and bigotry that deny black people's individual pain. Meanwhile, the collapse of individuality into a body of memorial time and metaphor persists.

The constant "truth" about interpretations of black pain in America is that black people disappear while their bodies are constantly renewed as memorials to suffering and as tools for lessons benefiting systems of American acculturation. Gerald Early, Marcus Woods, Linda Williams, and Robyn Wiegman author four studies that support this statement. These cultural theorists begin to bridge the gap created by the oversights of Morris and Scarry.

Early's interdisciplinary study, *The Culture of Bruising: Essays on Prizefighting, Literature, and Modern American Culture* (1994), uses boxing and other sports as metaphors for what he describes as "the philosophical and social condition of men." Early argues that the racial, class, and gender dynamics of cultural "bruising" wound and consume the individual in ways that result in a "human crisis of identity" (xiv). Published a year later, Wiegman's *American Anatomies* (1995) develops a similar theory—one that positions black bodies as signs for acculturation served as "narrative commodities" to a nation where racist exclusion and demarcation is ever present (41).

Following these studies by a few years is Woods's *Blind Memory: Visual Representations of Slavery in England and America, 1780–1865* (2000). In this text, Woods investigates semiotic codes that shape cultural and historical memory. According to his study, visual images of black bodies (and others) reorganize the past and sterilize it to eradicate unsavory elements, offering distortions, effacement, and erasure of racism and racial conflict by valorizing white reformers and rendering black people objects of passivity and suffering.

Williams's *Playing the Race Card* (2001) delves even more deeply into the role suffering black male bodies play in "the enduring moral dilemma of race" (xiv). Her text argues that the historical figure of Uncle Tom is kept alive in U.S. popular culture as a "major force of moral reasoning" because, in part, of the image's longstanding representation of moral fortitude in the face of racial victimization (xv). Williams, like Wiegman, presents suffering black bodies as catalysts in a crisis of moral legitimacy and identity. She suggests that the presence of the suffering black body presented through images of the American slave is "a partial attempt to explain the secret of American national identity in relation to that racial 'Other'" (6).

These cultural critics discuss the impact of black suffering on identity politics and racial marking in the United States but do not investigate black pain as distinct from black suffering. The prism I am calling *African Americans and the Culture of Pain* makes this distinction an effect of its reflections. Because pain is not always a long-lived experience, I investigate it as immediate, sporadic, intense, and, often, evidence of a fatal event, a mortal injury. While suffering garners sympathy and delays action, pain, by signaling the heightened presence of power or weakness, is action. Suffering, on the other hand, is defined in this text as a lingering, life-defining experience—an indicator of what Linda Williams calls "moral legitimacy" and something more (6).

While Williams contends that the "Othered" body she studies precipitates a "crisis of moral legitimacy" and defines the forms that model of the Other takes in popular culture (6), *African Americans and the Culture of Pain* explores and wrestles with how the pained black body becomes a resource for subverting a different type of legitimacy. National, not moral, legitimacy is the focus here. This text also moves beyond a discussion of images produced to reflect the visual memory of slavery, moral authority, and the stagnant claims of antiracist agendas so brilliantly challenged by Wiegman and Woods. I presuppose these contentions and move beyond them to focus on select visual and verbal imagery produced from 1930 to 2005 that reveals the value of black pain as a metaphor of exclusion and a container of non-American identities.[11] My ultimate goal is to expose the symbolic properties of black pain hidden beneath America's love-hate relationship with the black body.

Why Black Pain?

Although black people make up the largest *colonized* minority in the United States, they are not the largest minority group or the only racial group to suffer objectification, alienation, disfranchisement, and racially motivated brutality in America. They are, however, the only ethnic group whose skin color has been identified consistently with such happenings since the birth of this nation. Racial loathing associated with black skin has encouraged and developed the problems of racism in the United States for almost three centuries. This is the primary reason this study focuses on black pain and no other.

As internal colonized minorities, African Americans receive the least respect of all American citizens. For most Blacks, matters are as JoAnn Moody suggests when she claims, "Not all minority groups possess the same standing and regard from the dominant group in power. Immigrant minorities . . . frequently enjoy higher status in the eyes of the majority group than do internal colonized minorities who are in this country because of force, not choice" (65). The status of being an internal colonized minority sets African Americans apart from immigrant minorities in multiple ways. Moody explains further:

> Generation after generation, colonized minorities find that their ancestors' violent entry to this country continues to undercut their own status and relation with the majority culture and negatively influence their daily lives. Generation after generation, they feel oppressed and see their religions, their native languages, their intellectual abilities, and their substantial contributions to the development of the country under-estimated or scorned . . . If they are in the United States, they often feel that the American Dream—upward social mobility and wealth—is for others but not for them. (69)

Although the non-immigrant black person experiences this feeling in manifold ways, the often-attempted "incarnation" of racial stereotypes and claims of "animalistic humanity" coded through skin color, or race, instantly relegates all black people to a subhuman species considered inferior, stupid, lazy, criminal, immoral, undeserving, pitiful, violent, unsafe, and victimized—regardless of "actual" colonized status (Steele 134). The influence of this belief on the interpretation of race-based identities is vast. At first sight, often without provocation or reason, in part or whole, white people read black bodies this way; brown people read black bodies this way; black people read black bodies this way; and so do others. And, although they may exist, those who "never do" are rare.

There is no hiding from color-coded stereotypes and institutionalized racism in America. There are only second chances, and many Blacks never get that second chance. Recall, if you will, the murders of Michael Griffith, Yusef Hawkins, and Amadou Diallo, who many believe died because their skin was black.[12] By making hurtful stereotypes almost inescapable while also supporting and maintaining an infrastructure of institutionalized racism, body reading stigmatizes black people thoroughly—even jeopardizing the lives of those who are innocent of the stories their bodies tell.

It is easy to use the stories black bodies tell to deflect issues that might be socially and politically divisive. The circumstances of William J. Horton's national notoriety come quickly to mind, for instance. Because of a mistake made by those administrating the Massachusetts furlough program in 1987, Horton, a black man convicted of first-degree murder, was given an approved forty-eight-hour furlough. He escaped to Maryland where he raped a white woman as her hog-tied fiancé, whom Horton also stabbed, watched. George H. W. Bush, who was vice president at the time, used the incident and the image of William Horton (renamed using the less dignified, more threatening "Willie") to compromise the political reputation of the democratic candidate, Michael Dukakis. Dukakis, the Massachusetts governor at the time of Horton's release, lost the 1988 presidential election as a direct result of Bush's sensationalized commercial campaign.

The campaign had far-reaching consequences—especially for black people, whose image and body were linked then, as today, with a specific type of violent crime: rape. According to Kathleen Hall Jamieson, of the University of Pennsylvania's Annenberg School of Communications, "[t]he Republicans' use of Horton shaped the visual portrayal of crime in network news in ways that reinforced the mistaken assumption that violent crime is disproportionately committed by Blacks, disproportionately committed by black perpetrators against white victims, and disproportionately the activity of black males against white females. In other words, the Republicans' use of Horton shaped the visuals in 1988 network crime coverage in a way that underscored the Bush message" ("Subversive Effects" 55).

The black body is always already characterized stereotypically as belonging to the "brute," a criminal and illegitimate heir of U.S. citizenship whose presence is a national threat. As a result, William Horton easily became a symbol of America's *internal nemesis.* His image and his crimes refocused the presidential campaign away from potentially explosive issues like abortion and health care. As a bipartisan issue, the threat he represented united Republicans and Democrats around a common interest. The image of Horton as the nation's most ominous symbol of pain, rape, and murder served as a safeguard against arousing concerns that might have had a stronger potential for destabilizing the status quo or placing Bush on the losing end of the 1988 presidential race.

Another, even more stunning, example of a black body used to deflect concern from a potentially divisive issue occurred on March 6, 2001. That day, the *Miami Herald* reported a shooting at California's Santana High School by presenting information and a visual image external to the event that offered readers comfort and a renewed faith in the "safety" of American schools. Beneath a full-page story of the incident was an Associated Press listing of "Recent Shootings at U.S. Schools." Although race was never mentioned in the written descriptions of the eleven incidents recorded, the only photograph suggesting what the perpetrator of such crimes might look like was that of a black boy, Nathaniel Brazill. Brazill's crime was unpardonable but not characteristic of those his image was made to represent. He did not kill or assault others in mass but was accused of killing one person—his teacher. This fact was secondary to the work of reaffirming a mythology of a white, pain-free, and violence-free American suburbia.

Brazill's face was the face of black pain. As a metaphor of exclusion, violence, and hurt, it allowed those who were not black to assume a certain level of denial by accomplishing two things. First, it reminded them that loss through teenage murder and assault is most often (although stereotypically) a minority experience. We have learned to expect such horrific occurrences in the ghettoes and barrios where Black and Latino children die from gun violence almost daily. We do not expect it in white suburbia. Second, it suggests criminal behavior, such as murder, is distanced from those whose bodies, unlike that in the photograph, are usually not associated with such trauma. The correlation of a black face with stories of murder and assault convinces those hungry for some type of reprieve from fear and shock that shootings among America's white children are uncommon and that the incidents reported, the crimes contradicting that "fact," are flukes.

Toni Morrison calls African Americans "the common denominator" of race and race relations around which groups and disparate identities can unite. She explains,

> [B]lack people have always been used as a buffer in this country between powers to prevent class war, to prevent other kinds of real conflagrations. If there were no black people here in this country, it would have been Balkanized. The immigrants would have torn each other's throats out, as they have done everywhere else. But in becoming an American, from Europe, what one has in common with that other immigrant is contempt for me—it's nothing else but color. Wherever they were from, they would stand together. They could all say, "I am not that." So in that sense, becoming an American is based on an attitude: an exclusion of me. . . . It wasn't negative to them—it was unifying. (Qtd. in Amgelo 120)

Unity derived from phenotypic recognition and exclusion works within a process of Americanization that is color-bound and, often, hurtful. The second reason for focusing on black pain in this text, then, is to disclose its role as an actor in the construction of the typical or acceptable and *safe* "American."[13] James Baldwin explains, "No one was white before he/she came to America." They were Irish, German, English, French, and Spanish (among other nationalities). Even people identifying with particular ethnic and religious groups were not white before coming to America. "Jews," for instance, "came here from countries where they were not white, and they came here in part *because* they were not white" (Baldwin, "On Being 'White'" 90–92). According to Baldwin, being white is the result of entering into an exchange, purchasing a "ticket," and, thereby, accessing racial associations and privileges denied or not even considered previously. For these immigrant groups, construction of a legitimate American subjectivity and sense of belonging begins with race and is refined through various signs of exclusion and inclusion. Images of the black body in pain function as such signs.

Linda Williams claims the "melodramatics of racial suffering" have been "basic . . . to the very process of citizenship in American history" ("Melodrama" 15). Along these same lines, Richard Dyer states unequivocally that "a sense of being white, of belonging to a white race . . . [is] part of the process of establishing a U.S. identity" (19).[14] In other words, at the top of the chart defining what an "American" looks like, acts like, and *is*, we find an Anglo face; on the opposite end, we find a black one. Set in constant opposition, black and white have come to mean "other" and "owner" when we envision constructions of U.S. identity and success. The so-called economically and socially successful model minority, for instance, is as close to white in action and appearance as possible. He remains ethnically identified yet fully "American," male, and nonblack. In fact, the more successfully "American" a nonblack minority becomes, the more distanced from an association with blackness and its everyday markings of exclusion (such as pain).[15]

Consider Jennifer Lopez. Some of the choices she has made to advance and maintain her success as a performer distance her from African American and Afro-Latin identity associations, although her professional origins are in the black entertainment world. As Tace Hedrick and I discuss in "Women of Color and Feminist Criticism," "Lopez has had her dark hair bleached, straightened and thinned, and her normally curvaceous body has been trained out to produce a physically fit and lean body with the famous butt well under control. . . . [T]he only contemporary signs of Lopez' 'ethnicity' are her high cheekbones, her slight slanted eyes and her carefully managed, smooth light tan" (70).

Lightening her skin and getting "bad hair" under control are not the only signs indicating Lopez's distancing from blackness (whether intentional or not). She also broke with her boyfriend, the Black recording artist Sean "Puffy" Combs (Puff Daddy), later marrying a white dancer-choreographer whom she divorced before announcing her engagement to the white actor Ben Affleck.[16] Even black performers like Lil' Kim (whose wigs and blue contact lenses have placed her in the blond bombshell category with Marilyn Monroe and Mae West) and Foxy Brown have, at some point in their career, distanced themselves from the black body by "lightening up."

In addition to Blacks' status as the largest colonized minority in the United States, the most hated racial group, the "common denominator" in conversations about "minority affairs," and the possessors of a body against which others measure their ability to belong, there exists another reason for focusing on black pain. Black bodies have a history of being the most "visible" objects for pain's public consumption. In fact, the popular and recurring image of black bodies in pain as a normalized representation of suffering in photos, film, and other cultural products has come to position those bodies as material representations of pain. This misrepresentation of the black body ultimately assists in building the mythology of who is and who is not "American."

Pain's Legacy, Pain's Diminution, and Surviving Pain

This book is divided into three parts. The first, "Pain's Legacy," introduces the various and varied critical methodologies I use to substantiate, more thoroughly, the hypotheses outlined earlier in this introduction. More important, it moves into issues of hurt while addressing a question others asked frequently of me as I began researching this subject: "What pain?" In response, I define pain as a boundless perception woven intricately from experiences of physical, mental, and emotional wounding and trauma that threaten one's ability to move "safely" into "survival and wholeness" (Walker, *In Search* xi). It is any experience that threatens the soul and sets the stage for "soul murder" and racial hurt.

What psychologists call "soul murder" I regard simply (or, perhaps, not so simply) as the death of personal will, everyday living, and, consequently, life. I argue that there is an essential link animating each aspect of body, soul, and spirit as a tripartite unity. Since the 1960s, this link has been called *soul power*. It is the most effective motivating force behind one's ability to overcome wounding events and personal trauma, traverse harmful situations "safely," and, thereby, maintain wholeness. Soul power is the ultimate rescue from the repercussions of memorial time and bodily abstraction.

The first part of this text, "Pain's Legacy," distinguishes the experiential and political structure of black pain as a product of human vulnerability and a reminder of human mortality from the symbolic function of verbal and visual representations of the black body in pain.[17] As a metaphor of memorial time and the resonance of racism's timeless bodily abstraction, the latter is defined as *blackpain*, a term I coined especially for this study. *Blackpain* denotes the visual and verbal representation of pained black bodies that function as rhetorical devices, as instruments of socialization, and as sociopolitical strategy in American popular culture and literature. While *black pain* describes "whose pain," the revised word signifies the textual function and surplus value (supplemental function) of black bodies in pain.[18]

The symbolic implications of blackpain are built on the assumption that racially biased political and social dogma cannot be conceived as distinct from the bodies they segregate, define, and mark as "Other." Such dogma is intimately tied to those bodies, and in fact, it depends on them for sustainability and justification. As Morrison contends, "[T]he subject of the dream is the dreamer" (*Playing in the Dark* 17). Much like the slave master's power and authority depend on the slave's symbolic representation as an outsider and a failed social being—a socially dead, living being—so do those who have the power to define blackpain's symbolic function depend on it to validate their relationship to inherited power.[19]

Contemporary black people, existing on the margins of society, become conflated in images of blackpain with the stereotypical black body, which is assumed to be pained, terrible, and unsafe. Blackpain, then, is a symbolic and intrusive abstraction of black people as living beings. As such, it is essential to the mythic logic of a pain-free American identity. Like their slave ancestors, African *Americans* and their assumed pained existence are threats to this logic. Black people cannot be both Americans and pained. They are, therefore, the outsiders who can never be "let in," the ones who do not belong but who, by virtue of their pain, are failed Americans—socially dead "bodies" whose existence justifies the normal and stable logic of the pain-free, nonblack American.

Because popular images of black bodies in pain hide Black "Being" (human presence) and individuality beneath devastating racial markings, black bodies have gained multiple meanings and varied symbolic functions. Blackpain has a metonymic function as a sign of social, economic, and cultural woundedness that can be co-opted by anyone suffering in a manner associated historically with black people. First-wave feminists, for instance, who argued their plight as disfranchised women was like that of black "slaves," claimed an association with "black pain." They made such claims not because of some physical resemblance between the two groups or because they shared actual experiences of suffering, but because calling on the abstract meaning potential of black bodies was socially, politically, and economically expedient.

On another level of meaning—as a synecdoche—images of suffering, dismembered, or disfigured black bodies function within a negative symbolic index of social worth defining what an American is *not*. Meaning, in this case, is not derived from injury but is built on the injury's direct association with something larger than itself. It occurs as the pain and wounds inflicted on the black body become representations of racially circumscribed issues, fundamental beliefs, rituals, and events that inform national legitimacy.[20]

It is in this context that I must introduce a phrase, *white nation,* that will be useful when exploring notions of national identity and legitimacy. Coined in 1997 by the anthropologists Karen Ho and Wende Elizabeth Marshall, the phrase is intentionally provocative and is thereby poignantly useful in subverting claims of whiteness as "invisible, normative, and blameless." Following Ho and Marshall's lead, I define *white nation* as a "network of decentralized webs that deploy multiple processes—judicial, economic, linguistic, military/paramilitary—from varied sites to achieve an always contested hegemony" (212–14).[21]

White nation does not signify a nation belonging to a specific race of people. It is not the exclusive property of white people but of any individual or group supporting comprehensive systems and strategies that ultimately maintain white patriarchal power and subvert all others. Its expansive influence, cross-culturally and interracially, begs the (now clichéd) question: Can the master's tools dismantle the master's house? As Audre Lord reminds us in *Sister Outsider* (1984), the answer is a resounding "NO." Therefore, my use of the words *white nation* in a study about black pain is not intended to signify right-wing or far right-wing politics (although that is sometimes unavoidable), racist individuals, or radical groups.

Like Ho and Marshall, I intend to evoke pain-filled images of institutional racism and prejudice that, by their existence alone, function to maintain racist white dominance. My discussions, however, extend Ho's and Marshall's definition to include prescribed doctrines of naturalization that "Other" blackness by assigning the pained black body negative symbolic capital (economic and social worth).[22]

As a closing statement, my analysis of *The Green Mile* (1999) presents one way popular culture employs, as it cloaks, the implications of racialized social scripts that naturalize the negative symbolic capital of black bodies in pain.[23] This concept is developed further in the second division of this text, "Pain's Diminution," where I consider the role blackpain plays in black social activism and in individual acts of resistance. Social activists invert pain's negative symbolic capital and use it to point out the inhuman and unjust treatment served on black people and black bodies. Discussions examine how blackpain is resisted, co-opted, and used to challenge both racist constructions of black bodies in pain and America's everyday acceptance and simultaneous denial of white-nation sociodicy (which, like religious theodicy, is a justification or vindication for prescribed dogma).

"Pain's Diminution" begins by investigating select moments when Civil Rights advocates used black bodies to establish a critical break with racist violence, "dreadful pleasures," and white-nation dogma (Baldwin, "Going" 239). Examples are drawn from the appearance of blackpain in real-world social politics as well as in Ralph Ellison's *Invisible Man* (1952), James Baldwin's "Going to Meet the Man" (1968), and Billie Holiday's famous song "Strange Fruit." Discussions move from personal protests and declarations of war to warfare as I evaluate blackpain's symbolic implications in narratives that revisit real-world battles and circumstances of war. My subject texts, *Glory* (1989), *Rosewood* (1997), and *Men of Honor* (2000), expose black men's relationship to the politics of equality, protection under the law, and patriarchal power (respectively) by presenting blackpain as visible evidence of a vicious, but denied, race war.

In "Pain's Diminution" I also examine the belief of many African Americans that silence is a mechanism for surviving racial and gender hurt—even when silence fails to subvert threats of fatal physical injury. My discussions distinguish between inert silence, which can be wounding, and the liberatory possibilities of silence conceived as action. The latter I call "silent mobility." Through it, inert silence dissolves into a liberatory movement, an energy that allows the subjects of racial and gender hurt to redefine for themselves, their families, and their community the presence of weakness and the unsayable within painful experiences. Readings in this section explore how black writers negotiate the political implications of silence in relation to pain and conclude that black men use silent mobility to script pain as weakness leaving the body. Black women, however, treat both silence and pain as central to a crisis of truth—a crisis (defined differently in each text) that must be exposed and resolved continually if black women are to survive whole.

Male characters in the texts of writers like Richard Wright, Ralph Ellison, James Baldwin, and Ernest Gaines express courage by viewing pain as an avenue for expelling racial hurt. They employ powerful dispositions that release personal weakness and murderous rage for the sake of communal survival, pride, and solidarity. Weakness (including the experience of powerlessness and degradation) is expunged as individuals move through pain-filled silence toward a new definition of their experiences and their lives (or deaths). Instead of giving voice to pain or, often, even acknowledging its presence, black male writers focus on how their male protagonists use painful situations to replace the unspeakable wounds of racial hurt and personal loss with meanings and actions that sustain their identities as men and their communities as their eternal legacies.

Women authors, on the other hand, write in the same way Harold Bloom describes Freud as writing: they "refuse to be silent in the face of the unsayable" (113). As Elaine Scarry reminds us, pain is the unsayable. It is that which cannot be spoken, although it can be signified through supplementation. Black women writers acknowledge the presence of the unsayable experience, courageously using silent mobility as well as bold and, sometimes, violent "screams" to emphasize their attempts to give voice to it. Their most successful characters reject inert silence in order to confront pain, and the source of pain, with audacity. These writers grant their characters (and by extension, their readers) the courage to expose personal or communal crises of truth and, thereby, weaken pain's power to control or determine the fate of those it threatens. To explore how black women writers reach that outcome, I offer the final division of this study, "Pain's Expulsion." This section opens with an exploration of a few ways black women's writing during the period under survey defines and terminates inert silence's drive toward a crisis of truth.

I focus on the work of Toni Morrison and Gloria Naylor. These writers are examples of black women writers who enter the "bowels" of blackpain to flush out that which holds truth captive: racial and gender hurt. Both focus on the reasons and methods black women devise for survival. By placing emphasis on the self, they challenge the adage that black women should be self-sacrificing vessels of woundedness, prepared to carry not only their pain but also the pain of others. Black women are not "de mule uh de world," as Zora Neale Hurston's Nanny believed (29). This is a crisis of truth that characters in black women's texts do not always survive—although they try. By defining an acceptance of hurt as an alliance with death, black women writers, however, pose the possibility of survival and so free their readers to express hurt unfettered, resist its soul-murdering potential, and, if possible, survive its traumatic realization.

This discussion of survival continues in the following chapter as I explore the expression of pain through the church shout as well as the healing arts of conjurational spirituality and laughter. I examine what it means to share black pain as opposed to watching from the trees, so to speak, or observing its consequences passively. This final chapter of part 3 weighs the pros and cons of sharing pain in both public and private spaces and discusses how that sharing is accomplished. Ultimately, it offers a review of "magic" and religion as methods of healing used in African American folk culture. The division concludes with a discussion of laughter's healing power and its presence as a double-edged sword.

Presented more as a suggested area for further study than a detailed investigation, in this discussion I argue that laughter frequently opens pathways to healthful living while compounding subliminally the pain it attempts to soothe. Its duplicity hinders its effectiveness as an agent of healing rather than strengthens it. Much like silence, the use of humor by black comedians and others is often complicit with worldviews and fields of conflict that assign black bodies in pain a negative symbolic value. Therefore, I conclude that, although agents of comic production may enjoy an economically beneficial re-lationship with blackpain, the assurance of healing that those agents might hope to find in laughter must, in the end, be found elsewhere.

African Americans and the Culture of Pain is about the life of a metaphor that I call *blackpain*. It does not trace this metaphor's escalation over time, because blackpain exists outside of time. In fact, it is time—mythic time—and a me-morial to the wounds and traumas some Americans wish to deny and discard. Instead of gathering a list of events that mark stages of this myth's develop-ment, I offer an examination of it as a persistent and essential strategy of An-glo American nation building and power exchange. I offer it as a cognitive and affective training strategy, a hidden persuasion of U.S. socialization.

As a corrective to the associations and racial markings that produce such meanings, I suggest an oppositional approach to interpreting blackpain which demands that its challengers realize three things. First, we must acknowledge that "one cannot be a calm, cool and detached" observer of racial wounding (Du Bois, *Dusk* 67). No one escapes blackpain's victimizing hand. Once it is encountered, we are deceived by it, wounded by it, or moved to action against it. We choose. Second, as potential victims of racial harm, we must do the hard thing. We must disrupt the pervasive marking of race that codes black bodies in pain as an ordinary event of everyday life, a naturalized agent of American acculturation. And finally, we must seek out and speak out against existing cultural fields of conflict in which black bodies are inscribed with pain while being stripped of subjectivity. Throughout the following pages, I attempt to follow these rules of protocol as I examine the specular and symbolic value of pain that influences so deftly how Americans in the United States confront and interpret traumatized, discarded, and abused black bodies.

One

Pain's Legacy

"We don't just burst into the Negro Problem; that's voted bad form. We leave that to our white friends. We saunter to it sideways, touch it delicately because"—her face became a little graver—"because, you see, it hurts."

—W. E. B. Du Bois, *The Quest of the Silver Fleece*

1 | Overt and Symbolic Violence

Violation invites, teaches violence.
—June Jordan, *Civil Wars*

On April 23, 1899, just after Sunday morning church services, the white citizens of Newnan, Georgia, marched, with shocking jubilation, into what one reporter at the time called "the annals of the savage" (Ginzburg 19). Their aim was clear: to witness Sam Hose's lynching. Although suspicion and doubt accompanied accusations that Hose raped a white woman named Mattie Cranford, assaulted her children, and murdered her husband, Alfred, there was never a formal hearing or jury trial. Instead, Hose was dragged through the streets to a place where the rope and faggot awaited him. There was little concern for his guilt or innocence—even though Mattie Cranford attested to Hose's innocence, declaring the murder an accident and the claim of rape a fabrication. Her testimony did not matter. All that mattered was Hose's race and the lessons of mob violence.

Amid an atmosphere of carnival and hysteria, two thousand people watched neighbors and friends—drunk with power—tie the 140-pound, five-foot-eight black man to a tree and torture him until he died.[1] Every moment of Sam Hose's suffering, humiliation, and pain was documented, making it easy for newspapers from Georgia to Springfield, Massachusetts, and beyond to offer their readers a shocking, yet enthralling, glance at a "Sunday holiday in one of the most orthodox religious communities in the United States" (Ginzburg 19).

Some reports were comprehensively graphic. In *100 Years of Lynchings* (1962), Ralph Ginzburg documents the *Springfield Weekly Republican*'s report of the incident. Written in active voice, it places the reader in the front row as a witness of the event:

> They cut off [Hose's] ears, his fingers and other members of [his] body, and strip him and pour oil upon him while the spectators crowd desperately for positions of advantage in the great work of torture and death. As the flames rise about the victim people watch the quiverings of the flesh and the writhings of the frame, and shout back descriptions to the jostling, cheering hundreds on the outskirts of the ring. The Negro raises a cry of agony that can be heard far away, and in a supreme effort loosens the upper part of his body from the chain which binds it to the tree. The fire is deadened while he is being chained back, and the awful agony prolonged to the evident relish of the spectators. Then more oil and fire, and death at last comes to the man's release. (19–20)

In "Hellhounds," Leon F. Litwack adds a detail left out of the *Republican* report. He tells his twentieth-century readers that "[b]efore saturating Hose with oil and applying the torch, they cut off his ears, fingers, and genitals, and skinned his face" (9). This description makes the horrible even more unbearable and the verbally rendered image of Hose's death more ghastly.[2] Yet, there is something about this horror that intrigues and makes turning away difficult.

Reading these words, we join our nineteenth-century ancestors as witnesses to what could be described as America's voyeuristic relationship with black bodies in pain. We pass through the horror of Sam Hose's lynching, however, with the assurance that America is more civilized today, more compassionate. Like newspaper readers a century earlier who may have claimed a nonparticipatory role in the story they read, we can claim superiority to the hundreds who watched Hose die that Sunday in 1899. When James Byrd was murdered, we may remind ourselves, only three witnesses were present; only three men were caught in the whirl of mad pleasure found in violent expressions of power—not an entire community. Meanwhile, we misrecognize (Pierre Bourdieu's term for forgetting and denial) the power of pleasure within our current precarious, re-creative and recreational view from the trees (Bourdieu, *Outline* 21–22). Consider how a white University of Florida graduate student reading this story responded. "After I started the passage," she writes, "I found myself

"This is her first lynching."

having a strange feeling of an almost inability to turn away. . . . I would explain that reaction away by saying it wasn't 'pleasure' that I was getting but rather a total disbelief that this could happen. But [the] point is that that [in itself] is some kind of pleasure, and I find that to be a really thought-provoking, as well as disturbing, realization."[3]

Disturbing? Indeed. Yet this student's recognition of pleasure and her attempt to explain that pleasure away demonstrates the role denial plays in this drama. As we continue to watch or, in this case, continue to read and envision the horror of Hose's murder, denial provides ways for us to cope. It allows passage beyond the guilt of submission to a perverse pleasure. When reminded of racism's horror in this way, black people feel abused and wounded while sympathetic whites "show both concern and a measure of befuddlement at how other whites" can behave so dishonorably (Steele ix).[4] Others convince

FIG. 3. Chaos and mob frenzy are depicted in Paul Cadmus's *To the Lynching!* 1935, graphite and watercolor on paper, Sight: 20½ x 15¾ in. (52.07 x 40.01 cm). (Photograph copyright © 2000: Collection of the Whitney Museum of American Art, New York, Purchase 36.32)

themselves that people like Byrd's murderers are aberrations. It is easy to be-lieve that people no longer gather in hordes around saplings (or anything else) to enjoy public displays of human torture, degradation, mutilation, and death.[5] Unfortunately, this is our hope, not our reality. People gather in movie theaters and in the privacy of their homes around televisions throughout this nation where they watch such horrors occur every day.

U.S. popular culture encourages pondering the historical wounding of black bodies, and the buying public acquiesces. Audiences have flocked to *Amistad* (1997), *Mississippi Burning* (1988), and other historical dramas that offer black bodies bloodstained, swollen, silent, or twisted with pain.[6] Some patrons witness these films hoping to be informed, to gain knowledge, and, through it, cultural capital. Others are simply curious. The assumption is that cinematic recreations of the past reveal truth, which they usually do not. In-stead, they feed the public's desire to witness history. Audience members watch from the trees and enjoy a deceptive sense of distance and assumed educa-tional gain while allowing themselves a guarded experience of pleasure—or is it leisure?—surrounded by images of blackpain.

Misrecognition, or denial, during such moments masks awareness of social "lessons" communicated through blackpain. Sometimes it takes a jolt of sur-prise, an infusion of shock and a moment of personal crisis to move interpre-tation beyond racialized expectations, which often end with little more than finger-pointing and a "not me, but them" attitude of complacency. But why? What are the origins of these expectations and why is no one shouting, "No more!" Images of blackpain are so commonplace that the "buying" public no longer recognizes it as "grounded in social processes" (Holt 9).[7]

Thomas C. Holt maintains that through historical repetition, the "everyday life" of racial marking leads "seemingly rational and ordinary folk [to] com-mit irrational and extraordinary acts" (7, 8). We see this in the description and visual representations of the lynching of Sam Hose and James Byrd (the lat-ter is discussed in the introduction). Racial marking also leads ordinary and, often, unsuspecting folk to view and interpret the black body as an image of pain—a sign to be feared, hated, and avoided, particularly when confronted outside the protected arena of popular culture and literature.

The everydayness of these associations and reactions stems from long-standing interpretations of blackness that mark it as evil, dangerous, and painful. Writing in the eighteenth century, Edmund Burke comments: "[B]lack-ness and darkness are in some degree painful by their natural operation, independent of any associations whatsoever. I must observe, that the ideas of darkness and blackness are much the same; and they differ only in this, that blackness is a more confined idea" (415).

Burke qualifies his comments by using the black body as an example of confinement. He recounts the story of a boy who, after being healed from a lifetime of blindness, was frightened at the sight of a black woman. "The boy appears by the account to have been particularly observing and sensible for one of his age," Burke notes, "and therefore it is probable, if the great uneasiness he felt at the first sight of black had arisen from its connexion with any other disagreeable ideas, he would have observed and mentioned it."[8] Burke insists the boy's reaction was not due to any ideological associations made in reference to the woman. Instead, the "disagreeable" marking of blackness dominated her body and stripped it of any human resemblance. His assessments support Holt's assertion that racial marking naturalizes racist ideas and practices, making them "self-evident, and thus seemingly beyond audible challenge" (7).

Images in popular culture, both verbal and visual, developed from the eighteenth century until the present have molded the idea of blackness to the pain Burke associates with it by inscribing both on phenotypically black human bodies. Today the image of black bodies maltreated and in pain carries within it meanings that, even when absolutely horrible, are accepted, categorized, and forgotten almost at once. In an era of popularized multiculturalism and diversity, personal critiques that expose the social processes supporting and promoting the repetition of such ideas are denied, or even worse, received in ways that make challenging them seem unreasonable and even perverse.

As examples, I return in the following paragraphs to my introductory discussion of the *Dateline* story about Laci Peterson and the Showtime feature film *Jasper, Texas*. While *Jasper, Texas* employs images stripped of meaningful reflections on individual humanity, thereby encouraging the successful denial and "selling" of a pained black body, the image of *Laci*, America's girl next door, promotes and sells its more alluring opposite. Neither of these productions, however, provides a critique of the normalizing cultural politics they promote. Instead, they develop racial stereotypes along a biased continuum, thereby measuring human worth without opposing or challenging the assumptions of that continuum.

These comments are not meant to infer that the viewing public passively accepts the normalizing rhetoric promoted through images of the pained black body and the carefree girl next door. The images are resisted, negotiated, and opposed as individuals watch and interact with what they see. Unfortunately, in most cases, individuals do so while processing such images through a sieve of racial value and assessment externally determined, personally accepted, and continually reaffirmed. In other words, meaning is accomplished through ongoing "conversations" between normalizing cultural politics and individual negotiations of how they can or will accept normalizing paradigms and under what conditions.

Both the discomforting visual image of black bodies in pain and the more soothing image of pain-free white bodies amass value on a field of racial hierarchy.[9] This field of struggle is where contesting images and power relations are in constant play. If struggle is denied or rendered invalid by some implied or imposed judgment, the images are sustained as normalized paradigms of human worth. They maintain their assigned worth only as long as their functions within various social processes remain unacknowledged and invisible.

Readings such as those offered in the present discussion, for instance, expose the field on which racial stigma and ethnic devaluing is played. Like a football game or any other game played on an acknowledged field of conflict and action, covert game plans are exposed and countered when movement becomes visible. As a result, the possibility of resistance, change, and struggle rises. These possibilities are denied or rendered invalid in both the NBC newsmagazine program and the Showtime movie, as if the denial was a natural part of the action or reporting event.

In *Jasper, Texas* the portrayal of the New Black Panthers and the Ku Klux Klan suggests that any act of resistance existing beyond the realm of agreed-upon legal action is unnecessary.[10] The behaviors such groups represent in the film are offered as unreasonable responses to the mutilation and murder of African Americans. To validate this point, their aggressive and potentially violent presence and social agitation is the only symbol of struggle offered in the film. Individual citizens do not question or challenge the murder and neither do other groups. The presence of the Klan and the Panthers is read against the film's progressive portrayals of community self-help, racial collaboration, and "the law." In that context, civil disobedience and social conflict are rendered invalid. Struggle is rejected as a threat to communal order; by extension, any form of racially influenced resistance to the film's dominant social meanings is also invalid.

In the *Dateline* story, struggle is not challenged so directly. It is an undercurrent presented in the form of denied voice and visibility, competing forces always present yet unacknowledged. Although outrageous conflict, struggle, and violence lead to Laci Peterson's death, each is denied visibility in the *Dateline* interviews. Silence replaces discussion of the woman's mutilation, and, although we know she is dead, we are not faced with the violence of that death through descriptions or imagined details. Unlike *Jasper, Texas*'s treatment of Byrd's mutilation, there is no recreation of this event—not in this or any other program. Byrd's raced body is not given the same respect or "privacy." Why? One reason may be that American popular culture treats images of black bodies in pain as symbolic capital, not as private experiences. As such, we find them presented without respect to issues of "privacy." They are viewed as deprivatized assets within a U.S. symbolic index of race and belonging.

Both the creation of Laci as America's girl next door and the replication of Byrd's pained and mutilated body for display have exchange value within the social economies of American acculturation and systems of national heritage. *Dateline*'s creation of Laci is based on an understanding of worth agreed on within a social contract that allows the symbolic capital exchanged through her image to exist. Clean-cut and without disfigurement, Laci has cultural value that viewers want to claim, and do. Her body has worth that James Byrd's racially marked and historically defined body, even were it presented without disfigurement, can never achieve. His body exists within a field that is inextricably bound to slavery, Jim Crow, and lynching.

The players on this field are in motion constantly and have been since the boundaries of the field were drawn during the drafting of the nation's Constitution and the "three-fifths compromise" of 1776. This compromise, made between the nation's slaveholding and nonslaveholding state spokesmen, or "founding fathers," marks enslaved, black bodies as partial, fragmented, and therefore, "worth" less than the bodies of "free persons."[11] Although this part of the Constitution has since been amended and slavery abolished, the repercussions of its language and founding beliefs reverberate in the everyday practices of today's visual and verbal imagery. In many ways, the definition of black bodies as belonging to whole persons remains disbelieved and devalued.

We see the effects of this legacy in *Jasper, Texas* where the image of Byrd's body, fragmented and pained, "bears the curse of a negative symbolic capital" (Bourdieu, *Pascalian Meditations* 241). While Laci sells as a symbol of a desired American identity, Byrd's body sells as a model of what an American is not.[12] An American identity is not pained, torn, or mutilated; it is not fragmented and forced into wholes by calculating percentages. It is conceptually whole and wholesome. The visual image of Byrd's pained body is useful, then, only as a storehouse for those non-American identities, hyphenations, and partial "truths" that legitimize and give mythologies like that of *Laci*, America's girl next door, more value, more prestige.[13]

Cast as entertainment and aligned with a difficult-to-overcome system of race naturalization, the serious critique of racism and its history of wounding that appear to be the intent of filmmakers and producers of movies and television productions like *Jasper, Texas* can be misrecognized or "misperceived" (Bourdieu, *Outline* 21–22). This is why programs claiming to recall history, and thereby short-circuit forgetting and national illegitimacy, often fail to do so. At most, they force a realization that there is no comfortable place assigned to the meanings and emotions ignited by the concurrent union of pain and pleasure, race and wounding (Wiegman, *American Anatomies* 41).

What happens, then, when the spaces where agents seek pleasure are saturated by demands for witnessing black bodies in pain? What happens in the mind or in the socialization of the man, woman, and child sitting on the branches of the tree, watching murder and mutilation take place? What are the messages communicated when entertainment and pain are conflated and allied? What happens to delight when pleasure unexpectedly turns into hurt or when it is compromised by the brutality of xenophobic sadism?

According to Burke's meditations on the sublime, pain is stronger than pleasure. It is more intensely experienced because it is "stronger in its operation than pleasure." He continues, "When danger or pain press too nearly, they are incapable of giving any delight, and are simply terrible; but at certain distances, and with certain modifications, they may be, and they are delightful" (107). However, it is not always possible to achieve a comfortable distance from visually and verbally witnessed or imagined pain.

This is particularly true because history, even contested history, is always present in the body. It is inescapable and, as such, forces black people to become inextricably likened to or linked with historical black pain. This is another reason black bodies function easily as everyday living memorials to and signs of suffering, pain, and social abuse.[14] Filmmakers and writers often take advantage of this by placing black bodies in positions where they default to a symbolic value denoting nothing else. In *Mississippi Burning*, for instance, black bodies are fixed so intimately to notions of woundedness and the historical realities of it they have only to appear for pain to be communicated. Often in the film, that is all black characters do. They appear, then run or stand silently before the camera, not as individuals, but as a wounded, thoughtless, and pitiful communal body.[15]

During these moments, they have no voice, no story apart from that of an oppressed people void of connections with those nonblack agents who watch. They are almost as empty of human life and spirit as statues commemorating the dead. Within the symbolic discourse of black bodies in pain, these characters are just that: commemorations of death, emblems as easy to misrecognize as are ghosts. They are mere objects, "pain-filled" enough to condemn and ostracize. These unfortunate messages and codes of human disregard are easily met by a conscious or subliminal audience desire to gaze on the "Other" as a curiosity.

Racial Vulnerability

Violence against the black body does not end with overt acts of injury and murder, however. The lessons of racially motivated violation inform moments of *symbolic violence* also. According to Bourdieu, symbolic violence is "violence which is exercised upon a social agent with his or her complicity" (Bourdieu and Wacquant, *Invitation* 167).[16] This type of violation is not the same as the brutal exploitation and overt violence of lynching, yet both types of violence yield similar regulatory and disciplinary effects. Both are sources for racial hurt, psychological wounding, and, ultimately, soul murder.

While overt violence is often bloody, symbolic violence manifests itself through individual or communal acceptance of naturalized racial markings. In this way, symbolic violence works to legitimize strategies of exclusion and build the political, economic, cultural, and social capital of the status quo. It can also act as a mechanism to encourage containment of anything or anyone, group or individual, that the established social order deems unsavory or unwanted.

The silent acceptance of blackpain as a predictable cultural image (or metaphor) is symbolic violence enacted not only by Blacks but also non-Blacks. The pleasure of seeing Hollywood roles for black actors expand beyond servants, dancers, and clowns, for instance, is enhanced by the economic and social value gained from the expanded availability of jobs and professional images. These benefits lead some viewers (Black and non-Black) to hesitate before raising a hand of protest against the symbolic "tricks" they observe in films like *Mississippi Burning*. For these individuals, there may be a need to believe the stories as shown are achieving something good, even when those stories play by rules that reduce black bodies to signs of pain and suffering or impose corrective and disciplinary actions that categorize black people as worth less than those who are not black.

Silently accepting such images, however, is complicit to activities played on a field of wounding racial domination. It is symbolic violence. Spike Lee focuses on the wounds delivered via the complicity of silent acceptance in *Bamboozled* (2000). This satire of network television's racial prejudices and greed is also an indictment of black people's collaboration with the perpetuation of negative stereotypes in popular culture.

In the film, the Harvard-educated black writer Pierre Delacroix creates a blackface minstrel show in protest of an ultimatum given to him by his employer. His charge is simple: produce a successful "urban comedy" or find another job. The charge does not offer an opportunity for Delacroix to produce what he feels is important work. In fact, the request is received by Delacroix as racist. It falls too neatly within the boundaries of comedy as the only acceptable form of black entertainment. Unable to gain support for the type of work he feels is his best, Delacroix decides to reveal the true nature of the request by producing the most racist show he can imagine. When it succeeds, he does not admit his act of resistance. He does not "bow out" of the production but keeps silent about his feelings of woundedness and shame—ultimately committing suicide to escape the racial hurt his silence and symbolic violence have condoned. His actions dramatize the meaning and implications of symbolic violence while emphasizing its relationship to racial hurt and *spiritual wounding.*

Racial hurt is often misinterpreted and defined in pathological terms as docility or laziness, when in fact these "behaviors" are frequently evidence of spiritual wounding. Shelby Steele highlights this aspect of spiritual wounding in a theory he calls *racial vulnerability:* "Racial vulnerability is best thought of not so much as the wound of our oppression as the woundedness we still carry as a result of it—our continuing openness to inferiority anxiety and to racial diminishment and shame. This woundedness is not an inert pain; it is an active agent within the personality that pressures Blacks individually and collectively to see ourselves and the world in ways that protect us from our pain and doubt" (57).

Racial vulnerability is not an "inert pain"; it is spiritual woundedness in search of protection from overt and symbolic reinjury. It is a denial of pain's presence for the sake of self-preservation or pride. More important, it is a struggle to emerge from beneath the strikes of racially motivated historical assaults. In other words, racial vulnerability is like a sore deep within Black America that is eternally open and susceptible to reinjury. This injury is the site of spiritual wounding, the place where the crippling effects of "wounded-ness" reside and where the strength of personal resistance and voice must coagulate if black people are to survive whole.

For Steele, racial vulnerability leads to racial shame, which is distorted by a guise of victimization and externalized through false charges of racism (59). Steele's paradigm of social degeneration may be true for some Black Americans, but for many others, racial vulnerability remains an unexamined hurt, a deep wound—unacknowledged and, often, unknown. It is the source of self-alienation, slow spiritual decay, and collusion with soul murder, which is the subject of the following chapter.[17]

In the darkest moments of our nation's past, morality and ethics have been overturned by power dynamics, social processes, and racial tensions that often compel Americans to accept pleasure in viewing black pain and express passion through horrific acts of torture against the black body.[18] Promised access to a pleasure-producing inheritance of power and status, the individuals and communities referred to here engaged in distasteful, and sometimes even criminal, activities. History records their behavior as if there were no calculation or weighing of conscience strong enough to curtail submission to the communion, chaos, and savage passion of violent social action.

Sam Hose's lynching and physical violation a century before James Byrd's dragging death offers an example of a community's failure to recognize black people as people. Both murders, separated by a full century, speak to a lack of caring made acceptable by social processes and an history of "uncontestable" racial marking. This lack moves everyday folk to engage in irrationally violent action without regard for human life or individual dignity.

2 | Racial Hurt and Soul Murder

Chester Himes contemplates racial hurt and soul murder in his 1971 autobiography *The Quality of Hurt*. His description of hurt spans a broad but segmented field of pain typecasting. He writes:

> Up to the age of thirty-one I had been hurt emotionally, spiritually, and physically
> as much as thirty-one years can bear: I had lived in the South, I had fallen down
> an elevator shaft, I had been kicked out of college, I had served seven and one half
> years in prison, I had survived the humiliating last five years of the Depression in
> Cleveland; and still I was entire, complete, functional; my mind was sharp, my
> reflexes were good, and I was not bitter. But under the mental corrosion of race
> prejudice in Los Angeles I had become bitter and saturated with hate. . . . I had
> become afraid. . . . I was thirty-one and whole when I went to Los Angeles and
> thirty-five and shattered when I left to go to New York. (75–76)

For Himes, mental, physical, emotional, and spiritual pains are distinct experiences that can be compounded and perceived beyond sensation as a series of hurts the weight of which shatters, or wounds, the soul. Thirty-five years after the publication of his autobiography, many have adopted a similar understanding of the relationship between perception and pain. The big divide separating physical, mental, and emotional pain is nearly closed. According to David Morris, the segmented thinking or typecasting of the past now looks "like a gigantic cultural mistake, perhaps similar to the belief that the world is flat" (*Culture of Pain* 12).

Still, the remnant of pain's big divide causes one to ask pertinent questions of a study like this one. What kind of pain is under survey? Are we talking about the body's pain stemming from physical injury, or is this text about pain originating with the mind's confusion or the so-called wounded heart? An examination of questions such as these points out the false boundaries separating racial hurt from various sites or sources of pain.

Morris contends, "[D]ifferent sources do not necessarily imply different pains. . . . Pain is always personal and always cultural . . . [it] is never timeless, just as it is never merely an affair of bodies" (9, 25, 29). Like Himes, Morris draws a picture of pain that needs more than an acknowledgment of sensation to exist and have meaning. For both, pain exists meaningfully as long as it is perceived and has the potential to be interpreted socially, culturally, politically, and historically. What is not so clearly communicated by Morris is where the concepts of soul murder and spiritual wounding (suggested in Himes's autobiography) might fit in this revised understanding of pain.

Spirit and soul are often thought of as esoteric and metaphysical concepts. Therefore, pain associated with either is considered either nonexistent or peripheral to investigations of medical practice, sociocultural relations, and intellectual life. Such considerations of pain exist on the borders of belief systems that offer a speculative nod to the interpretation of sacred, symbolic, and religious connotations of spirit and soul without considering their meaning or value within the secular registries of human experience. This is perhaps why Morris describes the "redemptive, visionary implications" of pain as "actively at work in the modern world, like a *neglected* but potent sacred text" (125, emphasis added).

Morris's observation is particularly important to consider when examining the relationship between black bodies and the development of an American culture of pain. Spirit is soul—an essential element of a cherished African American "sacred text" known in folklore, literature, popular culture, and cultural mythology. Although soul is most often associated with a certain type of music (featuring James Brown and Aretha Franklin, among others), Himes describes it as an unabashed ability to "hurt too painfully" while traversing life-threatening assaults "safely" (351). "Having soul," in this context, means possessing the ability to keep both the sacred and secular power of one's "self" intact through sheer determination.

Soul is the glue that fixes the tripartite unity of body, mind, and spirit. As such it brings together the essential elements one needs to experience and survive pain. In *City of God*, book 14, Saint Augustine claims, "[W]e speak of bodies feeling and living, though the feeling and life of the body are from the soul, so also we speak of bodies being pained, though no pain can be suffered by the body apart from the soul." In this way, body, mind, and sprit are united through the centrality and immediacy of the soul. Consequently, the soul provides access to both experiences of pain and the will, or power, to live beyond those experiences. In this paradigm, victims of hurt may not be "safe" from pain, but they may emerge safely from an encounter with "painful hurts" by using the impulses and activities of a determined spirit.

Himes's autobiography shows us the face of debilitating trauma and its crisis of truth. Shockingly, the truth it hides is not found in experiences of pain but in the crevices of pain's face, so to speak. It exists in racial hurt. Pain is a personal experience, a feeling that is uniquely our own. Himes would have us believe we own it and can, thereby, control it. Racial hurt, however, is not something we own. Racial hurt owns us. It, not pain, attacks the soul and renders its victims wounded or worse—soul murdered.[1]

Soul Power

Soul power is will power on fire—a combination of hope and self-determination that influences how woundedness, pain, and injury are read internally, as well as how fully their negative potential is manifested externally. Through soul power one maintains control over personal responses to confrontations that create barriers to motivated living. Soul power is not fatigable. It cannot be taken away or conquered, but it can be killed or given away. Consequently, it diminishes only if those suffering symbolic and overt violence collaborate with pain and its champion to the point of being consumed.

Euphemistically, the product of such collaborations and complicity is called a *broken spirit*. Pain emanating from such brokenness weakens the will, makes courage volatile, overwhelms confidence, fuels anger; and, yes, it can kill. The historian Nell Irvin Painter, borrowing from psychology, uses the phrase *soul murder* to identify the consequences of spiritual brokenness. The "depression, lowered self-esteem, and anger" she attributes to "soul murder" are externalized expressions of an individual or community beyond the reach of "safely" surmounted conflict and woundedness.[2] It can also be the consequence of a soul, or souls, consumed by collaboration with institutional and cultural processes that cause black people physical, psychological, and emotional injury.[3] Painter argues that "sexual abuse, emotional deprivation, physical and mental torture can lead to soul murder, and soul murdered [people's] identities are compromised; they cannot register what it is that they want and what it is that they feel" ("Soul Murder" 16–17). As the product of various forms of illness, torture, and abuse, spiritual woundedness and soul murder breed hopelessness and urge forth the death of desire sometimes to the point of rendering victims members of the walking "dead," unmotivated and afraid (or, at the least, unwilling) to engage life.[4]

The Women of Brewster Place, published in 1983, demonstrates the potential danger posed by spiritual wounding and loss of soul power. In this novel, Gloria Naylor presents Ciel, a young mother and wife, whose experiences are so excruciatingly painful, so penetrating, that she wishes for death. After an abortion, being abandoned by her husband, and her baby daughter's fatal accident, Ciel "shuts down." Her condition results from painful "overloads" that force her to disengage on multiple levels of viability. She loses her desire to live (spiritual), her ability to cry (physical), and her concern for her body (mental). The narrator tells us:

> People had mistaken it for shock when she refused to cry. They thought it some special sort of grief when she stopped eating and even drinking water unless forced to; her hair went uncombed and her body unbathed. But Ciel was not grieving for [her daughter] Serena. She was simply tired of hurting. And she was forced to slowly give up the life that God had refused to take from her. . . . Her visitors' impotent words flew against the steel edge of her pain, bled slowly, and returned to die in the senders' throats. No one came too near. . . . A neighbor woman entered in studied certainty and . . . as she reached for the girl's hand, she stopped as if a muscle spasm had overtaken her body and, cowardly, shrank back. (101–2)

Ciel is committing suicide. Only the "steel edge" of her pain exists beyond the walls of symbolic violence she erects in her own soul. Perhaps she is lost in spiritual brokenness; perhaps she is not broken at all but willfully intent on being complicit with pain's ultimate end. Either way, the power and depth of her alienation from safety ward off attempts from others to save her. It is as if her inability to surmount pain safely also threatens their ability to "hurt too painfully" and survive.

Beyond recognizing it as a danger, Ciel's friends fail to connect with the overwhelming reality of her pain. More specifically, they fail to recognize its connection to what Naylor describes in the epigraph of another novel, *Linden Hills* (1984), as "that silver mirror God propped up in your soul." Repeatedly, they insist on fragmenting Ciel's experience, looking only at a small part of it instead of the whole. Unable to witness it all, they either withdraw or misread her behavior as an emotional response to her child's death and nothing more.

Only Mattie Michael, Ciel's friend and surrogate mother, recognizes Ciel's pain as full, deep, and deadly. Only she has the courage to reach beyond the familiar and bearable to touch skin "so hot it burned." Only she dares reach into the "nadir of [Ciel's] hurt," beyond the rubble of time, "Aegean seas," and "murdered dreams," to retrieve the instrument of this woman's torture—"a slight silver splinter, embedded just below the surface of [Ciel's] skin" (103). This splinter is evidence of an attack against Ciel's soul. Without Mattie's willingness to look deeply into Ciel's pain and acknowledge its soul-wounding potential, witness its "naked force" and "raw fires" instead of reading surfaces and isolated parts, Ciel would have died a victim of suicide by soul murder (102).

How prepared we are to cope with a hurt like Ciel's, to acknowledge and use *soul power*—that indefatigable source of personal will—as refuge against complicity determines pain's influence upon us. Sofia in Alice Walker's *The Color Purple* (1982) never goes as far as Ciel in her movement toward self-imposed or collaborative spiritual wounding and acceptance of soul murder. Instead, Walker gives her readers insight into how Sofia survives a soul-wounding experience safely. She does not relinquish her soul. Instead, she stimulates it through her imagination, which she describes as both pretending and dreaming. Sofia dreams, for instance, of securing revenge for the beating she suffers beneath the anger and disrespect of white men's overt violence. "I dream of murder, she say, I dream of murder sleep or wake" (76).

Still, her confrontation with wounding highlights spiritual networks linking physical, emotional, and mental fields of experience in ways similar to those we witness when we read about Naylor's Ciel. Although Sofia does not entertain suicidal thoughts or behave as if she desires death as Ciel does, she still acts in collusion with her own soul-wounding experience for several years. Her story is a testimony to how soul power influences "the making and unmaking of the world"—the stakes that Elaine Scarry claims are at risk for every pain victim (23).

Sofia's problem begins when she and her financially secure boyfriend, a prizefighter, take her children to town. The mayor's wife, Miss Millie, sees Sofia and her well-dressed children "looking like somebody," standing beside a car, which marks them as prosperous. Considering herself superior, she speaks to Sofia, complimenting her on her children's appearance, but in a condescending manner. Miss Millie then proceeds to remind Sofia of her place in the social and financial hierarchy of dominant society by asking Sofia if she wants to work as a maid. Sofia responds, "Hell no," and receives a slap from the mayor for her insolence (73).

Sofia rejects the roles racism dictates as appropriate for her. She refuses submission to white authority and behaves in a manner she deems practical— perhaps even soulful. Her rejection of her place within a community of role players, however, solicits an overtly violent response from the white men who gather around her. Celie, the novel's protagonist and narrator, says, "They crack her skull, they crack her ribs. They tear her nose loose on one side. They blind her in one eye. She swole from head to foot. Her tongue the size of my arm it stick out tween her teef like a piece of rubber. She can't talk. And she just about the color of a eggplant" (74).

After suffering this brutal beating, Sofia is sent to jail where she works in the prison laundry. Her final punishment for insolence and for the assumed prosperity Miss Millie observed in town is to work as the woman's maid, teach her to drive a newly purchased car, and chauffeur her in that car when necessary.

In both the film and the novel, Sofia's injury is communicated through a disposition of silence and bodily posturing that suggests the integrated nature of her physical, mental, emotional, and spiritual hurt. The novel describes her as "yellow and sickly"; her demeanor is described as being like that of a "slave" (75, 85, 86). For three years she does not laugh or act as if she is living in the world. The psychiatrist and trauma specialist Henry Krystal refers to this type of reaction as a *psychogenic death*, a "psychic closing-off" wherein "a mere vestige of self-observing ego is preserved" (81).[5] In the film, Oprah Winfrey, who plays the character, dramatizes Sofia's brokenness, or psychogenic death, by not only lowering her head but also slowing her steps. She assumes a mode of behavior, of standing, speaking, and not speaking, that reveals externally the character's submission to internal injury. For Sofia, resistance leads to physical assault, which then leads to a devastating mental acceptance (de facto symbolic violence) that threatens soul murder.

Like Celie, who accepts a continual wounding experience in her relationships with men, Sofia, who is confronted with devastating racial hurt and assault, is complicit with that wounding through silence. Unfortunately, she uses Celie's method of survival only to discover that acceptance of spiritual wounding is no answer to the threat of soul murder.

Celie struggles with spiritual wounding from the opening lines of the novel. In fact, her wounding is so severe its relationship to the living death of soul murder is suggested by the words deleted in the character's first letter to God: "I am." That dramatic inscription of death introduces Celie as the novel's "walking dead." The film version of her story actually places her in that role as she walks behind the wagon carrying her mother's casket. A small piece of the cloth hanging outside the casket lures the viewer's eye down as the camera pans toward the spokes of the death wagon's wheels. The spokes, moving inward, seem to beckon Celie to move deeper into the funeral march by joining her mother inside the casket. Celie ignores the beckoning. She does not lay down her life as Ciel attempts to do in *The Women of Brewster Place*. Instead, she endures the pain of spiritual assault daily, relinquishing her will to that of others while ignoring any personal desires she might have.

Her ability to abdicate self to spiritual woundedness is a model for Sofia, who "becomes" Celie during the most difficult moments of her imprisonment. "Every time they ask me to do something, Miss Celie, I act like I'm you. I jump right up and do just what they say" (75). But, after living for years with Albert, who is an abusive husband, Celie rejects her subject position as a self-deprecating, spiritually injured woman and reclaims her life by speaking out and announcing her decision to leave town with Shug Avery. Encouraged by Celie's decision to take charge of her future, Sofia not only imagines ways to survive—she does survive. Sofia finds the courage, the soul power, to resurrect herself. Her ability to do so shocks everyone:

> If you hadn't tried to rule over Sofia the white folks never would have caught her [Celie tells Harpo].
> Sofia so surprised to hear [Celie] speak up she ain't chewed for ten minutes.
> That's a lie, say Harpo.
> A little truth in it, say Sofia.
> Everybody look at her like they surprise she there. *It like a voice speaking from the grave.* (175–76, emphasis added)[6]

Spiritual wounding like Sofia's is a central cause of the devastating effects pain has on individuals and communities in many of the texts surveyed here. As the root of wilted desire and defeat, spiritual wounding often accompanies and may even precede the oppressive experience of racial hurt, which Himes describes as the cruelest wound and the deepest cut to bear. Both his and Sofia's experiences of racial hurt highlight spiritual wounding as a prelude to the soul-shattering potential of prejudice, hate, and fear.

Soul Food

Authors who align spiritual wounding with pain in African American literature do not always suggest death and silence as its eventual resolution. Sometimes spiritual wounding is depicted as an economically profitable and productive entity existing within various fields of racially codified value systems. The music industry is one of the most profitable of these fields, especially when we consider the role blues music plays in soothing spiritual woundedness. If willfulness and courage are basic concepts within soul power, then the blues, balancing on the sharp edge of both, is soul food. As Trudier Harris notes in *South of Tradition* (2002), "[s]inging the blues does not solve problems, but it does boost the spirit sufficiently to continue to deal with the problems" (14).

In *Blues, Ideology, and African American Literature,* Houston A. Baker Jr. comments that "the blues performance contain[s] lyrical inscriptions of both lack and commercial possibility . . . . creativity and commerce" (9). During the 1920s the blues industry flourished. While offering several weekly releases, labels like Victor, Gennett, Okeh, and Columbia experienced successful sales in the "hundreds of thousands" (Baker 12). For years, the blues grew as a trope of suffering synonymous with black pain. It was tangible, marketable, and, regrettably, appropriated in ways that compromised its authentic connections with the black phylogenetically conceived self. For many African Americans, the representation of the blues in various popular venues, including literature and film, became too closely associated with debased and perverse behaviors. For them, negative racial marking (the commerce and symbolic capital of the blues) ultimately rendered this music a source of shame—a site for denial and cultural misrecognition.[7]

Pain is a reckonable presence within the African American blues tradition, a communicated and sensed experience shared between singer and audience. It provides the blues with a powerful and authentic pedigree of meaning recognizable through texture, depth, tone and structure of voice, and engaged emotion. In other words, the blues embodies pain and gives it an articulated presence—a presence one can feed to the soul as fuel for tomorrow's pain-filled fights. In Gayl Jones's *Corregidora* (1975), for instance, Ursa, the novel's protagonist, gives voice to pain through her music. Experiences of personal and historical woundedness are not only heard as she sings, but they are also felt.

Ursa is physically, mentally, and spiritually wounded by her body's relationship with past and present acts of overt and symbolic violence. After a physical attack that ends in the removal of her womb, her voice is recognizably endowed with articulated pain and woundedness. Her friend Cat is the first to recognize the change. "Your voice sounds a little strained, that's all. But if I hadn't heard you before, I wouldn't notice anything. I'd still be moved. Maybe even moved more, because it sounds like you been through something. . . . you sound like you been through more now. You know what I mean?" (44).

Much later, Max Monroe, the owner of the club where Ursa sings, tries to name the thing that makes her voice so special. For him, Ursa's is a wounded, wounding, and enthralling blues voice. It is a presence with texture and substance. "You got a hard kind of voice," he tells Ursa. "You know like callused hands. Strong and hard but gentle underneath. Strong but gentle too. The kind of voice that can hurt you. I can't explain it. Hurt you and make you still want to listen" (96).

Pain's audible presence gives Ursa's career as a blues performer a boost. Everyone who hears her sing is attracted to her music and, by extension, to her (in some cases both sexually and emotionally). Ursa's blues speak from her soul and connect with other souls. In this novel, the soul is a safe space where emotions are stirred if not also conjured. It is a place where movement through pain to safety can be at once pleasurable, hurtful, and impossible to resist.

The novel makes clear the intimate relationship between soul power and the blues. Ursa's repertoire of songs, for instance, includes titles like "The Broken Soul Blues," which speaks unmistakably of soul wounding. "People always got real quiet on that," the narrator tells us (159). As audiences connect with the emotions and complex mental experiences of pain and pleasure that extend from Ursa's blues, there is silence. Sometimes there are even tears. The novel presents a forty-eight-year-old blues veteran who speaks of this as he compares Ursa to Billie Holiday: "You know you made me feel good sanging. You made me feel real good sanging. . . . You know the onliest other time I felt good was when I was in the Apollo Theater. . . . Billie Holiday . . . sang for two solid hours. And then when she finished, there was a full minute of silence, just silence. And then there was applauding and crying" (170).

Pain's presence safely and soulfully "mastered" is manifested in ways clearly linked to the blues singer's ability to perform the blues and, thereby, maintain not only a career but also economic security. Although Max is attracted to Ursa sexually, he rejects the urge to "have" her because it would not end well for his business. Ursa is "safe" from an undesired touch because she masters pain and returns it to the world outside her self in a "palatable" and profitable form—in her music. Max would not risk losing the financial benefits of her "soul food's" success for a moment of physical pleasure. For the blues singer and those who benefit from her or his song, pain equals money, pleasure, and power.

But there is a danger in becoming too connected with pain or too indebted to woundedness—even for the blues singer. The man described before as the blues veteran in *Corregidora* points out how this danger affected Holiday. "If you listen to those early records and then listen to that last one, you see what they done to her voice," he comments. "They say she destroyed herself, but she didn't destroy herself. They destroyed her" (170). Although this may be true, is it not also possible that her racial vulnerability overcame her ability to resist submission to symbolic violence?

According to Holiday's autobiography, *Lady Sings the Blues* (1956), which was made into a movie in 1972, the singer experienced physical attacks from Southerners who did not appreciate her brand of entertainment, particularly when she sang "Strange Fruit," a song about lynching. She also suffered racist rejection in the form of back-door entrances and broken romances. Indeed, "They" (and, by this, I mean primarily those who control the field of music and decide who will and who will not be a success) did contribute to Holiday's retreat into soul murder. "They" used her talent for profit and pleasure but forgot her humanity. Holiday, however, played a self-destructive role in her demise. She chose an escape from pain that had no power to accomplish its task. Instead of saving her, it threatened the one thing she had that could: her soul power. Holiday's spirit was attacked by racism's mortal wounding, but she died of complicity through drug abuse.

Mattie, in Naylor's novel, recognizes Ciel's suffering as a mortal wound existing beyond the range of what is considered "normal" mourning behaviors. She does not heal her friend by aligning their personal stories, analyzing the cause of pain, masking it with drugs, or otherwise misrecognizing it. Although a concern for and understanding of each potential source of misrecognition certainly assists Mattie's ability to retrieve Ciel from impending death, they are not central to her healing. To uproot and dislodge pain's overwhelming effects, and to help Ciel overcome it safely, Mattie connects with a history of woundedness and lost children, a past inscribed on Ciel's body and present within her dying soul. Ursa also connects with her history and survives it safely. She feeds her soul by giving voice and soul-cleansing expression to the pain that threatens it.

Apparently, Holiday was unable to do the same. She failed to dislodge or uproot racial hurt successfully because she failed to recognize and abolish a potential threat to her soul. By masking racial vulnerability and the threat of soul murder with drugs, she became complicit with them, allowing racial hurt to splinter her "silver mirror" to the point of death.

Blackpain

In the 1998 motion picture *Living Out Loud,* an intoxicated white woman ascribes the talents of an African American nightclub singer named Liz Bailey (played by Queen Latifah) to a racial and biological inheritance of pain. "I swear you make me cry," the woman says, "because when you sing it's not about just you, it's not about now. It's the whole black experience. You know what I'm saying? Because, you see, black people—African American people—when they sing sentimental songs it's not sentimental. Not sentimental. Right? You know why? It's because of the pain . . . because of the pain to back it up . . . it's the pain . . . you have the pain." Dispersed throughout the woman's speech, mocking her words and her assumptions, are the dismissive replies of Queen Latifah's character: "Oh yeah, . . . the pain, . . . Yes, I see. . . . I have the pain. . . . I'm just filled with pain."

Pain is the singer's role, the part she is asked to play in the drama of "living out loud." The white woman's comments offer no other reason for the singer's presence, no other reason to listen to her song. The only point of the scene is to emphasize the value of black people, specifically black artists, as living memorials to a pain-filled past.

Although the white woman in the scene appears ridiculous and unwittingly racist, her assumptions are not far out of line with the racial myths defining black bodies in America. For this woman, and many others like her, no matter what is occurring or what the circumstances of assembly might be, the individual whose body is black is always a reminder of the gruesome realities that sustain an impenetrable link between racial terrorism and black pain. The white woman, in acknowledging this, thinks she is vindicated, removed from the frame of those who cause racial hurt, when in reality, she is promoting a legacy of suffering that separates her from those with whom she is attempting to identify. Her verbal and visual assault amounts to overt violence.

She has wounded her victim with eyes that watch but see nothing beyond the mythical logic of black bodies as a metaphor for a legacy of pain.

Queen Latifah's character, with her flawless physical appearance and pain-free disposition, demonstrates that tangible evidence of African American suffering does not have to exist for a body-reading public to assume knowledge of black pain or be held captive to stereotypical perceptions about it. As much as we might like to deny it, sometimes when we see black skin, we assume the presence of pain. It is there either as a history embedded in the tones and texture of the flesh or as a mythology accepted as truth. This kind of image-reading allows the black body to function as a metaphor for suffering, injury, and pain (which I call *blackpain*). This perception and potential for meaning has evolved into a mythico-ritual logic (that is, intelligence drawn from the integration of history, myth, and ritual) that aligns black people inextricably with a pain-ridden legacy. It is a legacy once thought to influence and color everything African Americans create—particularly art and literature.

Irving Howe, the critic and editor of *Dissent Magazine,* falls victim to this logic in his 1963 essay "Black Boys and Native Sons." Howe claims black literature is produced beneath the pressure of "a pain and ferocity that nothing could remove" (qtd. in Ellison, *Shadow and Act* 111). For him, pain is a necessity in matters of black genius. It is the ultimate "truth" motivating black writing. Ralph Ellison responds to this accusation in "The World and the Jug" by challenging the prescriptive mandate:

> I must say that [Howe's comments] brought a shock of recognition. Some twelve years ago, a friend argued with me for hours that I could not possibly write a novel because my experience as a Negro had been too excruciating to allow me to achieve that psychological and emotional distance necessary to artistic creation. Since he "knew" Negro experience better than I, I could not convince him that he might be wrong. Evidently Howe feels that unrelieved suffering is the only "real" Negro experience, and that the true Negro writer must be ferocious. (*Shadow and Act* 111)

Chester Himes also comments on the willingness of white publishers to buy into and promote the stereotype of pain's inseparable connection to black creativity. Himes claims his resistance to the stereotype is why the publishing industry rejected his novel *Black Sheep*. He writes, "American publishers are not interested in black writers unless they bleed from white torture. I was beginning to bleed, but I had not bled enough by the time I wrote that book. This attitude might also apply to the white American readers of novels. I have never heard the phrase 'It's a beautiful book' applied to a book written by a black writer unless the black characters have suffered horribly" (72–73).

Hilton Als charges the publishers and editors of *Without Sanctuary* (2000) with the same narrowly focused acceptance of black people as pained. Als claims his role as a cliché is the only reason he was invited to write an introductory statement for the volume of lynching photography.[8] "In writing this . . . I'm feeding, somewhat into . . . 'white euphoria,' which is defined by white people exercising their largesse in my face as they say, Tell me about yourself, meaning, Tell me how you've suffered. Isn't that what you people do? Suffer nobly, poetically sometimes even? Doesn't suffering define you?" (40) Als describes himself sarcastically as the player of assigned roles, the "fool" in collusion to be displayed for the pleasure of "white folks." In other words, he is the voice and body of blackpain.

As suggested in the introduction to this study, living a pained existence is "un-American." *True* "Americans" are constructed as virtually pain-free individuals who live in economic prosperity and political authority while helping others move beyond the painful realities of unfortunate circumstances. These circumstances assume a racial specificity that provides those who are not black a superficial means of escaping responsibility for and ownership of certain types of experience. For them, black bodies are not only memorials to black pain, they also serve as vessels for all the disposed, diminished, and denied experiences rejected by white-nation principles and belief systems.

One way these systems preserve a pain-free national image is through the maintenance of the black body as an absent presence within the state—a substantive, monitored, and contained vessel of pain. Such beliefs circumscribe a world and a people unmade symbolically as human beings, as U.S. citizens, and as individuals by pain's incomparable grip. According to this mythology, the only purpose for such a person's continued existence is to serve as a receptacle for other people's suffering (and sexual perversions), an "other" existing to support a nation's belief in its pain-free status. This could never be more poignantly communicated than in the 1999 film *The Green Mile*.

The movie presents a stereotypically large, infantile, frightened, and ignorant black protagonist, named John Coffey (played by Michael Clarke Duncan), who is on death row for the murder and rape of two little girls. In "Melodrama in Black and White: Uncle Tom and *The Green Mile*," Linda Williams rightfully describes the film as falling within the "mainstream of the negro-philic Tom tradition—that is, in the tradition that privileges sympathy for the unjust suffering of black victims. . . . [and] a Christ-like and Tom-like black acceptance of racial injustice" (16). Although this is an astute reading of the film, another exists. The cultural politics of *The Green Mile* not only ask its viewers to accept "a melodramatic misrecognition of virtue," as Williams insists, but they also offer a cinematic design that insists readers misrecognize and deny the regulatory action and mythology of exclusion sustained through the film's interplay of blackpain and black virtue (19).

The film falls into the recently popular "magical black man" category because of Coffey's peculiar magical powers.[9] He can absorb into his body the suffering and disease of others, healing them of pain and saving them from the threat of death. This is what he is attempting to do when arrested for rape and murder. He is trying to revive two dead girls. Although a "crazed" or "mad" white man (who is executed later for another offense) was the one who killed them, Coffey tells everyone he was trying to "take it back; but it was too late." He was trying to "take" death and injury "back" into his body, which, as we can see, is where it belongs in the symbolic system of blackpain. The statement interpreted this way—that he takes back what is rightly his—suggests that both death and injury are somehow inherent to his existence and to the collective black bodies he represents. Coffey is convicted of murder not because of overwhelming evidence but because everyone misinterprets the meaning of his confession. To them he is a black man explaining what happened after he raped and killed two little white girls. That he was neither the little girls' murderer nor their rapist has little bearing on his fate. The head prison guard, Paul Edgecomb (played by Tom Hanks), is the only one to correctly interpret Coffey's words, but even he permits the man's uncontested execution.

The audience is forewarned of this ending when Percy, the evil and most inexperienced guard in the movie, introduces Coffey's arrival on death row by yelling repeatedly, "Dead man walking." At this point in the film, we do not know the black man's name or why he is doomed to die. All we know is that his sentence has rendered him empty of life. He is a body, walking to its final destruction. It is from this metaphorical lifelessness, a spiritual death, that the audience gets its first glimpse of the character as an icon of blackpain—a sign representing America's desire for a pain-free existence. The black man's magical talent—one he uses to free several white characters of pain, suffering, and disease—makes clear his usefulness to the nation-state.

Coffey takes into his body the pain and illnesses of everyone associated with the state prison system (that is, the nation-state). He cures Edgecomb's painful urinary tract infection, making Edgecomb sexually virile and disease free — purified. He also heals the warden's dying wife of cancer. When a white inmate dies painfully in a botched electrocution, Coffey feels his pain as he has felt none other. The characters assigned to view the execution run from the horror they witness, knowing the inmate is suffering in a manner they cannot bear to watch. But as the camera shifts from Coffey to the execution chamber and back, we realize the white inmate feels nothing. Although his body jerks, he is silent. Blow by blow, Coffey takes the man's pain into his body until anything touching Coffey (including the air around him) is fired with the explosive energy of pain. The force of it is so strong that we might conclude Coffey absorbs into his body both the dying man's pain and the sin of the guard, Percy, who intentionally botches the execution.

In all except this case, Coffey's magic concludes as he releases the absorbed pain in pellets that explode from his mouth and float into the air like bees from a hive. He is weakened by the experience, but he survives. After the electrocution, however, only part of this happens. Because the inmate dies, he, like the little girls, cannot receive a pain-free "existence." Although Coffey tries to contain the man's pain and "take back" death, human mortality defeats his efforts. As the inmate lies still (and on fire) in the death chamber, Coffey feels "mighty tired" and folds himself into a fetal position to rest. His "rebirth" upon waking does not free him of his responsibility and task as pain's vessel, however. He continues to function as the leveler of white suffering until his own execution, even endowing Edgecomb with a gift of longevity by simply touching him. When Coffey's usefulness as a receptacle of pain ends, he is disposed of — thrown away without reprieve.

John Coffey is never presented as an individual, a man whom we know. Neither do we feel a need to know anything about him. He enters the movie a stranger and remains a stranger throughout the story. By its end, we know nothing about his history, his family, his work, his likes and dislikes, his age, or his desires. We are not sure where he comes from or how he came to be near the girls he is accused of killing. And because of his abnormal size and unusual talent, we wonder if he is human at all. Instead of entertaining this possibility, the film asks us to read into Coffey's existence only those things we have been told. First, Coffey is a "dead man walking," a body void of "real" life, functioning as a depository for white (male and female) Americans' pain, suffering, and criminal misdeeds. Second, he exists within the "house" of the state (the penitentiary), but he is not a subject (employee) of the state. Third, his only "job" (his only reason for being) is to cleanse those who are in danger of being bothered by virtue of their inability to escape pain's grip. And fourth, he is the "cancer," the infection, the unwanted and uncontrollable growth that somehow found its way into a world dominated by the pure and worthy; he must be expunged.

Even a mouse, freed magically from pain and inevitable death, is worth more than this man, for the mouse gains his life and immortality while the black man who granted his stay (as in stay of execution) is killed. The white world controlling Coffey's destiny sentences him to death for crimes he did not commit and purges itself of disease, blame, and discomfort by using him as a container for its pain; he is then discarded like a used bandage. Although his story is fictional, it is a frightful reminder of how unjust and horrific U.S. "justice" can be when we refuse to see beyond myths and racist fictions.

According to Linda Williams, the film "rescues white Americans from the guilt of putting the innocent black man to death. . . . What is striking . . . is the remarkable extent to which the establishment of white virtue rests upon a paradoxical administration of pain and death to the black body so that white people may weep" (*Playing* 20–21). However, because the mandates of containment and image control (agreed on by the subjects of this nation) define black people as the inheritors of pain, something more is at stake.

Popular perceptions linking black bodies to a legacy of pain compromise, and sometimes diminish completely, the power of the human voice and will to support and encourage soul survival. Under its weight, black artists and everyday folk, like John Coffey, become memorials to pain and receptacles of a nation's unwanted injury and illness—both social and physical. While Coffey loses his life, Liz, in *Living Out Loud,* loses her individuality. Both are victims of a naturalized communal association with pained bodies.

Unlike Ursa in *Corregidora,* Liz is not perceived, in the scene discussed earlier in this chapter, as the owner of a powerful and soul-feeding voice. Unlike Billie Holiday, her song is not soul food, at least not to the white listener speaking to her. The white reader of the black body in the scene misrecognizes the singer's niche as a healer and provider of soul food. Liz becomes instead an image of pain operating very much like the black woman in Edmund Burke's story, which confines to black bodies the assumed and inherent pain of blackness (discussed in chapter 1).

Even closer to Burke's proposal is the "pain killer" in *The Green Mile,* John

Coffey. The black body is an icon of blackpain functioning primarily as a myth-ology of substitution and containment. The film, therefore, provides insight into how blackpain defines and cleanses the white nation and its constructed image of U.S. citizenry while concealing the realities of African American lives and individuality—rendering such knowledge both superfluous and unneces-sary. Like Coffey, blackpain provides a space where experiences converge to dominate meaning and life. Within that space, "[p]ain defines both voice and body, the speaker and the spoken" (Davis 396).

In this way, the black body remains a site of compromise and containment: compromise of human dignity and life and containment of unwelcome or un-American experiences. Racial wounding persists under these conditions and with each strike of human abstraction brought on by the imposition of memorialized pain, soul murder and social death occurs. Without a Mattie Michael to rock us past the memory of ancient wounds and racial hurt, heal-ing evades us.

Frequently, cultural representations intended to revise misrecognition, calm racial vulnerability, and soothe the alienation of personal hurt fail to do so. Why? I suggest that when the representation of the black body is too closely tied to a history of terror, suffering, torture, and national woundedness, it can-not break free. When life and Being are made subordinate to physical vulner-ability and suffering, the body is bound, as an abstraction, to pain. It becomes *blackpain,* a metaphor void of soul. Being and, therefore, soul are made sub-ordinate to body. It is impossible to experience or recognize the healing rem-edy of soul power when there is no soul offered for consideration.

Two

Pain's Diminution

De only way tuh keep a lie frum gittin' foun' out is tuh stop tellin' it.
—Bert Williams, "Bert Williams Joke Books"

3 | **Personal Protests and War**

> I will sometimes go to sleep crying. I think about what he must have suffered. I ask the Lord why did he have to suffer? If they had just shot him, that could have been so much easier to bear. And in one of those question sessions, the Lord showed me, revealed to me, the way he looked was the personification of race hatred. That is what race hatred looks like—Race Hatred is Ugly.
> —Mamie Till Bradley, quoted in Plaines, *African American Holocaust*

In September of 1955, Mrs. Mamie Till Bradley, the mother of fifteen-year-old Emmett Till (whom she called Bobo), challenged America's commitment to justice and equality by revealing to the world what racism had done to her only child. Her decision to "show the world" provided one of the most profound images of blackpain associated with the mid-twentieth century Civil Rights Movement. Karla Holloway comments that Bradley's "insistence made certain that the ravages of racism, etched into her Bobo's poor, dark body, would inscribe the cultural moment" (*Passed On* 130). To do that, she had to expose her pain, not through language, but through the power of the gaze, for, as she admitted, she could never put into words the horror and hurt she felt on first seeing her baby's lynched body:

> [W]hen I saw [his face] the right eye was lying on his cheek. His tongue had been choked out by the weight of the fan [that weighted him in the Tallahatchie River] and the barbed wire that was around his neck was still attached to the fan, parts of both ears were missing. . . . The back of the head was practically separated from the face area. The mouth was wide open. You could only see two of the three remaining teeth. . . . I realized that here's a job that I got to do now and I don't have

time to faint; I don't have time to cry. . . . I got to make a decision and my decision was that there is no way I can tell the world what I see. The world is going to have to look at this. They're going to have to help me tell the story. (Qtd. in Malcolm R. West 16, 15)

Bradley's decision to let her son's broken, mutilated, and bloated body lie in an open casket for four days gave over 600,000 people an opportunity to share her pain as they filed past his casket or viewed his face, unrecognizable as belonging to a child, in magazines and newspapers across the nation and the world. She challenged symbolic violence by allowing the world spectatorial access to her (and her son's) pain. Because of her actions, "Emmett's death gained a transcendent metaphoric value," a value that moved others toward action (Dyson 196).

Bobo's corpse became a trope representing race hatred. As a result, blackpain became, in this case, evidence of racism's sadism and the symbol of a nation's shame that encouraged Blacks and Whites to join forces against racism and do something to disempower notions and attitudes that condemned a child to such a horrible death. Till's body subverted its intended use as an instrument of discipline and control initiated by the racists who lynched him and, as a consequence, fired the indignation of millions. In this way, shame and guilt (perhaps even a bit of aversion to being a silent accomplice of racism's barbarity) influenced an event broadly acknowledged as the catalyst of the modern Civil Rights Movement.

This was possible because most people have an irresistible and almost always justifiable desire to look on such horrors from a distance. The emotions, sense of moral obligation, and guilt such desires can create within those who watch or gaze on the results of horrible behaviors are valuable to social activism—but only if the horror is recognized and accepted in ways that lead to remorse and change. If remorse and change are stimulated via the gaze, blackpain functions as a powerful resource for the advancement of civil rights and justice. Seeing is confirmation, and, in many cases, visual confirmation is enough to transform complacency into moral outrage and fear into action— as in the case of Emmett Till. Michael Eric Dyson comments that the visual exposure of Till's body gave his death the force needed to "galvanize a people perched on the fragile border between heroism and fear to courageously pursue meaningful and complete equality" (196).

But when does seeing for the benefit of confirmation and reflection violate its own boundaries and move into an arena of perverse pleasure? Is there a role for guilt in moments when visual reflection becomes voyeurism? And what is the difference, anyway? This chapter considers these questions while also reviewing a few instances in literature and popular culture when black-pain emerges as an instrument of social activism, personal protests, and war.

Defining Guilt

As a tool in the arsenal of civil rights activism, black suffering solicits action through guilt. Sometimes guilt is nothing more than the recognition of the vilifying potential of inaction. I call this *civilizing guilt*. On other occasions, guilt emerges from moments of scopophilic pleasure. This type of guilt is more personal, more private, and therefore, more easily ignored as guilt than any other. Civilizing guilt, for instance, occurs once the witness of blackpain actively couches what he or she sees in terms of privilege and disadvantage, right and wrong, moral and immoral, pride and shame. It encourages the perpetuator of harm, as well as the agent of vicarious assault (those who witness black pain but do not participate directly in it), to respond by changing the circumstances of inequality and injustice through social action. Self-indulgent or scopophilic witnesses to blackpain, however, respond to scenes of inequality and inhumanity with selfish preoccupation, pleasure, and denial. Their actions in response to what they witness are most often self-protective and self-absorbed.

In "Three Essays on the Theory of Sexuality," Sigmund Freud defines watching as a pleasure and the individual watched as an object of curiosity. According to Freud, "The force which opposes scopophilia, but which may be overridden by it . . . is shame" (251). Since shame means the overthrowing of scopophilic pleasure, and vice versa, those who reject shame for pleasure are guilty of enjoying the spectacle of pain's horror, if nothing else. No adult escapes the choice suggested here. From Freud's perspective, only children are "essentially without shame." Only they experience scopophilic pleasure in its spontaneous, and thereby shame-free, manifestation ("Three Essays" 269).

Scopophilic guilt, then, is not guilt at all, but the residue of guilt. It is what remains when an individual recognizes and then denies the shame of viewing the pained or suffering "Other" as an object of curiosity, the victim of a pleasurable and controlling gaze. Unlike the witness experiencing civilizing guilt, this witness of blackpain reads (and dismisses) the guilt of inaction through a narcissistic lens that sees nothing of the humanity within those who suffer.

Neither do such witnesses see a need to become "too involved" or make any effective or, possibly, self-transforming changes. They sense that watching uncritically the suffering of pained black bodies poses a threat to their ability to remain innocent and shame free. They may even feel pity for the victim of violence and abuse but reject such feelings by denying that they exist. Instead of recognizing guilt and shame as possible charges against themselves, those guilty of scopophilia misrecognize blackpain as nothing more than entertainment or as an opportunity for satisfaction, visual pleasure, "easy innocence and escape from judgment" (Steele 88).

"Strange Fruit"

Diverse reactions to visual representations or images of black pain appear in documented responses to Billie Holiday's "Strange Fruit." Altruistic images set beside racism's sadistic horrors and presented in this song have proven blackpain's ability to move people to activism and to pleasure at the same time—thereby forcing a decision between the two types of guilt I just described. In New York's integrated nightclub Café Society, audiences listened to Holiday's rendition of this song and felt the chill of its subtle call to action. As an articulation of blackpain, or what the record producer Ahmet Ertegun called "a declaration of war" and Holiday called her "personal protest," "Strange Fruit" motivated activists during the 1940s to take a stand against lynching (Holiday 84).

"The germ of the song," Holiday says, "was in a poem written by Lewis Allen [Abel Meeropol]. I first met him at Café Society. When he showed me that poem, I dug it right off. It seemed to spell out all the things that had killed Pop. . . . I have to keep singing it, not only because people ask for it but because twenty years after Pop died the things that killed him are still happening in the South" (84). The irony of using "Strange Fruit" to honor a loved one and encourage activism is that the measure of its effectiveness depends on the listener witnessing a verbal image similar to, if not also duplicative of, the very activity Holiday condemns. "Witnessing 'Strange Fruit' at Café Society [was] a visual, as well as an auditory, experience" that called on the listener to watch the body of a lynching victim as it decays against a Southern landscape (Margolick 49).

Holiday closed each set with the song. Before she began, the lights were dimmed and all service stopped. Waiters, cashiers, and everyone else stood or sat quietly. A single spotlight glowed and seemed to suspend the singer's face against a darkened stage. No one in the audience was allowed to leave or speak while she performed the song. According to Holiday, "the waiters made a habit of going up to the noisiest characters and saying 'Miss Holiday is afraid you aren't enjoying yourself. Pay up and go'" (Margolick 50). When Holiday finished singing "Strange Fruit," she left the stage quietly and did not return—regardless of how loud or how sustained her curtain calls were. Such attentiveness to atmosphere and stage direction gave Holiday's performance a solemnity that summoned the physiological, psychological, cognitive, social, and behavioral components of the human pain experience.

The lyrics to "Strange Fruit" forced audiences not only to witness imaginatively but also to participate in the horrible spectacle of a world where one might stumble on a poplar tree and find, hanging from its strongest branch, a lynched black body. As Holiday sings, the audience is encouraged to experience the "Scent of magnolia sweet and fresh and the sudden smell of burning flesh." The song's use of irony strips any trace of a human spirit from the memory of the black body in pain. Each line juxtaposes natural and unnatural experiences of sight, smell, and taste. Holiday's poignant description of torture and overkill forces listeners into the roles of voyeuristic witness and recreational consumer of racist terrorism. The singer comments on the sometimes crude misinterpretations of the song that emerged because of its popularity and scopophilic value as entertainment: "One night in Los Angeles a bitch stood right up in the club where I was singing and said, 'Billie, why don't you sing that sexy song you're so famous for? You know, the one about the naked bodies swinging in the trees.' Needless to say, I didn't." Holiday describes this woman and others like her as "squares and cripples" (84).

The truth of Holiday's words can and did also move those hearing the song beyond an understanding of it as entertainment. Instead of being "sexy," her words indict audiences for their inability or unwillingness to intervene against the unnatural consequences of hate and human disregard. By emphasizing the terrorism and trauma visited on the natural landscape of the South and the bodies of black people, the lyrics call for the recognition of civilizing guilt and human sensitivity. Holiday recalls an experience in a club on New York's 52nd Street that demonstrates the remarkable power of the song to strike a responsive cord in both her audience and in her:

> I finished a set with "Strange Fruit" and headed, as usual, for the bathroom. I always do. When I sing it, it affects me so much I get sick. It takes all the strength out of me. This woman came in the ladies' room at the Downbeat Club and found

me all broken up from crying. I had come off the floor running, hot and cold, miserable and happy. She looked at me, and the tears started coming to her eyes. "My God," she said, "I never heard anything so beautiful in my life. You can still hear a pin drop out there." (85)

This woman's description highlights the image's potential as a source of scopophilic guilt. She was moved to act on a self-reflexive impulse, grounded in innocence—an act free of self-judgment—when she followed Holiday into the ladies' room. "I never heard anything so beautiful . . ." the woman says. The song has a different effect on Holiday, who, by singing it, draws a picture of violation so criminal it wounds and condemns as the visual it recalls solicits and encourages civilizing guilt. Holiday is at once pleased with her ability to conjure the scene and convicted physically by it. In other words, she is made to feel a sense of guilt in its creation. Sick, she leaves the area where the body she imagined and produced through song "hangs" shrouded in silence. I propose it is her racial vulnerability and the recognition of her body's association with blackpain's symbolic capital that weakens Holiday's spirit, rendering it "broken up" and in need of repair. For her the performance is not "beautiful" but symbolically potent and thoroughly wounding.

Suspended between the deceptively soothing tone of Holiday's voice and the horror of lynching, listeners are riveted to the image of a black body rotting in the sun. Perhaps they are not quite sure what to do with the feelings the image solicits within them. The words of Holiday's song encourage her captivated (if not also captive) audiences to experience a range of emotions, extending from bitterness and incensed humiliation to denial, guilt, and fear. For some, these emotions were soon dismissed as the residue of intense pleasure and entertainment. For others, they settled in a wave of antilynching activism.

The visual representations of the black body in pain and the political economy of the gaze can be used to level difference, encourage outrage, and intensify activism against social injustices. It can also be a call to reconciliation or a charge to remember both the ugly and the beautiful within human interactions. There are, however, more sadistic effects to consider.

Secret Pleasures

Instead of being hopeful of healing and change, some witnesses of black bodies in pain are consumed by a voyeuristic desire for visual confirmation of white subjectivity and superiority. For these individuals, blackpain identifies those who belong within particular spheres of influence and "camaraderie" and those who do not. In other words, blackpain defines those whose U.S. citizenship and power within the white nation are legitimate and those for whom this is not the case. Ralph Ellison makes note of this in *Invisible Man* (1952), where the American voyeur is a solid white citizen who just happens to be racism's most unsuspected victim.

In a scene known as "the battle royal," a desire for the voyeuristic pleasure of witnessing blackpain spins out of control—at least for the black boys who are literally shocked by the depth of its thirst and moral abandon. A group of successful white educators and businessmen entertain themselves by watching ten blindfolded black boys fight for money. In *The Culture of Bruising* (1994) Gerald Early claims that "prizefighting is a remarkable metaphor for the philosophical and social condition of men (and, sometimes, women) in . . . mass society" (xiv). This is certainly the case in Ellison's novel. The spectacle concocted by the white business men in "the battle royal" is a metaphor for the insurmountable difficulties facing Blacks who wish to achieve an American identity, or anything else that is American, while pain (real and imposed) controls and centers their actions and opportunities.

The invisible man finds himself a pawn in the white men's games because of the abilities that distinguish him from the stereotypical Black "norm." He is a talented public speaker who sees himself as an up-and-coming Booker T. Washington—a leader with dignity, pride, and confidence in the American Dream. We see him as a boy with a future, a past, a family (his grandfather is mentioned twice in the scene), an education (he is a high school graduate), desire, expectation, and the ability to feel shame and pride. We are able to see the invisible man as a human being who is fighting to achieve a self-defined reality and an unchallenged American identity.

In the scene, a "magnificent blond," who dances for the intoxicated white men hungry for fulfillment of their voyeuristic pleasure, represents America and its desirability. According to the invisible man, who steals a glimpse of her as she stands before him, the only thing she wears is a "small American flag tattooed upon her belly [just above where] her thighs formed a capital V" (19). On the surface, the woman's role in the text is that of an erotic dancer, but in a more broadly defined schematic her presence conforms to the contours of subjectivity and to the ownership white male superiority demands. In other words, she represents that which the black boys can never have: freedom to touch, hold, enjoy, and claim an American identity. This privilege belongs to white men, who, after the woman's performance, fondle her and toss her into the air. She and the country her body represents belong to them. Only they can control and share its promise and beauty as they wish. That the woman leaves the room with "terror and disgust in her eyes" tells us how miserably these men fail to do either responsibly (20).

In her nakedness the woman not only represents the United States but also the availability of the American Dream and its promise to fulfill the desire of all legitimate citizens who have "vision." I use the word *legitimate* because the invisible man and the other black youth are viewed as illegitimate Americans, and for this reason they are denied the pleasure "she" promises. Instead they are teased, tempted, and frightened by her presence. The invisible man explains, "[T]he big shots [were] yelling at us. Some threatened us if we looked and others if we did not" (19–20). Either way, the "big shots" maintain control of the gaze. By denying the black boys ownership of a freely determined return gaze, they prevent the boys from claiming any part of what the woman represents.

Before and during "the battle royal," the white businessmen and educators threaten and encourage murder, mutilation, and, of course, pain. The invisible man recalls that "[t]he harder [the boys] fought the more threatening the men became" (24). As "the battle royal" ends, the men direct the invisible man and the other boys, dazed and drenched in blood, to collect their "pay," which the men toss on a rug. The invisible man describes this harrowing moment in detail:

> I lunged for a yellow coin lying on the blue design of the carpet, touching it and sending a surprised shriek to join those rising around me. I tried frantically to remove my hand but could not let go. A hot, violent force tore through my body, shaking me like a wet rat. The rug was electrified. The hair bristled up on my head as I shook myself free. My muscles jumped, my nerves jangled, writhed. But I saw that this was not stopping the other boys. Laughing in fear and embarrassment, some were holding back and scooping up the coins knocked off by the painful contortions of the others. The men roared above us as we struggled. . . . Ignoring the shock by laughing, as I brushed the coins off quickly, *I discovered that I could contain the electricity* — a contradiction, but it works. . . . Suddenly I saw a boy lifted into the air [by the white men], glistening with sweat like a circus seal, and dropped, his wet back landing flush upon the charged rug, heard him yell and saw him literally dance upon his back, his elbows beating a frenzied tattoo upon the

floor, his muscles twitching like the flesh of a horse stung by many flies. When he finally rolled off, his face was gray and no one stopped him when he ran from the floor amid booming laughter. (27, emphasis added)

The invisible man learns several lessons during his experiences in "the battle royal." The most important one he learns through courage and shrewd thinking. When encircled by white men who block his escape from the elec- trified rug, the invisible man finds he is faced with the same fate as the boy who ran from the room in pain. He avoids it by rolling away from the men's clutches and moving through the experience of pain while using laughter and his mind to contain its effects. He comments that pain "seared through the deepest levels of my body to the fearful breath within me and the breath seared and heated to the point of explosion. It'll all be over in a flash, I thought as I rolled clear" (28). To survive the pain of electric shock, Ellison's protagonist learns to "control" it.

Instead of being controlled or contained under surveillance, the invisible man inverts the meaning of the experiences and events. First, he steals an un- monitored glance at the naked woman, thereby assuming the power of those with "vision." Then, he uses that power to control and restrict his experience of pain. As impossible as it sounds, "the battle royal" teaches him that the most effective way to emerge whole from moments of torture is to absorb its pain into the deepest levels of his body, where its effects are curtailed and contained "to the point of explosion."

Unlike *Invisible Man*, James Baldwin's "Going to Meet the Man" privileges the triumph of scopophilia over shame and guilt by exploring the thoughts of the one who tortures. In this short story, sadistic arousal is achieved by watch- ing a victim's reaction to pain. Violent demonstrations of power, which, in the story, stimulate marital sex, begin in scenes between a white deputy sheriff named Jesse and a young black man whom he calls "boy." The violence on black bodies continues throughout the narrative as the author uses flashbacks to call forth the sexual connotations and symbolic capital of blackpain.

The young black man, "boy," is the assumed leader of civil rights protesters who refuse to stop singing and protesting their unjust treatment as citizens during a town "voter" registration. Because he refuses to instruct the group to stop singing, he is beaten horribly and taken to jail. Jesse recalls the incident, and others, as he lays beside his wife unable to perform sexually. He recalls beating the young man, touching his testicles with a cow prod and kicking him in the jaw as blood runs across the jail floor. Even as he watches and recognizes a living body lying before him, he fails to categorize that body as human. "This ain't no nigger, this is a goddam bull," he thinks as he hovers over the "boy." The narrator tells us that when the "boy" is unconscious, Jesse becomes aroused at the sight of his tortured body (233).

The victim of violence in Baldwin's short story is much like the victims in Ellison's "battle"—pained, abused, and observed for the benefit of another man's pleasure. This young man, however, is seen by his tormentor as an animal with the power to withstand severe physical attack. His jailhouse tormentor, Jesse, also like the white men in Ellison's novel, experiences a sadistic pleasure connected to his ability to wound and watch the pained results. Jesse's pleasure is enhanced, however, by a childhood memory he later identifies as the lynching, castration, and ultimate destruction of a black body.

In his memory Jesse recalls a moment of human recognition and narcissistic reflection: "He saw the forehead, flat and high, with a kind of arrow of hair in the center, like he had, like his father had" (246). This moment of reflection contributes to the narcissistic nature of Jesse's scopophilic encounter with blackpain and, in this case, so does the juxtaposition of the mother's beauty with the beauty of a black body in pain. The narrator explains, "[Jessie] watched his mother's face. Her eyes were very bright, her mouth was open: she was more beautiful than he had ever seen her, and more strange. He began to feel a joy he had never felt before. He watched the hanging, gleaming body, the most beautiful and terrible object he had ever seen till then" (247).

The "strange" stimulation described here as "joy" that the child, Jesse, feels when looking at his mother is immediately transferred to the sweat-covered body of a tortured black man. Following this recognition and juxtaposition of blackpain with the mother's physical allure and beauty, Jesse witnesses the black man's castration by knife. In that moment he recognizes the threat and the possibility of his own castration. In true Freudian fashion, he is instantly alienated from the mother and aligned with the father, his father, whose "face was full of sweat, his eyes were very peaceful. At that moment, Jesse loved his father more than he had ever loved him. . . . Jesse's father took him by the hand and, with his mother a little behind them . . . they walked through the crowd, across the clearing" (248).

A bond is built between father and son through the "secret" pleasure of blackpain, which Jesse describes as "the key to his life forever" (248). This pleasure violently forces Jesse through the oedipal experience and builds, for him, an association of black male genital violation with feminine allure and, by extension, sexual attraction and pleasure "forever."

The end to these early morning reflections is the revival of sexual desire and performance. As Jesse lies next to his wife, his thoughts drift again to "the boy in the cell; he thought of the man in the fire; he thought of the knife and grabbed himself and stroked himself and a terrible sound, something between a high laugh and a howl, came out of him and dragged his sleeping wife up on one elbow" (249). Having been unable to perform sexually earlier, the deputy sheriff is now able to satisfy his wife as never before. His pleasure exists alongside the desire for self-elevation and a psychological, perhaps even subliminal, transfer of immoral vision, control, discipline, and potency from the site of blackpain and scopophilic pleasure to sexual performance.

There is an almost unavoidably voyeuristic quality in America's relationship with black bodies in pain, which Jesse's experience highlights. The attraction or psychological cachet of excitement, when drawn to the extreme, is explosive. For Holiday, the explosion is internal, confusing, and physically exhausting. Ellison's text focuses the readers' experience on the explosive possibilities and explores methods of controlling it. James Baldwin describes the explosion from the point of view of the tormentor. For his protagonist, Jesse, it is "a curious and dreadful pleasure" rooted in sadistic sexual arousal and release ("Going" 239).

In each of these texts, blackpain is communicated as a presence and an influence that defines beauty, draws out secret desires, and validates father-to-son legacies. Black characters receive a legacy of pain and communal struggle while white characters receive power and sociopolitical power. Yet, even within this structure of racially controlled and predetermined outcomes there exists the threat of an explosion. Its repercussions are not so well controlled—the explosion of social activism, resistance, and a realization that both are part of a denied reality guardedly called an American race war.

Baldwin hints at this threat when he writes that the old men who were once what Jesse is now—enforcers of white-nation law—behave differently than they did when Jessie was first learning his profession. Now they are fearful of the unknown, especially since "[e]xplosions rocked the night of their tranquil town." The unspoken question surrounding the thunder of those explosions is who controls them. Who lights the fuse that rocks each night's violence? "Each time each man wondered silently if perhaps this time the dynamite [intended to destroy black property and black life] had not fallen into the wrong hands"

(237). The victims of black pain have the capacity to fight back and can be moved to resist racist domination through violence and organized warfare. Knowledge of this makes the old men's fears even more terrible. Baldwin's narrator explains that the white men "could not possibly know every move that was made in that secret place where the darkies lived. . . . [T]hey *knew* that some of the niggers had guns. It stood to reason, as they said, since, after all, some of them had been in the Army" (237, emphasis in the original).

"Going to Meet the Man" speaks directly to the warlike possibilities in the field of racial struggle. The author and his characters are aware that beneath every war this country has ever fought is a metawar of race, a subfield of constant resistance and secret battles, wartime trauma and personal sacrifices. Baldwin writes, "They [black and white men] were soldiers fighting a war [World War II], but their relationship to each other was that of accomplices in a crime. They all had to keep their mouths shut" (238–39). They are America's secret bearers.

The psychoanalyst Dori Laub discusses a similar role shared by Holocaust survivors. He comments, "Survivors often claim that they experience the feeling of belonging to a 'secret order' that is sworn to silence" (67). This "order" is similar to the one Baldwin creates in the statements quoted in the previous paragraph. Laub maintains that the "truth" of Jewish dehumanization by way of Nazi persecution is what keeps survivors silent. He writes, "The implications of this imaginary complicity and of this conviction of their having been chosen for a secret mission are that they believe, out of loyalty, that their persecution and execution by the Nazis was actually warranted" (67). Baldwin's characters are certainly keeping a secret of dehumanization; however, they are also maintaining the situational delusion of an America populated by equals. Baldwin's protestors are the young ones whom Laub describes as being able to see that the emperor has no clothes—the ones who are not "conforming by staying within the confines of the delusion." His soldiers, however, are the keepers of a delusion.[1]

No one besides other American soldiers can know their shameful secret. They cannot reveal the lie at the core of their union as comrades for democracy. Thus, the "thrilling silence," shared by both black and white men, cloaks the reality that during World War II they were engaged in two wars—one fought at home and one fought in Europe (238). This secret moves the text beyond the bonds of undisclosed pleasures, which Jesse shares with his father, only to redefine that bond in war terms at the conclusion of the story.

In the metawar of race and racism, the greatest enemy American soldiers must battle, according to Baldwin's story, is one "of terror . . . unreadable and inaccessible to themselves." Baldwin tells us this terror arises from a "past, [which] while certainly refusing to be forgotten, could yet so stubbornly refuse to be remembered" (238). The great secret of racism's metawar and its role in the development of white-nation sociodicy, then, is the dependence of both on African American collusion and denial. Beneath that secret and its masking of racist horrors lay the vulnerabilities of America's claim to equal treatment and national unity sheltered, silenced, and relentlessly contested.

War

Elaine Scarry contends that "*it is when a country has become to its population a fiction that wars begin,* however intensely beloved by its people that fiction is" (131, emphasis in original). On August 31, 1989, in Brooklyn's Bensonhurst division, this possibility emerged from a domain of secrets and intuitive terrors in a dramatic, although not physically threatening, way. This day is identified by some as the "Day of Outrage" when nearly eight thousand people marched down Flatbush Avenue in protest of Yusef Hawkins's murder. Hawkins, a black teenager, had been shot and killed by a mostly white gang eight days earlier for being where his murderers thought he should not be. "Whose streets? Our streets! What's coming? War!" the marchers chanted as they moved through Bensonhurst. The march ended and no other battle cries were heard—at least not in Bensonhurst.

In *The Coming Race War? and Other Apocalyptic Tales of America after Affirmative Action and Welfare* (1996), the University of Colorado law professor Richard Delgado spends a great deal of time contemplating this issue. Delgado argues that because of the losses minorities suffer beneath diminished support for affirmative action, reduced welfare benefits, and dismissal of multicultural programs in colleges and universities, America will undoubtedly face a race war before the end of the twenty-first century. He claims that because Americans of European descent will cease being in the majority by midcentury, leaving African Americans (and other minorities, particularly Hispanics) to control the vote and, therefore, control various centers of power, this move toward "war" will be intentional. To prevent the transference of power and the resulting political domination of those currently considered minorities, Delgado warns, radical leftist and white "opinion-makers" are "gearing up for a fight" (120). "The cruder elements are arming, while conservative churches are preaching a return to early values—thinly veiled references to race—thus laying the theological basis for a race war" (125).

Although Delgado cites "rollbacks, which go far beyond those necessary to save the budget or provide the poor with an incentive to work," as the primary causes of war, he admits that they do not improve black poverty or eliminate the need to police racial justice (126). That is not the goal of such policies and laws. The true goal is to "save America as a white society." Speaking as a member of a colonized American minority, Delgado claims that supporters of white-nation sociodicy try to achieve this objective by "increas[ing] minority *misery* to the point we react, to the point violence breaks out" (120, emphasis added). I described this breaking point earlier as a point of explosion.

Delgado argues that minority rebellion will give the power-holding subjects of the state reason to employ drastic means of control in escalating degrees until a system of apartheid exists. If rebellion in the form of civil unrest and war flourishes across America, as it most likely will under such restrictions and acts of blatant racism, not even the Supreme Court will be able to protect minority rights. According to Delgado, that distinguished body of mostly Caucasian men can and will override both the Bill of Rights and the Fourteenth Amendment to preserve the "compelling state interest" of a white-governed, white-dominated society (121).

Delgado's arguments are provocative; however, they misrecognize the very social processes that I believe constitute America's race war. Anticipating a race war to come sometime in the near or distant future requires a prerequisite of denial. To view an American race war as "coming," we must forget history and deny recent acts of murder and terrorism that prove African Americans are constantly under siege. We must blind ourselves to cinematic and literary docudramas, produced during the last two decades of the twentieth century, which offer war as a metaphor for American race relations. We must ignore, for instance, the filmmaker John Singleton's use of war as an organizing theme in *Rosewood* (1997). In this film, two men (one black, one white) join forces in a battle against foes who destroy a prosperous black town.

Drawn from historical events, the film captures the warlike dynamics of racial conflict that resulted in the massacre of citizens living in Rosewood, Florida, on January 5, 1923. Characters openly compare the events in which they are engaged to battle by claiming, "We're in the trenches now," as they arm themselves to fight. In the tradition of soldiers, they salute during the film's denouement in honor of a battle well fought. And, although the strain of racial distrust exists between them, their relationship offers clear and obvious clues to the film's use of war as a metaphor for race relations in this country.

Other films present the race war more subtly. *Mississippi Burning* is one of these. When Mr. Ward (Willem Dafoe), the lead FBI agent in the movie, calls for one hundred men to search a swamp for the bodies of three missing civil rights workers, his colleague, Mr. Anderson (Gene Hackman), comments, "Don't do it, Mr. Ward. You gone start a war." Noting the history of violence and animosity between the races that preceded the workers' disappearance, Mr. Ward answers, "It was a war long before we got here." Indeed, the race war is more an American tradition than a future possibility. It is a legacy handed from father to son and mother to daughter for two-and-a-half centuries. One of the heroes in the film *Rosewood,* a character called Mann (Ving Rhames), draws attention to this legacy as he assigns a little boy the role of lieutenant in the war in which they are engaged—thereby emphasizing the father-to-son and generational inheritance that is the American race war.

In literature, characters like Tyree Tucker, a mortician in Richard Wright's *The Long Dream* (1958), confront the realities of death and survival by casting both against the backdrop of an American race war. Tucker explains in terms of war the lynching of a young black man to his son, Rex (or Fishbelly, as he is called most often in the text). "Son, this is race war, life and death. . . . They [white-nation advocates] fight us in the street, in the church, in the school, in the home, in business—they fight us everywhere" (66). The battles Tyree references are fought on a subfield of social and political struggle where the race war is omnipresent. Its battles, persistent although often mystified, are denied as such, yet they emerge in everyday life with causalities like Yusef Hawkins, and the numbers continue to mount.

Cinematic and literary recreations of historical moments do little to soothe the intensity of these battles. Instead, they help define what is at stake while refining the boundaries of battlefields that seem to expand daily. On occasion, they may even buttress the race war's political necessity—particularly when the stories told are framed as narratives about a war within a war. Filmmakers and writers rescript history as narratives in which war sets the stage for American race relations and blackpain marks the limits of both patriarchal power and legitimate exchanges of that power from father to son.

John Singleton's film *Rosewood* (1997), Carroll Case's novel *The Slaughter* (1998), the 1989 motion picture *Glory*, and the director George Tillman's *Men of Honor* (2000) demonstrate distinct ways fictionalized histories of African American suffering are formulated as fact, "packaged" for public consumption and inserted into cultural memory. In each text the instability of white-nation patriarchal control, rules of subjectivity, and social monitoring are concealed by the presence and symbolic capital of blackpain.[2]

Lacan's "phallic order" governs the socializing events in these texts. Beneath scenes "retelling the stories of history" lay narratives filled with socializing connotations and restrictions that work to empower white men, culturally and politically, over all others. My subject texts use violence to mask the exchange of power and patriarchal partnerships. Violence minimizes awareness of the naturalizing processes that support white patriarchal hegemony and its racially organized "logic of socialization" (Tate 195).

In *Rosewood*, for instance, sex and sexual stereotypes conceal the story's negative intraracial politics and symbolic violence. Both are banished to the margins of this race war as the male representatives of the story's white and black communities reject the body of Jewel (Akosua Busia), a very dark-skinned black woman. John Wright (Jon Voight), the white storekeeper and her lover, who joins the black community's cause in battle, refuses to protect her. Her body, rejected, cast aside, and apparently raped by the community's white invaders, is never mourned. She is a symbolic sacrifice for cross-racial male bonding and a symbol of colorism's painful consequences.[3] Hers is also the body of blackpain through which a message of gendered exclusion from the ownership and inheritance of power is communicated. Although the film represents a victory in the race war for those who escape or survive racial violence, this victory distracts viewers from black women's defeat in terms of gender socialization.

Race-war violence in relation to black women in this film is excess, cloaking a message of black female negation while confirming male alliances and the continuity of patriarchal inheritance as it moves from fathers to sons. Not even the death and "burial" of Sarah Carrier (Esther Rolle), the dark-skinned black woman killed at the massacre's start, honors or empowers black women. Instead, her death provides a means of escape for her son, who hides in a discarded piano box beneath (behind) her corpse until he is able to join the other men in battle. In this black director's film, Sarah Carrier's body functions as a sign of and sacrifice to blackpain. It is a site for sanctuary that conceals a black son's racial vulnerability. Because she dared speak the truth about a white woman's charge of rape against an unknown black man, Sarah represents the revelation of truth silenced and denied. Both she and the hidden truths she represents are the now-dead things that threaten no one. In this role, she and the pain her (now harmless) body symbolize offer safe passage for her son through the horror of war. Since there is no father from whom he can inherit power, Sarah, as mother and sentinel, sneaks him safely past the white "guards" of patriarchal control and domination. The result is his assurance and security as an inheritor of the victor's reward.

Much like scenes of violence in combat films, violence in films depicting the metawar of race and racism can be used as cloaking devices for diverse socializing activities and messages. Susan Jeffords explains in her much-anthologized essay, "Masculinity as Excess in Vietnam Films: The Father/Son Dynamic of American Culture," that "scenes of violence in combat films, whether as fighting in battle, torture, prison escapes, or explosions," are

> the point of excess, not only for the filmic narrative but for masculine subjectivity. Because the continuous progression of (social) narrative depends upon the stable positioning of power as affiliated with the father, exchanges of power between fathers and sons or transferences of power in which the son becomes the father cannot be openly articulated. As breaks in that narrative continuity through productions of excess as spectacle, combat sequences provide deferring arenas from such exchanges and allow transferences of power to occur, at the close of which power relations, though altered, appear continuous and stable. (990)

Unlike most war stories, however, the violent activities in the texts surveyed in this chapter invert the function of surplus violence in terms of patriarchal power and its exchange. *Rosewood, The Slaughter, Glory,* and *Men of Honor* present blackpain as spectacle and as victory. It is a surplus suggesting the presence of power and its possible exchange between white and black men. The negative symbolic capital of blackpain as surplus, however, fails to honor this promise.[4] In fact, it communicates just the opposite by actually maintaining and defending established boundaries covertly.

Blackpain provides white and black men with avenues to alliance in these texts. It redefines vulnerabilities as strengths and disproves racially determined pathologies. And, although there seems to be a power exchange or an accommodation made toward racial unity in each, there is none. The status quo remains unchanged, although challenged, while progress toward the goals of power exchange, patriarchal authority, and inclusion is suggested but never fully achieved.

Glory

The very desire for patriarchal authority appears to be absent in *Glory*, directed by Edward Zwick. This film was the first successful attempt to set before an American audience the Civil War and the accompanying metawar of race. Based on letters written by the twenty-five-year-old white regiment commander of the all-black Massachusetts 54th Volunteer Infantry, Colonel Robert Gould Shaw, and the 1973 commemorative book *Lay This Laurel* by Lincoln Kirstein, the film depicts battles from both the American Civil War and its metawar of race. This is a film worth celebrating for its daring portrayal of black Civil War soldiers and for the pride its revelations have brought to African Americans, many of whom learned of this history only through the film. Yet, *Glory*, like so many other dramatizations of black history, fails to develop black characters as inheritors of patriarchal power.

The soldiers' characterization—particularly that of Sergeant Major John Rawlins (Morgan Freeman), Private Jupiter Sharts (Jihmi Kennedy), and Private Trip (Denzel Washington)—effectively demonstrates the commitment of the black men who fought in the Civil War. But neither the fight against racism nor their desires for an inheritance of power are the focus of the film. Instead of hearing the soldiers' thoughts about the race war or seeing, extensively, how the men whom black characters represent fought against wartime prejudices, viewers gain insight into the strategies of war and the race metawar as engaged in by Robert Shaw (Matthew Broderick), the film's hero. Through *Glory* we learn how a white man balances the demands of both a national conflict and the day-to-day battles of a racial conflict during the Civil War.

We see Shaw violently oppose the army's dismissal of the men's need for shoes and contest the vandalism in which they are forced to engage, but we do not see the men protest these inequities or unethical behaviors for themselves. And although Rawlins reports to Shaw about the men's need for shoes, and Private Trip encourages their protest against a salary discrepancy, we see little else from the black soldiers in the way of protest or effective resistance against racism.[5]

We do see these men grow, however, into dedicated soldiers and warriors for the protection and advancement of American freedoms. Private Jupiter Sharts, who cries when being a "man" becomes too difficult, grows in courage and refuses to return home after being injured. The others meet death with courage. Before their final battle, they hum an evocative melody in witness to the valuable sacrifice they are about to make for the cause of freedom (a sacrifice of life). Through their emotional and physical pain, we learn of their courage. We also learn that their desire, as presented in this film, is not for equality but, as Rawlins testifies in the pre-fight scene, for "freedom" and an honorable, pain-relieving death.

Private Trip, who does not even merit a first name, is the primary black character protesting unwarranted neglect and suffering. Besides the pay incident, in which he is the central motivator of resistance, we witness him seeking food and female companionship at the risk of being deemed a deserter. The punishment he receives for this poorly conceived act of resistance does little to bring full humanity to the development of this character, however. He is whipped like an animal. The result is a persona the audience sees as an erring adolescent. It is a degrading experience, soliciting viewer compassion for his pain and for his loss of masculinity. Eventually, Rawlins tells him that his attitude, if left unchanged, will prevent him from being anything more than a "nigger." Trip's pain is a metaphor for the pain of all abused slaves, and as a result, it renders his role in the war, and the role of all black soldiers in this film, no different from that of the slaves they meet as they march toward their deaths. His role as "rebellious nigger," we are told, gives him little chance of reprieve from this fate.

One reason for this imbalance may be because the film is based on Shaw's letters and not the thoughts of the black soldiers. Although there were other letters available, none were used to explore the complexities of the metawar–Civil War dyad in terms of a black fight. Corporal James Henry Gooding, for instance, sent letters home for publication in his local newspaper, the *Mercury* of New Bedford, Massachusetts. He even wrote a letter to Abraham Lincoln in protest of the pay discrepancy he and the other black soldiers faced. His eloquent plea gives us a picture of how the black soldier saw and experienced the metawar of racism at this time.[6]

Despite Gooding's eloquence and conviction, there is no mention of him, his resistance to racism, or his letters of protest in Zwick's film. In *Glory,* the race war is not a war to be recognized or fought by Black Americans but by their white advocates, saviors, and heroes. The bodies of black men who attempt self-appropriation and self-defense are rendered pained and punishable. We see this played out as the soldiers, whose feet are wounded for lack of cover, beg for shoes and are punished for acting independently to reduce personal pain while Shaw is allowed to rage against those who deny his soldiers relief from such pain and moments of compromised dignity. Private Tripp, for instance, is charged with absence without leave and whipped when he attempts to secure personal comfort. Shaw, however is never punished for his insubordinate behavior when he destroys the "sacred temple" where the prized footwear is stored. In fact, both his behavior and his assumed protection from retribution are archetypical with Christlike undertones.

His impassioned act of "fatherly" protection is not rewarded. When Shaw and "all" his men die at Fort Wagner, the question of who controls patriarchal power is answered and the denial of its apparent transfer to black sons (even sons who are soldiers) is confirmed—and the attempt at transfer is punished. In this film, the white father never relinquishes power to the black *son*. The idea of such a transfer, as well as the "traitor" (Shaw) who dared attempt it, is buried when we see the soldiers' and Shaw's bodies dumped into a collective grave.[7]

The Slaughter

This type of disrespect for the bodies of black soldiers surfaces again in the dénouement to a Southern myth documented, examined, and revised in literature a century after the Civil War. The story of the massacre of the 364th Infantry Regiment at Camp Van Dorn in Centerville, Mississippi, has long been considered little more than a myth—a bit of Southern folklore. Whether the whispering behind locked doors is more than that—whether the massacre really occurred—has yet to be determined. There has been much suspicion and doubt, however, about its existence as strictly "myth." Events and conflicting attitudes leading to the alleged massacre are manifold, but perhaps the most important, in terms of this study, originates in black people's characterization of their circumstances in the United States as like being in a war.

Edna McKenzie, the historian and journalist, reflects on this period in U.S. history for a PBS documentary titled *The Black Press*. She recalls the attitudes of the press and the people for whom it spoke during the late 1930s: "We were at war and in war you don't have friendly relationships. You're out to kill each other. . . . We were trying to kill Jim Crow and racism and the lynching that was going on, that had gone on all century." This position is validated and supported by the *Pittsburgh Courier*'s instigation of the Double V campaign during World War II.

"Victory at Home, Victory Abroad" was the goal for black soldiers who viewed the world war as an extension of the ongoing race war they faced in the United States. The paper and the nationwide supporters of the Double V campaign considered the violence and terrorism of racism more than isolated events. They considered them combat strategies of a powerful foe. By encouraging pride and giving it a name, the *Pittsburgh Courier*'s call for Double V was a battle cry taken so seriously that some black soldiers reportedly burned its insignia (the interlocking double Vs) into their chests (O'Connell "Mysterious 364th," pt. 2).

The campaign was meant to encourage the fight against racism by building the morale of all African Americans during a bloody era tense with racial hostilities. According to Corporal Wilbur T. Jackson of the 512th Quartermaster Regiment in Camp Van Dorn, "All the white farmers and civilians [were] armed at all times and [seemed] to want a pitched battle with Negro soldiers" (O'Connell, "Mysterious 364th," pt 2). These hostilities climaxed in events shrouded by mystery and denial. According to eyewitnesses and investigative reports, ranging from those of journalists and other writers to rumors and declassified documents, a tragedy of monstrous proportions occurred at Camp Van Dorn in 1943. Some think of the events that summer as "minor incidents." Others remember only a skirmish, perhaps a riot. I describe it as a metawar.

Carroll Case documents the summer's events in a docunovel titled *The Slaughter: An American Atrocity* in which he claims the U.S. Army gunned down 1,200 black soldiers, then hid the atrocity by burying its victims in mass graves and ice-packed railway cars. (Witnesses confirm that railway cars carried the bodies of at least fifty executed black men from the camp.) In a 1999 report, the U.S. Army responded to Case's book by denying that anything happened to the soldiers. But by April of the next year, their "facts" were proven incomplete and inconsistent, if not also intentionally misleading and contrived, lending reason for suspicion. Using evidence drawn from declassified army records and intelligence files from the national archives (extensively edited) recovered by the NAACP, the journalist Ron Ridenhour and other investigators suggest that at least part of Case's fictionalized docunovel is, perhaps, more than fiction (O'Connell, "Mysterious 364th," pt. 2).

Their findings reveal first that a mysterious fire in 1973 destroyed military personnel records crucial to any investigation of the incident. Second, materials on which the army based its 1999 reports are unavailable to the public and researchers. Among these are confidential medical records maintained by the Surgeon General, records that explain or describe injuries pertinent to the alleged massacre. Third, Malcolm La Place, the regional headquarters clerk for the 364th Regiment, maintains that he documented everything happening in the camp, including the disappearance of several black soldiers. This "Regimental Journal," however, shows no entries during most of the regiment's stay in Mississippi (from its arrival at Camp Van Dorn until November 4, 1943). Fourth, La Place claims his name is forged on journal pages the army reports to have recovered from 1942. His charge appears valid, since records show he did not join the service until 1943.[8]

Because of the inconsistencies and eyewitness accounts surrounding the fate of the 364th Regiment, many consider Case's book a record of truth—at least the first part of it, which contains documents supporting his charge of foul play and murder. The army, however, remains skeptical, admitting only that four black men died while at Camp Van Dorn, and not as the result of a massacre condoned by the army. The facts, however, place even this in question. Geoffrey O'Connell reports that "[w]hatever happened to the 364th in the summer of '43, in December the regiment's remaining men were relocated to a far-off camp in the Aleutian Islands [1,500 miles off the coast of Alaska]. It was then that their personnel roster began to show signs of hemorrhage. Records show that between 800 and 1,000 of the 3,000 men left the 364th before the war's end. In other words, from June 1943 until Japan's surrender, about one soldier's name per day disappeared from the 364th's roster" ("Mysterious 364th," pt. 2).

Similar facts and supporting documents are presented in the first fifty-four pages of *The Slaughter*. The second part of Case's book, subtitled "The Evangeline File," is a fictionalized story featuring a white man's investigation of the "massacre," which ends with the same misleading ambiguity and display of blackpain as *Glory*. This occurs mainly because its author leaves the promising ground of documentation and factual analysis to develop a mystery novel filled with all the intrigue, murder, money, rape, and love of a dimestore paperback.

Instead of using the information uncovered through investigations and research to build an oppositional testimony about possible overt violence against the black soldiers, Case writes a fictionalized tale aligned with stereotypes and dominant, or hegemonic, manipulations of blackpain. Through it, he reduces the story of the black soldiers' murder to little more than the desire of a white male protagonist to sell a novel about the tragedy (as well as movie rights), win the love of a beautiful woman, and purchase a Porsche.

Case claims he wrote "The Evangeline File" in an attempt to make the soldiers' story easier to accept, not so raw and painful. He explains: "It is such a terrible, ugly tragedy, and there is an innate human hesitance to admit what actually happened. By putting it in a vehicle of fiction, it somehow makes it easier to face the truth. My ultimate goal is to finally tell the story so that wrongs can be righted and justice be done. It is my tribute to the soldiers who are buried in the red clay hills of Mississippi" (40). True as this may be, the "docunovel" actually does nothing to clarify the events or diminish the politics of speculation and doubt surrounding the men's "disappearance."

Case may have had "good intentions," but the story he tells adds to the men's tragedy by stripping them of their humanity and any future claims they and their "sons" may have had to patriarchal power. Although the novel is supposedly about their deaths as an "American Atrocity," the black soldiers do not make an appearance until the epilogue to the novel. Instead of being the focus of their own story, they are an afterthought. Even then, they are not given the dignity they deserve. Carl Brady, the novel's white protagonist, finds their bodies, "rows and rows of bodies," 796 feet below the ground in a salt mine filled with "briny tasting air" and "bloody footprints." Case describes the blood as "dried to a black crusty substance" (295). He continues his dehumanizing attack on the men as he describes their bodies: "Brass belt buckles now had a patina, and the bloody, bullet-ridden olive drab uniforms had turned to sepia. More than 50 years of entombment in an airtight salt chamber left the cadavers almost perfectly preserved. Their skin, once dark, had turned an unusual shade of blue, giving the appearance of thick leather stretched over bone. Eyes as black as marbles stared into nothingness. Still cast on their faces were the grotesque expressions of terror" (299–300).

The men are never presented as men; they are cadavers with leathery skin and marbles for eyes. They are bodies frozen with death and the bloody evidence of historical pain. Case does not free them or the story of their deaths from ostracism and banishment because he does not allow his protagonist to see this as a possibility. Bradley does not find any proof of the soldiers' lives as men. There are no signs of inheritors who could benefit from the freedoms World War II protected or the power and pride secured through the legacy of the Double V movement. Bradley finds no pockets holding pictures of children or wives, no rings signifying marriage or educational accomplishments, no letters from home. Nothing. There are only shiny brass buttons, olive uniforms, and black bodies grotesquely wed to pain and terror.

Instead of "imagining" the mystery solved and the guilty punished, Case abandons the real drama of murder and intrigue already present in the story, fictionalizing and replacing it with a tale that banishes the black family into obscurity and absence, making impossible a transfer of patriarchal power from father to son (or daughter, for that matter).

"The Evangeline File" uses the rape of a little white girl (in no way connected with the soldiers) as a substitute for the violence done to the black men and their families. The substitution devalues the trauma of the soldiers' deaths and denies the legacy of empowerment they were offered via the Double V movement. It cloaks the image of Black reproduction and national inheritance beneath a feminine, although white, image of powerlessness and victimization. The race of the child appears insignificant within these contexts until the overlay of hegemonic assumptions is considered.

Case's use of a white child encourages readers to develop or "imagine" an acceptable cause for outrage. It is important that the child is white because traditionally (and stereotypically) her race lends more credibility to the depth of public outrage Case intends to solicit. This outrage can then be transferred to the cover-up of the soldiers' murders. It validates punishing those responsible for the black men's deaths by soliciting sympathy through the horror of a little white girl's rape. Once sympathy is established, it is transferable to all characters who are wounded or stripped of personal dignity and physical rights.

Toxie, the white man who rapes the little girl, has been hired to keep the murderous deeds of the past undiscovered. He achieves this task by killing a black couple whose investigative interests in the case might lead them to the truth. Murder silences both them and the possibility of truth being recovered. It also abolishes their plans to "start their family" once the investigation is concluded (236). As a result, Toxie is immediately connected to individuals outside the text who murder and are thereby responsible for compromising the plans and legacies of black families. More importantly, he is connected to those involved in silencing black voices and covering up the "massacre" Case claims to fictionalize.

This, however, is not enough. The reader must agree that a harsh form of retribution is in order for those who obscure truth, compromise decency, and violate innocence. The rape of a child by a white man stirs the reader's emotions and provides justification for any penalty Toxie (and by extension, others like him) might suffer. Near the end of the novel, Ray Jean, the little girl's sister, burns Toxie alive. His death is not payment for murdering the couple (i.e., for destroying the lives of black couples and families, or for destroying their ability to win access to patriarchal power) but for raping a white child who, in the novel, is an icon of "American" values—specifically those of truth, moral- · ity, and justice. Her rapist is toxic. He is a poison threatening to spoil, if not kill, the image of America as wholesome and pure.

In many ways, Case's use of supplementation in "The Evangeline File" follows the racist biases Richard Wright reveals and condemns in *Native Son*. After Bigger Thomas is discovered as the murderer of a young white woman, Mary Dalton, the coroner in charge of her inquest uses the body of the black woman, Bessie Mears (whom Bigger also killed), as a substitute exhibit for Mary's incinerated one. Bessie's body is not swapped for Mary's. It is merely a visual "stand-in" for it—an exhibit used as a substitute for the human victim of murder. Although "a pile of white bones" (much like the pile of dead bodies in Case's book) is presented to the jury as Mary's corpse, Bessie's "raped and mutilated body" is used to prove Bigger Thomas committed the ultimate crime against Mary—rape. The function of the supplement in this case is explained clearly in the novel: "'It will help shed light upon the actual manner of the death of the deceased [meaning Mary],' the coroner said. . . . They were using [Bigger's] having killed Bessie to kill him for his having killed Mary, to cast him in a light that would sanction any action taken to destroy him. . . . The black girl was merely 'evidence'" (279–80).

This string of connections and substitutions is similar to the flow of supplementation found in Case's novel. In fact, we can easily paraphrase the quote using names and circumstances from "The Evangeline File": Case is using Toxie's having raped a white child to kill Toxie for the role he played in killing the truth of the soldiers' deaths.

The jury cannot see Mary's bloody and broken body; they see instead a set of bones cleaned and whitened. They are, however, shown Bessie's "bloody and black" body (282). To the jury, Bessie's corpse is an object offered to justify the toughest penalty possible for a black man who "raped" and killed a white woman, then burned her remains. The fact that Bigger did not rape Mary means nothing, especially since gender and his role as the two women's murderer links them. Through these links Bessie's rape becomes Mary's, a crime for which Bigger must pay the harshest penalty. Similarly, Case uses the rape of a white child to cast Toxie, and those like him, in a light that would sanction any action taken to destroy him.

As "evidence," Bessie's body is an abstraction, an emblem of pain, and as a symbol of pain it becomes Mary's body, but only in the manner of her suffering and death. The fact that *Bessie* died of her wounds is of little consequence.

Likewise, the black couple in Case's novel are not configured as individuals but as an emblem of blackpain (the body as memorial). The little girl who is raped does not function in the same way. She is not used to represent the black men's suffering, or anyone else's pain, but to solicit an emotional response from the reader—a response that will alienate the reader, any reader, from Toxie. The assumption, of course, is that his role in covering up the mass murder of black soldiers will not solicit anyone's disdain.

Men of Honor

Transference of another kind is present in the motion picture *Men of Honor* (2000), directed by the black filmmaker George Tillman Jr. The transfer of power from father to son is a primary theme in this film. Tillman resists presenting an emotionally "touching" story (such as the one *Glory* tells) or presenting dispirited, pitiful, or helpless characters like those found dead at the end of Case's novel. *Men of Honor* insists that its viewers wrestle with the question of deserved suffering, a question films and literary works honoring white heroes of minority causes rarely ask—or, if they do ask, it is not without the cover of a vindicating white hero's quest. Usually, however, such works avoid the question in a swell of heart-wrenching episodes depicting black helplessness and victimization.

Carl Brashear is not a victim. Throughout the movie, his character, played by Cuba Gooding Jr., fights the race war with grace, facing insurmountable obstacles with style and, well . . . *honor*. He is verbally abused, called "out of his name," almost frozen to death in a subzero lake, and crippled in an on-deck accident. Yet, he rises above each racist moment and physical injury to succeed as a navy man. If this film was not based on the life of the first African American U.S. Navy Master Diver's experiences, his heroism and determination in the face of undeserved suffering and excruciating pain would be hard to believe.[9] If the director had not given the character representing Brashear the respect and human dignity he deserves, no one would care. There would be no concern for whether he (or anyone for that matter) deserved or did not deserve the cruelty and pain he suffered. And, as a result, advocates of the white nation would be relieved of their duty to redress the role they or their ancestors may have played in inflicting similar pain.

Instead of characterizing Brashear as a black body rescued by a white friend or some other white savior, Tillman presents the story of conflict between two navy men (one black, one white), both of whom, by film's end, are equally heroic.

The parallel development of these men's lives begins when Brashear's father, Mac Brashear (Carl Lumbly), gives him a radio with the letters *ASNF* carved into one of its panels. Neither Brashear nor the audience knows the acronym's meaning until much later, when Chief Billie Sunday (Robert De Niro) decodes it and inscribes it on the panel: "A Son Never Forgets."

This moment of sentiment follows several episodes of harrowing struggle between the two men and marks the end of their conflict. Although each moment of their fight depicts a battle similar to the battles other black men faced during this historical period, the acronym introduces another theme—one like that identified by Susan Jeffords as characteristic of American Vietnam War films. Jeffords writes that these war films

> narrate the exchange, transference, or continuation of power between father and son, the defining parameters for the definitions and determination of the masculine subject in American social relations. . . . Whether those relations are failed . . . corrupted . . . or fulfilling . . . the dynamic and intention of the father/son relation remains the same: to define and determine power as existing only in and through the exchange between father and son, and to insure that alternate sources of power—in Vietnam films, women, Vietnamese, and blacks; feminism, communism, and revolution—are denied and defeated. This is what American Wars—whether fought "at home" or "in country"—are about. (987)

In *Men of Honor,* the father-son relation shifts from a powerless, poor, and hardworking black father, whose opportunities have been limited by racism and lack of education, to a poor, hardworking white father whose opportunities as a inheritor of white privilege have lifted him from the blistering work of a dirt farmer to military power and prestige. This film narrates the means by which power can be transferred to a black son during a time when black ambition was often forced to succumb to racism and the horrors of a relentless race war.

Brashear possesses the fortitude and desire to succeed. He is able to face racism's horrors without compromise and without injuring others. He saves the lives of several white comrades and, in one case, loses his leg doing so. He accomplishes each success and passes each test in spite of a white "father's" reluctance to relinquish power to a son (or potential inheritor of power) he has been taught to deny and defeat. As each challenge arises, Brashear must withstand bodily wounding and immeasurable pain to win his right to an inheritance constantly denied him. Violence and excess in the form of blackpain impedes the transfer of power in this film.

Through three central conflicts involving Brashear and Chief Sunday, the oedipal process and power transfer between father and son are developed. This transfer of power, although important, is not the only one affected by acts of violence and moments of great pain, however. There is also a violation of racial boundaries that traditionally restrict and dictate who can and cannot hold power, thereby limiting who can and cannot become "the father" (in Lacanian terms).

As mentioned earlier, both race and gender are excess in race-war narratives. Each form of excess masks the operations of the father-son dynamic in matters of power's transfer and each represents a potential site of resistance to white patriarchal power. For a transfer of power to occur in these texts, there must be a severance with the maternal and its limits, as well as a violation of the limits race (or, rather, racism) imposes.

Jeffords admits that gender is only one of the primary ways "patriarchal structures are enacted" but justifies her exclusive examination of it by reading transference of power as a form of male-enacted violence. She comments: "though the son may replace the father, the son is not the father. It is in response to and as a deterrence of this contradiction that narrational violence is produced" (992). While I agree, in terms of the race war, a different narrative is necessary. In race-war texts, the struggle that produces violence emerges through a tradition of consistency, restriction, and denial (not contradiction) that claims the black son may not replace the white father or become the father. To counter this tradition and deter its consequences, the prospective heir to power must first gain and then exceed a gendered and racial material existence.

This means that any contradictions—like the mother—must be rejected. In *Men of Honor* this rejection occurs gradually as Brashear's mother, Ella Brashear (Lonette McKee), fades into nothingness. From the beginning of the film, Brashear's mother is a background figure. She never emerges as essential to the story. We are last reminded of her when Brashear receives the news of his father's death (or we assume it is she who tells him). She has no voice in this scene. We only hear one side of the conversation—Brashear's.[10]

With the mother securely absent from the plot, Brashear and his paternal nemesis enter their first major conflict. The surface objective of this conflict is to win Brashear's Anglo-American friend reentry to the diving program (the character is expelled because of his alliance with Brashear). Thus, Brashear is depicted in this scenario as a white man's "savior." There are two other events taking place, however. First, Brashear must face a challenge that determines which of the two men, Brashear or Chief Sunday, is more potent as a paternal figure. Second, in the challenge scene, Brashear is reborn as the "son" of a dying white father.

Both men don diving helmets filled with water. In this state, they must overcome the desire to inhale. If they do not, they die—both as a living Being and as a potential threat. The challenger who fails to keep desire under control loses potency and is emasculated through demonstrated weakness. Chief Sunday faints and, thereby, loses potency. This symbolic release of life—with a stream of blood flowing from the nose—gives birth to an invigorated Brashear, who does not take off his helmet and inhale until he is assured his opponent has failed. Brashear emerges potent and, at the minimum, symbolically reborn. Chief Sunday becomes the source of that rebirth—the imaginary "father" who may provide Brashear passage into the arena of white paternal power.

The second major conflict between the men continues the theme of rebirth and endurance. After surviving several minor insults and assaults (even saving a man's life and watching a coward receive a medal for it), Brashear is almost murdered. The school's captain, "Mr. Pappy" (Hal Holbrook), orders Brashear's death to prevent him from completing the training program. To complete the program and become a U.S. Navy diver, Brashear has only to assemble a flange while immersed in a lake that one diver describes as being "cold as a well-digger's ass." Since time is not a factor in his ability to pass, the exam is little more than another challenge of will and endurance.

Standing on the lake's floor, Brashear awaits the start of his exam. In hopes that he will quit, Chief Sunday orders the bag containing Brashear's tools cut and thrown into the water. The tools spread across the dark lakebed. It takes Brashear nine hours and thirty-one minutes to retrieve them and complete the assigned task. When he emerges from the water he is shivering and gray from the pain and discomfort of his ordeal. His physical discoloration suggests the instability of race and marks it as a point of excess, masking the very real possibility of failure and miscalculation inherent in the field of white patriarchal power exchange.

To receive the white father's power, however, that father must accept Brashear as a "son." We know this requirement is achieved when Chief Sunday decodes the acronym carved on the radio. Brashear's father's parting words, his final directive, provide a means for interpreting the scene. He begins his speech before giving Brashear the radio. "Get in there and *fight*, Carl. Don't take promises. *Bust they ole rules* if you have to. And when it gets hard—and it will—don't quit on me. *Ever*! Now go on. Don't come back here. Not for a long time. . . . [He gives Carl the battery operated radio.] *Charge it when you get where you going.*" The italicized material in this quote guides my reading. First, the words *fight* and *ever* speak of the race war Brashear continues to fight throughout the film—without end. Second, the command to "charge it when you get where you going" instructs Brashear to remember (i.e., recharge), while the mandate to "bust they ole rules" signifies his duty as a solider and agent of change in the American race war.

Brashear arrives at his destiny; he gets where he is going on the day he passes the diving school's final exam. Because he passes, against the captain's orders, Sunday is demoted and sent to another facility. Before going, however, he provides the "charge" (memory) Brashear needs to hear his father's voice. By filling in the blanks of the ASNF acronym so that it reads "A Son Never Forgets," Sunday renders it and the black father's final lesson readable, complete, and decisively useful. Sunday not only provides the language Brashear needs to achieve understanding but also gives him permission to continue to "bust they ole rules."

According to the Lacanian formulation of subjectivity, identity and "the logic of socialization" are achieved through language (Tate 195, n. 11). This Lacan calls "the Law of the Father." When the acronym ASNF is decoded, Brashear moves beyond a fragmented preoedipal, prelanguage consciousness into the Symbolic or the Law of the Father. The move from acronym to the words *A Son Never Forgets,* then, provides the language necessary to achieve the contradictory, yet successful, blending and shifting from the "ole rules" of one father to that of another. Through this decoding, Brashear enters the world of patriarchal power with full understanding of its demands and complexities. "A son never forgets." With this knowledge of the codes in hand, he can now face the final oedipal conflict, which is, in part, a confrontation demanding his complicity with or rejection of a white-nation context for experiencing and encoding blackpain. As a subject or recipient of patriarchal power, he can now influence blackpain's meaning and its role in the American race war so that it speaks beyond pain. It speaks of *his* "fight" and *his* right to honor. To do this he must reject complicity and master the white-nation politics defining blackpain. In other words, Brashear must "break" the Father's Law, the Father's "ole rules" and signifying codes.

After the surrogate white father decodes the acronym, we never hear of Brashear's birth father again. The father's role is assumed by Sunday, and the transference of power is almost complete. The son has earned a right to the father's power, but the son has not "become" the father. Additionally, Brashear does not own, and therefore, cannot pass on, the power he has earned. The announcement, in the New Year's celebration scene, that Brashear's wife, Jo (Aunjanue Ellis), is pregnant addresses this concern.

It is important to note that while the news of Jo's pregnancy validates Brashear's *potency*, Sunday appears in a similar New Year's party scene that confirms his impotence. As he interacts with others who represent the Father's Law, specifically Captain Hanks, Sunday is "castrated." Hanks has been in conflict with Sunday from the moment we first meet him. After Sunday is relieved of his duties and demoted, Hanks denounces him publicly, ridicules him openly, and insults his wife. By the end of the New Year's celebration scene they fight—an act that signals a second struggle for paternal authority—this one between an older and a younger white man.

In fact, this struggle frames the entire narrative, constantly hinting at the instability and vulnerability of the white patriarchal process and its club of exclusive power exchange. The first scene of the film presents Sunday, beaten, bruised, and cuffed, sitting between two younger white Navy men, who offer him no respect. One laughs at him and reminds him he is no longer a "Master Chief" but a "deserter." Although Sunday is actually only "absent without leave" owing to a drunken binge, labeling him a deserter reveals his subject position as a traitor to his race—a man who allowed the "enemy," a black man, to gain power in a battle he should have lost. As the taunting continues, Sunday notices Brashear on a television monitor, preparing to retrieve a lost nuclear warhead. Realizing all he has lost, Sunday later cleans up and engages in a battle with Hanks to reclaim his dignity and his masculinity.

This occurs in the final scene of the film, which positions Brashear and Sunday in a two-tier father-son dyad set in opposition to the state and its authority. Defending his ability to continue as a navy diver after losing his leg, Brashear demonstrates his right to ownership of paternal power and the honor due a navy man. At the same time, Sunday defends his masculinity by proving his "decision" to relinquish power to a black man is not only his right as a potent paternal figure, but an exceptionally wise and honorable "choice." Both men prove their point by placing blackpain as a sign of endurance on display.

Masculine endurance and blackpain operate as excess, with the black body acting as a site that masks power's ultimate transference. Ironically, it is also the site where legitimate patriarchal authority is determined and established. Lauren Berlant's comments about the relationship of disembodiment and power are helpful here. "The white, male body is the relay to legitimacy, but even more than that," she adds, "the power to suppress that body, to cover its tracks and its traces, is the sign of real authority" (113).[11] To become a true authority, a true broker of power, Brashear must transcend his body; he must hide its traces (its blackness) and its pain. Sunday acts as his legitimating relay.

Wearing an extremely heavy diving suit, Brashear walks twelve steps toward Sunday, who is barking commands steadily—a demonstration of the power Brashear will later own and transfer to his son. The final few steps he accomplishes on a broken prosthetic leg. He sweats, pants, and struggles to rise above the body and the excruciating pain he experiences in it.[12] He struggles to rise above the image of himself as blackpain, part of a collective for whom suffering is a normal state of being and a primary sign of "not belonging." Only if Brashear can escape the social constructions that bind him to his body and the cultural politics that bind that body to pain and exclusion will he be able to achieve total subjectivity and clear ownership of paternal power. Once he realizes this task, Captain Hanks, the ultimate symbol of the Father's Law, concedes and pronounces Brashear the winner in a battle of will, strength, and endurance.

Brashear and Sunday salute as the scene ends. Sunday leaves, once again a full man, with his wife clutching his arm. Brashear, now the owner of patriarchal power, grips the shoulder of his son as if securing him or pinning him beneath the wing of that power. This move suggests the continuation of the father-son dynamic and the necessarily unchallenged dominance that stabilizes the hierarchy of that relationship. Standing, unredeemed, along the outskirts of both relationships is the black woman, Jo Brashear. Her absence, her subordination, to the father-son dyad is necessary for the promise of a future where transference of power from black father to black son is possible.

The black body in pain is not only the product of racist violence in film, literature, and in the social real; its surplus value is used to mask activities that threaten to expose power's most unsuspecting and impossible exchange (whether successful or not). The readings offered in this chapter focus on two uncommon characteristics cloaked by blackpain's surplus: black ownership of white patriarchal power and the transfer of that power to a black son. Within this context, blackpain is "excess as spectacle" as well as a metaphor of containment used by the advocates of white-nation sociodicy to cloak fields of conflict where the instability of white patriarchal power and the processes of its exchange are exposed and challenged.

There is nothing unique about Carl Brashear's ability to withstand the racism he faces and win the rewards he seeks. Many others have demonstrated the same courage as he. Many men and women have had the courage to withstand extreme pain and use it to their advantage. For Brashear, such courage is gleaned from the perfection of survival techniques shared by black people for centuries. The determination and willful endurance of what I have been calling *soul power* subverts the "ole rules" of white-nation ideology to create avenues and venues for a revision of power's exchange. Mamie Till Bradley called on soul power, and so did Billie Holiday. Both women demonstrated how soulful determination and courage transforms the world in which we live. It is through this soul power that black people, violated and pained, emerge safely—renewed and ready for tomorrow's perils and promises—even when the hope of survival is dominated by difficult odds and outdated rules.

4 | **Silent Mobility**

There is . . . an American Negro tradition which teaches one to deflect racial provocation and to master and contain pain. . . . to deal with it as men at their best have always done. It takes fortitude to be a man.
—Ralph Ellison, *Shadow and Act*

George Tillman's *Men of Honor* presents a heroic tale not because its protagonist, Carl Brashear, reaches his goal of becoming a navy diver but because he reaches this goal while moving silently through and beyond increasingly difficult circumstances. Although silence is an important survival strategy in his journey to success, Brashear does not achieve his victories because his relationship to it is inert or somehow natural. Neither is it a sign that he is dismissive of the prejudice and assaults he suffers. He is not considered a "man of honor" because he is more moral or deserving than his peers. He is recognized as a man and a "master" because he is able to endure extreme suffering while maintaining personal dignity.

Brashear chooses his battles carefully, remaining cognizant of, but quiet within, hurtful moments where there is no benefit to using his voice. Through the dignity his silence secures, he survives racism safely and achieves his goals magnificently. Like Brashear, the character named Mann in John Singleton's *Rosewood* also uses silence to survive racism safely. He exceeds human expectations for overcoming pain when he endures, not one, but two lynching attempts—both after he is hung and assumed well on his way to "the valley of death." In the second attempt, he is so silent he escapes the noose while his tormentors stand just a few feet away engaged in a brawl.

These stories suggest that pain can be conquered and used as a source of empowerment only if borne silently and with mobility. This silent mobility allows the individual to endure painful, difficult, and unjust atrocities with an uncompromised sense of dignity. It is a movement beyond suffering that acknowledges racial hurt without public expressions or personal submission to the limitations pain imposes. In the films just mentioned, silence is an act of resistance, inversion, and subterfuge that contains the limitations pain imposes and eases its effects at the point where endurance and racial hurt collide. At the point of explosion, Brashear and Mann invert the power of potential defeat through silent mobility, advancing their agenda against the odds while turning black pain into personal power. While others gaze at their bodies' movement toward abstraction and blackpain, these men move themselves beyond the image and toward pain's defeat.

Some find this move beyond recognizing pain easier than others. In *The Quality of Hurt*, Chester Himes (from whom I borrow the term "racial hurt") contends that achieving silent mobility is easiest if physical pain is all he has to endure. He reports that the brutality of the police officers who hung him upside down and beat his ribs and testicles with the butt of guns stuffed in felt hats was of little consequence when compared to the hurt he experienced from racism's persistent wounding. Himes describes the beating as "too much pain and not enough hurt" (56).

When he experiences pain in isolation of hurt, Himes controls it until *he* decides to "mumble" a confession. However, he finds the two, pain and racial hurt, experienced cumulatively and in concert, more difficult to control. For Himes, racial hurt is the thing to be avoided, beat back, and survived. It leaves him with scars and a profound rage that strengthens his awareness of himself as a man who "hurt too painfully" (351). For him, the weight of racial hurt threatens to violently break the boundaries of pain's containment.

There is duplicity in the relationship between blackpain as symbolic capital and silence as cultural capital that helps the wounded transcend the body's pain. This duplicity can make silence "read" as complicit with acts of social injury on one hand while offering the assurance of strength and dignity in the face of excessive cruelty and racial hurt on the other. How and where black men and women draw the line distinguishing silence that is complicit with racial hurt from silence that subverts moments of painful victimization and soul wounding depends on each individual's ability to contain pain beyond the point of explosion.

But what happens when it is no longer possible to contain pain? What happens when racial hurt explodes, or when the collisions occurring at the point of explosion spin out of control? This chapter addresses these questions while investigating the potential dangers and responsibilities inherent in an African American tradition that assumes silence as a personal apparatus containing and, thereby, disarming both blackpain and its most terrible cousin, racial hurt.

On April 30, 1836, the *Alton Telegraph*, an Illinois newspaper, reported the lynching of an unnamed Missouri slave whose response to torture transformed pain into personal empowerment and moral triumph. It is reported that the man attempted to sing and pray when flames touched his body but fell silent as fire began to consume him. He remained silent for an extended period, thereby thwarting the pleasure of the crowd, who awaited audible confirmation of suffering in a spectacle of torment, a carnival of pain.

By silently enduring pain, the unnamed slave deprived them of this pleasure. Perhaps he decided he could gain honor for himself and his community by choosing to experience death through the "safety" of a *bodily hexis* that was culturally and historically defined by black people as not only safe but also morally and ethically superior to the behaviors of white-nation advocates and aggressors.[1]

By using silence to at once become and challenge the subject position of the pained black body demanded by his tormentors' political mythology, the unnamed slave gained access to blackpain's symbolic capital. His silence redefined the meaning of his experience by bringing to it a level of human dignity and moral fortitude far superior to those who looked on and, perhaps, felt shame but did nothing. His choice of when to speak gave his death another measure of dignity. More important, he demonstrated soul power by rejecting complicity with a spectacle of human suffering. Instead, he honestly admitted his pain and soberly, without crying, asked for its end.

The reporter tells us that "[a]fter the flames had surrounded their prey, his eyes burned out of his head, and his mouth seemingly parched to a cinder, someone in the crowd, more compassionate than the rest proposed to put an end to his misery by shooting him, when it was replied, 'that it would be of no use, since he was already out of pain.' 'No, no,' said the wretch, 'I am not, I am suffering as much as ever shoot me, shoot me'" (Mattison 54). His plea did not meet a favorable response, however, and he died without uttering any other sound. In stories such as this, silence emerges as a defensive strategy, a mobility that allows torture victims some control over the way they experience and navigate moments of pain and racial hurt. It is a way of rising above victimization, if only symbolically.

Even though such fortitude is documented in reports of lynching from various sources, it seems impossible that anyone not suffering a physical impairment or illness could remain silent when burned alive or surgically cut without anesthesia.[2] Yet, such evidence does exist. Ralph Ginzburg's *100 Years of Lynchings* (1962) presents several reports of black people who chose to "contain" pain through silence.

According to articles Ginzburg collected from the *Baltimore Afro-American* and the *Washington Eagle* (among others), a man named John Henry Williams of Moultrie, Georgia, surprised the mob witnessing his lynching in 1921 by singing. The *Baltimore Afro-American* reported: "For a time the winds carried the flames and smoke directly in his face so that he could not speak. Later the winds shifted and members of the mob, unaffected, recognized the hymn he sang as, 'Nearer My God to Thee'" (Ginzburg 152). Williams, who had been made to eat his own castrated flesh, was defiant toward his tormentors and gave them little satisfaction. When asked if he had any last words, he responded with perfect disdain. Even though he was "[c]astrated and in indescribable torture he asked for a cigarette, lit it and blew the smoke in the face of his tormentors" (153).

A similar act of defiance and personal triumph occurred in 1933. Lloyd Warner remained silent while his murderers doused him with seven gallons of gasoline and set him on fire. The *New York Herald-Tribune* reported his reaction in a matter-of-fact manner. There was no need for anything more: "Warner was still alive. He was burned alive. He didn't cry out" (Ginzburg 207).[3]

Although many tortured African Americans were unable to remain quiet while suffering incredible pain, the stories of those who did are part of a behavioral script that defines suffering in silence as a source of dignity, courage, and ennoblement. It is evidence that one's will is stronger than racism's inhumanity. This belief might appear to buy into mythologies that claim Blacks do not feel pain the same as Whites. Because of this, silent suffering can be considered complicit with racism and symbolic wounding. Within an African

American culture of pain, however, it is not collusion at all. Instead, it subverts collusion, turning it inside out.

As a fundamental belief, "which does not even need to be asserted in the form of an explicit, self-conscious dogma" (Bourdieu, *Meditations* 15), suffering in silence was once so ingrained in black culture that it might be described as a behavioral-based cultural unifier. As a unifier and a defining element within an African American culture of pain, suffering in silence binds individuals to their communities through an agreed-on mandate for uniform behavior, a bodily hexis that raises the sufferer to the level of hero and martyr.

In both African American communities and cultural production, suffering without complaint or pleading offers black people a claim to moral superiority over those who inflict pain. Many believe it makes them more spiritual, more worthy of God's favor. But, like white-nation advocates who claim dominance based (in part) on tenuous mythologies and stereotypes, African Americans who accept these meanings find an assurance of superiority dependent on the presence of blackpain as symbolic capital.

This behavioral mandate is certainly why Ellison's invisible man swallows the pain of repeated electrical shock (even laughs at it) until it "seared and heated" his breath "to the point of explosion" (28). His culture demands he does so. This culture of pain directs those it claims to never react to racist cruelty and, thereby, never allows the hurt that gnaws the spirit and tortures the flesh to extend beyond one's self. It is a belief coded by an unwritten "law" demanding that sufferers never admit to the oppressor or even to themselves that silently enduring the wounds of racism's terrorism is self-destructive (symbolic violence). Instead, one must glean from the experience the strength to survive or die with as much dignity as this limited form of control allows.

African American responses to pain in the form of silent endurance have emerged, historically, for good reasons. Foremost is the desire to survive, to get along. Black mothers and fathers in the United States have always insisted their children learn how to "suffer through it" silently—*it* being any discomfort they might face during an encounter with racism (from emotional hurt to physical and spiritual wounding). Before integration, this was believed to be the only way of surviving in the apartheid South. To do otherwise was to invite pain, dismemberment, and, possibly, death. As bell hooks explains in *Killing Rage: Ending Racism* (1995), to complain, to express rage at the "myriad abuses and humiliations black folks suffered daily when we crossed the tracks and did what we had to do with and for whites to make a living . . . was suicidal. Every black person knew it" (14–15).

The cultural mandate for silence is not a belief in submission, however. Quoted in an essay in James Allen's *Without Sanctuary*, the Alabama farmer and sharecropper Ned Cobb claims, "he never submitted. To 'get along' . . . he learned 'to humble down and play shut-mouthed.' He knew to play dumb when the situation demanded it. And although he 'got tired of it,' he learned 'to fall back,' to take 'every kind of insult'" and wounding (Litwack 31). He learned to avoid the threat of death safely.

For many black people, being silent during moments of racial hurt has nothing to do with gaining power or economic and social parity with agents of white-nation authority (the passive resistance of the Civil Rights Movement notwithstanding).[4] It is a survival technique. In fact, Ralph Ellison maintains that this mandate for silence "is a tradition which abhors as obscene any trading on one's own anguish for gain or sympathy" (*Shadow* 111). Its benefits lie beyond that realm of personal influence. Survival is one such benefit; honor is another.

Silent suffering is honored cross-culturally. Individuals who accept silent suffering as valuable often revere the "redemptive, visionary implications of pain" (Morris, *Culture* 125). The suffering of Christ during his crucifixion, for instance, is uplifted in Christianity as a model of redemptive faith's perfection. It is a perfection gained, however, in the face of undeserved punishment and religious prejudice.

We find another example in Saint Sebastian, who lived in the third century after Christ's crucifixion and survived a brutal murder attempt only to succumb to death after an even more severe beating. As a model of martyrdom, his body is a popular subject for painters. In major museums, depictions can be found of him "half-naked, arms bound behind him, his legs and torso stuck with arrows. . . . a handsome male body . . . [with] up-raised eyes . . . Sebastian suffers with his gaze consistently lifted upward" (Morris, *Culture* 127). His eyes turned toward heaven appear to transcend and accept pain at the same time.

A third example is the erotic spiritual pain suffered by Saint Teresa of Avila (1515–82). Her experience of pain was so deep, so intense, she could not speak. She reports a dream in which an angel plunges an arrow deep within her heart. Although experienced in a dream, Saint Teresa's pain is real and provokes a moan from her in response. Saint Teresa and Saint Sebastian exemplify silence as a time-honored instrument or sign of growth and transition essential to experiences of visionary and mystical pain.

For African Americans, honor in silent suffering is neither visionary nor mystical, at least not in the same way and certainly not exclusively. The pain referred to here is earthbound in design, source, and consequences. It brings with it an honor gained on a field of racial conflict in which silent obedience and assent are roles assigned to African Americans as internal, colonized "captives" and subordinates. Black culture, particularly black male culture, reaches beyond that role by claiming connotations associated with the dominant culture's use of silence and silent suffering as signs of masculinity and strength (both spiritual and moral). Black folk culture denies the racialized naturalization of America's mythico-ritual belief in black inhumanity and the pained black body, replacing that "logic" with one alienated from racial indicators and markings.

For instance, in Ernest Gaines's *A Lesson before Dying* (1993), the protagonist, Jefferson, earns the right to be called a man because he dies without protest, outcry, or fear. Accused of a murder he did not commit, Jefferson stands trial. During the trial his lawyer, speaking from a racist disposition, strips him of all humanity and equates him with a hog. Supposedly in Jefferson's defense, he asks: "Do you see a man sitting here? . . . No, gentlemen. . . . A thing to hold the handle of a plow, a thing to load your bales of cotton, a thing to dig your ditches, to chop your wood, to pull your corn. That is what you see here, but you do not see anything capable of planning a robbery or a murder . . . What justice would there be to take this life? Justice, gentlemen? Why, I would just as soon put a hog in the electric chair as this" (7–8).

Jefferson believes this dehumanizing analogy and is wounded psychologically by it. His grandmother, however, does not believe it and wants Jefferson to prove it false. "'I don't want them to kill no hog,' she said. 'I want a man to go to that chair, on his own two feet'" (13). The bodily hexis implied here is one accomplished through stature, pride, and silence, not fear or any other display of racial hurt.

The entire book articulates the lesson of gaining pride, honor, and dignity in the face of an unjust and painful death. This Jefferson achieves. "Tell Nanna I walked," he asks the sheriff. "And straight he walked . . . Straight he walked. I'm a witness. Straight he walked," Paul, the sheriff, reports to Grant Wiggins, the man who provides the lessons Jefferson needs to "die like a man" (254). In this novel, silent suffering and honor are so tightly aligned that when Jefferson dies, he does so surrounded by silence. The only sounds heard during his death by electrocution are two jolts of electricity from a generator. There are no screams, no protests, and no evidence of pain—physical or otherwise.

Notably, at the novel's end, the teacher who guided Jefferson to knowledge of himself as a man stands facing a classroom of black children and cries. This is not a feminization of the character. The bodily hexis he employs is one redefining pain as weakness leaving the body: "I turned from [the sheriff] and went into the church. Irene Cole told the class to rise, with their shoulders back. I went up to the desk and turned to face them. I was crying" (256). Crying does not empty one of masculinity, the last lines of this novel seem to suggest, particularly if you are among a community of Blacks who share with you the experience of racial hurt. It is, however, unmanly and undignified to share emotional signs of racial hurt and pain with those existing beyond that community. Grant shows no sign that he is wounded while talking to the sheriff; yet, while standing before his fiancée and the classroom of children, he feels safe enough to touch his woundedness—but only through the silence of tears that cleanse and renew.

James Baldwin gives an example of the relationship between being a man and facing personal pain in "Going to Meet the Man." He suggests a resolution to the potential for symbolic violence inherent in acts of silent suffering. The character, a civil rights protestor identified simply as "boy," refuses to silence his comrades' mournful singing and is punished. During this punishment, he experiences what Himes has described as "too much pain and not enough hurt" (Himes 56). As a result, the "boy" gives voice to pain but resists submission to racial vulnerability and racial hurt. This way he gains personal power and self-respect.

The narrator tells us, "The boy rolled around in his own dirt and water and blood and tried to scream again as the prod hit his testicles but the scream did not come out, only a kind of rattle and a moan" (233). Like Saint Teresa of Avila, the "boy's" pain is so great he can only moan. Although the "natural" response to intense pain is to scream, Baldwin does not permit his male character to scream in response to the sheriff's racist abuse. Instead the "boy" separates pain from hurt and demonstrates that separation by responding to each differently. While pain solicits a soulful moan, hurt brings forth a venomous rejoinder and a threat: "'those kids ain't going to stop singing. We going to keep on singing until every one of you miserable white mothers go stark raving out of your minds.' Then he closed the one eye; he spat blood; his head fell back against the floor" (233). The character rejects racial hurt by choosing to voice his resistance to it and its source. In this way, he keeps hurt at a distance. This distance gains him dignity in the midst of an undignified and indignant situation.

There are two interpretative prongs of blackpain's symbolic capital present in the way Baldwin accomplishes this. One prong subverts the social worth of silence (as just demonstrated), while the other celebrates the redemptive and moral worth of silent mobility. By not allowing this black male character to cry or scream in response to his white tormentor, Baldwin not only helps the character demonstrate masculine endurance, but he also aligns himself and his text with an African American cultural mandate for facing pain in silence. Through silent mobility the "boy" described in this text becomes a man as prescribed within both black and white cultures. Through the moan, he demonstrates fortitude and an acceptable measure of resistance. He is a man—albeit a man existing along the borders of a dominant culture that excludes him from equitable treatment and citizenship.

Jesse, the "boy's" tormentor, reinforces the character's status on the border of white society by calling him a bull: "His foot leapt out, he had not known it was going to, and caught the boy flush on the jaw. *Jesus*, he thought, *this ain't no nigger, this is a goddamn bull*" (233, emphasis in original). The description indicates strength but does so in a manner that relegates the black man to the position of a strong male beast existing painfully on the borders of a social sphere that rejects him and, perhaps, fears him. He isn't even recognized as a "nigger," which, in Jesse's world, is a step closer to being human. If we adhere to Jesse's definition of the term, those achieving that title can occupy space *within* the social structure, which is supportive of the white nation's development and maintenance. They are the "good niggers."

Jesse, who cannot persuade the singers to be silent or engage the young black man's cooperation in soliciting their silence, reminds himself that "there were still lots of good niggers around—he had to remember that; they weren't all like that boy this afternoon; and the good niggers must be mighty sad to see what was happening to their people. *They would thank him when this was over.* In that way they had, the best of them not quite looking him in the eye, in a low voice, with a little smile: We surely thanks you, Mr. Jesse. From the bottom of our hearts, we thanks you" (236, emphasis added). Jesse expects the wounded community to act as agents of "good will" and thank him for his brutality and prejudice.

Because silence, or, rather, denial, is part of the role assigned to black people within a white-nation sociodicy, Baldwin's juxtaposition of cultural "laws" is rife with opportunities for collision between complicity and subversive action. Black subordinates, or "good niggers" as defined by Jesse, *appear* to accept the roles assigned them by using silence to solicit favor from white-nation advocates. This violation of the cultural mandate as described by Ellison is, like silence, dual in nature. While gaining favor, agents also frustrate the desires of those who watch and anticipate a very different reaction to racial hurt. Baldwin documents the dual nature of achieving favor in this way by presenting it (as exemplified before) with such irony as to expose the performed nature of the silent bodily hexis of a "good nigger."

There is a similar expression of performed agreement in *A Lesson before Dying*. Gaines's sheriff is proud and "honored" to announce the success of Jefferson's silent walk to death, describing the electrocuted man as "the bravest man in that room today." Grant, however, does not validate or become complicit with expressionless and silent suffering. For him, being brave means little when one is dead. "Maybe one day you will come back and tell them [the black children] so," Grant says in response to the sheriff before leaving him (256). His silence, like the silence of the "boy" in Baldwin's novel, is different from the shuffling performance of complicity Jesse expects from "niggers." Grant does not thank the sheriff for Jefferson's "brave death." He does not thank him for the community injury and racial hurt that death causes. His silence subverts the possibility of complicity. His tears do not represent a submission to pain. The bodily hexis of pride evidenced in standing tall suggests that they are a sign of weakness and racial hurt leaving the body—a purging of submission.

The collusion of silence with racial subordination, suggested in Jesse's expectations for "niggers," leaves black communities without transformative power and social influence in the larger society. When such behaviors fail to break radically with racially assigned social dispositions, they fail to be oppositional. However, if the "subordinate" uses a performance of agreement to renegotiate relationships within that structure, silence can be duplicitous. In other words, by adopting a subordinate's silence—which is silence that does not challenge racial hurt—the person suffering claims a space within the dominating social structure. Thus, a man can demonstrate his manhood by suffering silently while blackpain as symbolic capital functions within a white-nation sociodicy to align him and his silence with an already assumed subject position of racial subordination.

Interpretative Communities

In Richard Wright's *The Long Dream,* Fishbelly contemplates his self-worth as a racial subordinate. His ability to recognize and reconcile his body's relationship to blackpain as symbolic capital inverts assumptions of worthlessness associated with black people in white-nation ideology. "[C]uriously, he felt that he was something, somebody, precisely and simply because of that cold threat of death. The terror of the white world had left no doubt in him about his worth; in fact, that white world had guaranteed his worth in the most brutal and dramatic manner. Most surely he was something, somebody in the eyes of the white world, or it would not have threatened him as it had" (157–58).

Through Fishbelly's considerations, Wright exposes the external forces influencing black men's self-perception in this text, not by examining a character's reaction to pain, but by investigating the character's understanding of his value within a system that finds security in the threat of black pain and racial hurt. Wright denies the ability of pain to destroy this community's ability to move through silent mobility into language. Lynching and the constant threat of emasculation, castration, and death inflicts racial hurt on an entire community in *The Long Dream.* Through reinterpretation, Fishbelly becomes an agent of self-definition because he, not those who threaten, defines what the imminent danger of racial hurt means.

Doctor Bruce's examination of Chris Sims's lynched body is another way this novel brings language and reinterpretation to the world of those racially hurt or in jeopardy of hurt. According to the literary scholar Jeffery Geiger, the autopsy allows communal racial hurt to speak louder, and thereby become more interpretable, than personal pain:

> Because Chris can no longer speak, his experience is brought into language by a figure who must simultaneously translate and interpret the text of the crime as it is inscribed in his wounds. . . . As the doctor proceeds with an inventory of physical violence and violation, the loss of Chris's humanity becomes a metaphor for the displacement of human and cultural relations in the black community. This shift entails the loss of Chris as a "him," to be replaced by an "it," even erasing the linguistic markers that determine him as a gendered being. (200–201)

Chris's lynching becomes interpretable only through a discourse about its effects on and relationship to the community from which he is stripped. Wright does not offer the character's mutilated body as a sign or symbol explaining the rationale of the events that inscribed them. Instead, he offers them as an experience of "palpable pain, felt through a community of witnesses" (Geiger 199).

Chris's experience of pain (what Geiger calls the character's "internal trauma") can only be speculated about in terms of what it "must have" felt like or what he might have experienced (201). Doctor Bruce, frustrated by an inability to manipulate and explain Chris's pain scientifically, resolves the question through a cultural mandate and bodily hexis that foregrounds unacknowledged suffering. "My guess is that when three thousand screaming white men trap you and you know you're going to die, you're not worried about a little pain. . . . If I'd been Chris, I'd've been praying that I wouldn't be scared, that I'd die like a man" (77, ellipses in original).

From the doctor's perspective, the ability to contain pain (through silence and ignoring it) for the sake of achieving control over a defining moment of manhood is more important than explaining the extent of Chris's suffering. His hypothesis also suggests that achieving a bodily hexis of silent endurance and claiming its cultural capital for oneself and one's community is more important than contemplating or reacting to extreme torture and racial hurt. This philosophy reverberates throughout the black community where the disciplinary threat and communal, racial hurt of lynching is ever present. Reactions to both are contained and controlled until silenced. We are told, for instance, that "*The Clintonville Times,* the two-sheeted, Negro weekly published by the high-school principal, devoted a black-bordered column to Chris's funeral, but refrained mentioning the cause of his death" (83). The source of disciplinary action (or what Robyn Wiegman calls "panoptic surveillance") and, ultimately, racial wounding is not mentioned in the article.[5] Lynching and racial hurt are contained and redefined as a sacrifice for communal survival.

Fishbelly's father, Tyree Tucker, offers insight into the social meaning and communal consequences of Chris's lynching. "It's a good thing he's dead. . . . [T]here can't be no peace in this town 'less they git their *blood*! When white folks feel like that, somebody's got to die! . . . We can live only if we give a little of our lives to the white folks. That's all and it's the truth" (70–71). Chris's death—not his wounds or his pain—is necessary for peace. In fact, Tyree interprets Chris's role as scapegoat to be the only assurance of continued life his community has beneath the demands and blood-thirst of a racist society.

Although pain does not achieve meaning in this novel, the cultural capital obtained by surviving it silently does have meaning. The novel's construction adheres to the cultural politics and importance of confronting pain with silence. Wright not only does not allow the novel's black community to witness Chris's lynching, he also does not allow his readers to share in Chris's experienced pain by detailing the lynching as it occurs. Instead, he allows Doctor Bruce's wound-reading "autopsy" to suffice. In this way, Wright duplicates for the reader the manner in which black people, who are not usually witnesses to lynching as it occurs, begin to envision and reconcile it. He also distances his readers from the actual moments of injury and thereby avoids representing lynching as a sensational, specular event.

In place of the spectacular, Wright offers the scientific. He places a corpse, beaten and mangled, before a doctor, who, in a slowly measured and emotionally distanced manner, gives voice to its wounds. Instead of emphasizing the experience of pain, the autopsy serves as a boundary separating panoptic surveillance, a "specular scene," from the wound as a site of interpretation (Wiegman, *Anatomies* 13). Today we call this *forensic science*, which is popularly described as a tool allowing the bodies of the dead to "speak"—but only to those who understand their language.

Such communal "sharing" is essential to the interpretation of racial wounding that denies the relationship of pain to suffering in black male–authored texts. Even though Doctor Bruce is able to interpret the language of Chris's corpse, his reading of that body does not, and, in fact, cannot, speak as Chris would. It does not encapsulate the gravity of a tortured man's suffering—only Chris could do that. Wright, however, does not give us an opportunity to hear from him.

Even when Wright does allow the victim of a brutal beating to narrate the event and describe his pain, in "Fire and Cloud," we are denied full exposure to pain as suffering. At the most intense moments of his beating, Dan Taylor, the victim in this story, ceases to feel: "He was taut, but not feeling the effort to be taut. . . . He relaxed and closed his eyes. . . . He groaned. Then he dropped his head and could not feel any more" (390). His groan is more a release of pain than an expression of it.

Wright honors that moment of release in *The Long Dream* by leaving it in its completeness, untainted by verbal descriptions that imagine or assume to "know" what Chris suffered. To this end, the doctor's scientific reading of Chris's wounds replaces an actual rendering of the event and impedes any false encounter with descriptions that, through counterfeit, diminish recognition of racial hurt as the lingering terror of lynching.

This is not to say that such images in literature "alienate" readers from an experience of the event. They do not. It is difficult, for instance, for a reader, especially an African American reader, to be alienated totally from the experience of black pain that such descriptions solicit. As an informed member of an interpretative and experiential racial community, he or she is drawn into such images. Instead of experiencing pain's transfer away from self to an external object, as might be the case for an uninformed or nonblack interpreter, such descriptions offer an encounter with the historical remembrance of pain. In such circumstances, the simple recognition of the site where a lynching occurs can bring one inside the painful events, especially if that recognition awakens communal "knowing" and remembrance of racial hurt.

Trudier Harris offers a similar reading when discussing Wright's poem "Between the World and Me" (first published in 1935 in *The Partisan Review*). Harris writes:

> On the literal level of the poem, the speaker presumably takes a walk in the woods and uncovers the scene of a lynching and burning. He views the evidence of death and identifies vicariously with the lynched/burned man. He imagines himself in turn being killed by a white mob. In his observation and choice of details, the speaker recreates on one level the motivation and atmosphere for the lynching, ones grounded in historical black experience in the United states. . . . The speaker is alone, but he is alone with the community of his race. Individual black tragedies become racial tragedies. (*Exorcising Blackness* 99, 101)

The descriptions of lynching that Wright offers in the poem create an umbilical effect that connects experiences across time and space. The experiences themselves are imagined and claimed by individual readers. The closer the reader is to a self-aligned identity with the description (and victim), the more intense the experience. These are experiences of choice, but they reveal the symbolic potency of blackpain, the effects of which are "real" whether the observer sees its images firsthand or imagines them as the result of an encounter with collective memory.

Wright's decision not to render the lynching scene in *The Long Dream* and Gaines's decision to reveal the release of racial hurt through tears in *A Lesson before Dying* are similar acts of assurance. These writers (and many other black male writers) do not focus on the felt experiences of black pain as a physical reality. They do not offer "too much pain and not enough hurt." Instead, they examine pain's relationship with racial hurt and, while doing so, they

inscribe a message of hope for each community's "safe" survival. Their characters respond to pain in ways that protect themselves and others within their
interpretive community from further assault. Most often, their characters are
swayed from contemplating pain by a creed of masculinity that says it is unmanly to admit the sting of racism, uncover its deepest wounds before the
curious eyes of strangers, and thereby make oneself and one's children vulnerable to a hostile world.

Some black male authors demonstrate their protagonists' manliness by
moving them from pain into silent mobility as a disembodied, communal sign
of survival, safety, and empowerment. The invisible man, for instance, gives
voice to racial hurt throughout Ellison's novel. He becomes ultimately a "disembodied voice" rising out of underground hibernation and into the world's
chaos. He still speaks, however, for those in his interpretative community who
find safety and empowerment "on the lower frequencies" where silent mobility exists (581). Other authors depict manliness at points within the text where
blackpain's disciplinary action is subverted and a black man's punishment for
voice through loss of life leads to martyrdom. Bigger Thomas in *Native Son* expresses racial hurt explosively through murder and is executed, while Ernest
Gaines's Charlie Biggs in *A Gathering of Old Men* (1971) is killed after finding
his voice and proclaiming thunderously, "I'm a man. . . . I want the world to
know I'm a man" (186).

Both characters become martyrs for the benefit of communal survival.
Each breaks with white-nation expectations and demands for a submissive
and self-deprecating black silence to "overcome" or transcend the body's pain.
They denounce racial hurt and move beyond it. Unfortunately, like Jefferson
in *A Lesson before Dying* and Chris in *The Long Dream,* Bigger and Charlie are
claimed by death. Those deaths, however, achieve the profound honor of
martyrdom, an honor that, in black male–authored texts, stands as a mark
of personal growth and communal subsistence.

Rage: "A Just Response to an Unjust Situation"

In *Native Son,* Bigger Thomas's personal downfall is his inability to expel
racial hurt in a socially healthy and interpersonally productive manner. Bigger's emotions spin out of control as endurance and racial hurt collide, producing rage and panic. For Bigger, silence explodes in a boundless fear that
reverberates violently to end the life of two women, a violence his lawyer describes as "hot blasts of hate" (327).

Bigger serves as black literature's original example of stereotypical "black rage" unleashed on an unsuspecting white body. His story suggests that the inert (or submissive) silence white-nation cultural assumptions assign and expect of black people (whom Jesse described as "niggers") wounds the spirit. Beyond that, such silence allows others an opportunity to appropriate and control the interpretative politics of pain's eventual (and often "explosive") release. Wright aligns black rage with the release of pent-up frustrations and denied racial hurt. Bigger's lawyer, Max, explains in his defense that "though his crime was accidental, the emotions that broke loose were already there" (330).

Although Max argues Bigger's case extensively, the critical relationship of rage to racial hurt and black pain is made most evident by Bigger's adherence to a cultural mandate for silent mobility. Before his execution (which is not depicted at all in the novel) he tells Max, "I ain't going to cry. . . . Just go and tell Ma I was all right and not to worry none, see? Tell her I was all right and wasn't crying none" (358). In this way, Wright's novel follows a script that rejects pain and fear—even the fear of death—for the more manly influence of silent mobility.

Bigger admits feeling alive for the first time because he allows himself to experience his fear and anger deeply, passionately. For him, the rage they produce is freeing. It needs no confinement. Only tears need confinement and then only if they would be exposed and interpretable to a white audience. Tears in this novel are not merely evidence of weakness leaving the body, as they are in *A Lesson before Dying*. Because of the interracially public nature of Bigger's execution, they are also potential evidence of defeat and submission to racial hurt. Bigger's rage is public—the subject of interpretation in newspapers and among white lawyers—but he protects his pain and racial hurt from the interpretations others might impose. He reclaims silent endurance but not in the same way as he does before Mary's murder—not as inert silence.

Through silent mobility, Bigger is able to subvert the power others, especially those within the dominant social structure, have to interpret his relationship to blackpain. Because of his silent mobility, for instance, Max, who reads the character's violent frenzy as a product of society's murderous preconditioning, is not allowed to interpret Bigger's most painful racial hurt. During his final meeting with his client, Bigger admits he "felt things hard enough to kill for 'em." The exact nature of these things is never revealed to Max, and as a result, the clarity and "wisdom" he shared earlier in the courtroom vanishes. Bigger's tearless confession denies a display in which he, as a man, disappears into an abstract image of blackpain. Denied a final visual confirmation of a life lived in unmitigated suffering, which Bigger's crying and exposed racial hurt would provide, Max "grope[s] for his hat like a blind man" and leaves the jail (358). Bigger does not own his public rage, but he maintains control over and ownership of his personal "truth" (whatever that might be) by refusing to expose or contemplate it publicly.

Expressions of black rage in African American literature are not reserved for men. Sofia, in Alice Walker's *The Color Purple,* is one of its most pitiful victims. As mentioned in chapter 2 of this work, she admits to a rage that survives years of spirit-breaking confinement in prison: "I dream of murder, [Sofia] say, I dream of murder sleep or wake" (76). This is *killing rage,* a meeting of pain and racial hurt, which the cultural scholar and public intellectual bell hooks admits, in *Killing Rage: Ending Racism* (1995), to having experienced firsthand.

After a day of observing incidents in which black women are repeatedly confronted by racism, hooks is brought to tears. She describes being infuriated by a cab driver who asked her to leave his cab (he did not want to drive her to the airport) and enduring the paternalistic sass and disrespect of white airline ticket attendants who acted as if they did not want to serve her. She remembers boiling at the embarrassment and public humiliation her traveling companion suffered so that a white man could take her first-class seat, and admits crying after she observed a black woman, whom she did not know, relinquish her ticketed seat in coach to another white man. Of her response to these events, hooks writes: "It was these sequences of racialized incidents involving black women that intensified my rage against the white man sitting next to me. I felt a 'killing rage.' I wanted to stab him softly, to shoot him with the gun I wished I had in my purse. And as I watched his pain, I would say to him tenderly 'racism hurts.' With no outlet, my rage turned to overwhelming grief and I began to weep, covering my face with my hands" (11). She hides her tears from view; yet, they flow as her chosen method of relief—her only reasonable and immediately available means of diminishing racial hurt.

Although experiencing "killing rage" is always intense, neither hooks nor Sofia act on it by committing murder. The coping strategy hooks adopts is to write about her feelings until she finds something powerful and empowering to grasp—something that renews her power. Sofia, however, does nothing and in this way is complicit in her own oppression. Instead of giving voice to racial hurt and thereby expelling it, she uses fantasy to cloak the emotional truth of her personal desire to harm those who wounded her.

Wright documents a chilling story of a woman who submitted to her encounter with killing rage. In his autobiography, *Black Boy* (1945), he writes:

> One evening I heard a tale that rendered me sleepless for nights. It was of a Negro woman whose husband had been seized and killed by a mob. It was claimed that the woman vowed she would avenge her husband's death and she took a shotgun, wrapped it in a sheet, and went humbly to the whites, pleading that she be allowed to take her husband's body for burial. It seemed that she was granted permission to come to the side of her dead husband while the whites, silent and armed, looked on. The woman, so went the story, knelt and prayed, then proceeded to unwrap the sheet; and, before the white men realized what was happening, she had taken the gun from the sheet and had slain four of them, shooting at them from her knees. (83)

Wright admits not knowing if this story actually happened; for him, it is an "emotional truth," a way to keep his "emotional integrity whole." He explains that the cloaks of fantasy and creativity from which the retelling of such stories (true or not) originate hide from public scrutiny a desire to kill. During his youth, they were "a support that enabled [his] personality to limp through days lived under the threat of violence. . . . [T]hey were a culture, a creed, a religion" (84). Wright's use of stories about killing rage as emotional truths is a healthy buffer for pain and, perhaps, a cloak for secret plans and future actions. Unfortunately, it provides little beyond imagining oneself free of racist assault if those plans and actions are not productively channeled. Wright comments that the fantasy of resisting racist assault, which the woman's story provides, sustained him. It did not heal his fears or calm his disgust for the inert silence his life's circumstances demanded. Wright's ultimate response to these emotions was to imagine Bigger Thomas, a man whose actions depict submission to killing rage as an ineffective method for securing social change and emotional integrity.

To contain rage and shore up a claim to emotional integrity, hooks also wrote. Her goal, however, was to expose racism as the motivating force behind black rage. She cites William H. Grier's and Price M. Cobbs's *Black Rage* (1968) and the reading Cornel West gives on the subject but rejects them both. According to hooks, both readings fall short of a healthful and healing treatment of rage. They both fail to recognize black rage as an emotion arising from pain and frustration—an emotion that, when denied or misrecognized, is complicit with racism. Writes hooks:

> Even though black psychiatrists William Grier and Price Cobbs could write an entire book called *Black Rage,* they use their Freudian standpoint to convince readers that rage was merely a sign of powerlessness. They named it pathological, explained it away. They did not urge the larger culture to see black rage as something other than sickness, to see it as a potentially healthy, potentially healing response to oppression and exploitation. In . . . *Race Matters,* Cornel West includes the chapter "Malcolm X and Black Rage" where he makes rage synonymous with "great love for black people." West acknowledges that Malcolm X "articulated black rage in a manner unprecedented in American history," yet he does not link that rage to a passion for justice that may not emerge from the context of great love. By collapsing Malcolm's rage and his love, West attempts to explain that rage away, to temper it. (12–13)

For her part, hooks does not temper it. She does not rationalize it away but reformulates it until it has a productive presence. She admits to being shocked by her killing rage but refuses to submit to the mandates of a tradition that would insist on her silent acceptance of it. For hooks, rage is "a just response to an unjust situation" (30). It is the unavoidable consequence of racial hurt. According to her, black silence leads, at best, to a narcissistic rage, which is not "safe" and is certainly not concerned with transforming a system of inequity. Instead, it is concerned with achieving a ceaselessly elusive, individual parity within that system. Containing pain or masking it behind emotional truths that calm the impulses of killing rage (those acted on and those left to fantasy) does not provide security or protection. Instead, these routes to overcoming racial hurt devour the spirit and threaten the psyche.

Although hooks does not advocate murder, she does support attending to what she describes as the "complexity and multidimensional nature of black rage . . . the psychological displacement of grief and pain into rage . . . and the psychological wounds it masks" (27). Her resolve is to engage a militant rage mobilized for strategic resistance that will privilege change and "constructive empowerment," not pathology and denial. As a form of constant and open public discourse, such strategic resistance will challenge the white-nation sociodicy while exposing moments when Americans participate aggressively in "white supremacist capitalist patriarchy" (29).

Suffering in silence is not a uniquely male tradition (or, for that matter, an exclusively Black one). Black men, however, honor the tradition as a sign of masculinity that validates their right to patriarchal power and respect as heroes and masters of their own fates. In their texts, silent mobility moves both the victim of racist assault and his community beyond recognition of pain toward strategic resistance and oppositional readings of racial hurt and blackpain. By avoiding submersion beneath scripts that provide "too much pain, not enough hurt," the writers reviewed in this chapter assure their male characters' dignity and spiritual wholeness. In both films and in novels, silent mobility stills fear, tames pain's disciplinary action, and defies white-nation control while providing models and methods for surviving racial hurt safely.

Although there is symbolic violence in inert silence, the stilled presence of pain and fear at the root of silent mobility in African American culture is life affirming. It is the only route to safety, which, by the way, is only secured if all within the community of potential harm are safe. Narcissistic engagement and self-concern do not lead to safety. They are complicit with racial harm in their disregard for others. Similarly self-absorbed are those who reject silent mobility for inert silence.

In fact, silent mobility is not necessarily silent at all. It is loud, calculated, treacherous, awesome, and disturbing. Absent of oral expressions of pain and fear that diminish acts of resistance, silent mobility defeats racial hurt by responding to it, exposing it, and conquering it. As an act of resistance, it provides a degree of control that garners honor and communal respect while calming the threat of killing rage that the containment of pain often engenders. To overcome the potential of a harmful explosion, silent mobility uses private voices and public discourses—like the singing in "Going to Meet the Man"—to transform the interpretative conditions under which pain is considered and racial hurt articulated.

Silent mobility, then, means overcoming the fear and pain that keep resistance at bay by ignoring them and exposing their source. Regardless of race, everyone offended by racism must actively choose whether to be complicit with it or resist it. If the choice is resistance, then inert silence must be rejected, and, recognizing that "all our [inert] silences in the face of racist assault are acts of complicity," we must expose each wounding moment for what it is and move beyond it (hooks 19).

Three

Pain's Expulsion

Action is the natural antidote to both denial and despair.
—Patricia Romney, Beverly Tatum, and JoAnne Jones, "Feminist Strategies for Teaching about Oppression"

5 | Writing in Red Ink

Their voices blended into a threnody of nostalgia about pain. Rising and falling, complex in harmony, uncertain in pitch, but constant in the recitative of pain. They licked their lips and clucked their tongues in fond remembrance of pains they had endured—childbirth, rheumatism, croup, sprains, backaches, piles. All of the bruises they had collected from moving about the earth—harvesting, cleaning, hoisting, pitching, stooping, kneeling, picking—always with young ones underfoot. . . . When white men beat their men, they cleaned up the blood and went home to receive abuse from the victim. . . . They were through with lust and lactation, beyond tears and terror. . . . tired enough to look forward to death, disinterested enough to accept the idea of pain while ignoring the presence of pain. They were, in fact and at last, free.
—Toni Morrison, *The Bluest Eye*

In "The Laugh of the Medusa" (1975), Hélène Cixous advances the idea that women's strength is derived, in part, from "the gestation drive—just like the desire to write: a desire to live self from within, a desire for the swollen belly, for language, for blood" (346).[1] This is a powerful statement undermined only by its association with an illuminating pen of whiteness, a pen that marks out the primary vehicle of rememory, transference, and voice in black women's texts. Black women writers take their "mother's milk right along with [their] sister's blood," and with this revised recipe for writing, they liberate their characters' black flesh from moments of racial hurt and pain (Morrison, *Beloved* 153). For them, the desire for blood, then, is not a desire for gestation but rather a desire to acknowledge pain by giving voice to the voiceless and flesh (or spirit) to the fleshless.[2]

The preponderance of stories about captivity, mutilation, pain, and death in black women's literature is daunting. Who, for instance, having encountered Alice Walker's *The Third Life of Grange Copeland* (1970), Octavia Butler's *Kindred* (1979), or Gayl Jones's *Eva's Man* (1976), can forget the murdered Mem Copeland lying in "a pool of blood," Dana Franklin's violently severed left arm, or the imprisoned Eva Media Canada's oral castration of her lover? Images such

as these sadden and even horrify us, but for black women writers and their readers, these events represent a struggle against socialized codes and values that
denigrate subjective realities, hopes, and dreams. In each case, red emerges and
spreads as blood flows freely from and around bodies experiencing physical
and psychological wounding. The wounds expose characters' struggles against
both gendered and racial hurt. Usually, this spilling of blood intensifies moments of liberation and is often their prerequisite.

Images of bodily destruction in black women's literature bring into sharp
focus that which postmodern attitudes and black historical mandates have successfully disassociated with any possibility of sociocultural meaningfulness—
our pain. Cross-culturally, women are taught to deny their suffering and feel
so ashamed of scars that they hide them beneath makeup or remove them with
plastic surgery. Much like men, women are told they will be stronger, better
beings if they endure pain silently, ignore it, or medicate (and meditate) it
away. Women become likable and employable if we deny the need for deliverance from the wounds no one but ourselves see, or care to see. The pain black
women in novels, such as those just mentioned, experience cannot be ignored.
Neither can its significance be diminished or its call for deliverance silenced.

Like a magnifying glass placed against the wounded spaces of private lives,
the physical and psychological injuries suffered by the characters of black
women's fiction assist readers in acknowledging and understanding their own
pain. The blood readers envision flowing from mutilated or injured fictional
bodies offers safe passage beyond real-world suffering and fear. For the female
reader, pain, no matter how different from that read about, is somehow validated and justified as it is witnessed or unveiled through a literary surrogate.
The security found in witnessing yesterday's sorrow from a secure distance becomes available for personal ownership, and the failures of that past, fictionalized, provide the lessons that empower an audacious will to do more than
survive. It provides the audacity to be victorious in the face of oppositions and
social divisions that threaten an inevitable and painful defeat.

Cixous denounces the instruments of such a defeat and suggests that
women's greatest weapon against them is writing the body in laughing rhythms
and white ink. The freedom and subversive nature of writing as proposed by
Cixous suffocates beneath the weight of blackpain. Although inspiring and
liberatory for some women, Cixous' gendered metaphors do not consider the
plight of those held captive by gendered and racialized fictions. They do not
provide a remedy for black women writers who reach for that pen of illumina-

tion to find that the flow of mother's milk has dried up or been stolen. "[T]hey took my milk," Sethe in Toni Morrison's *Beloved* (1987) reminds us. "Held me down and took it" (17, 16). When we view blackness and mother's milk as more than metaphors for unknown territories and the unmasked jouissance of subversive writing, we cross the boundaries separating that which cannot be explored from that which cannot be spoken.

On this path, the "goods" of mothering the self and others extend from a loss of body and body parts. It comes from spilling blood and identifying that which is lost or injured as a sacrifice for life. One of the clearest examples of this type of giving appears in Morrison's *Sula* (1973). Eva Peace, a woman accused of not loving her children, sacrifices her leg for their financial security. When her daughter, Hanna, questions Eva's love, "Eva's hand moved snail-like down her thigh toward her stump . . . No. I don't reckon I did [love you]. Not the way you thinkin' . . . what you talkin' 'bout did I love you girl I stayed alive for you" (67, 69). Eva's wound memorializes a great sacrifice. It is a reminder that blackpain is both symbolic capital and real capital. In Eva's case, body wounding may not function easily as the sign of a "good" mother's love, because it is more than that. It is the source of goods. Eva "stayed alive" for her children. She did not run from potential death and certain pain. Neither did she helplessly embrace nor silently endure wounding. Eva accepted personal agency and claimed the right to speak out and take legal action, thereby turning pain into profit.

Hanna's definition of love cannot encompass the concept of bodily mutilation as a gesture of love and a gift for life. She hungers for proof of affection, not love. The mother she thinks she needed as a child could "tickle [her] under the jaw and forget 'bout them sores in [her] mouth" (69). As a young, widowed black mother, Eva could not afford to pet her children. Like so many black mothers, she was too busy helping them survive.

Morrison explores this line of inquiry further as she tells the story of another mother considered less than "good." Sethe is a woman whose "good" mother's milk (meaning, her ability or opportunity to mother "sweetly" and provide her children sustenance) is stolen. Morrison presents her as "riveted . . . between the Medusa and the abyss"—to borrow from Cixous (Morrison, *Beloved* 339; Cixous 341). Having escaped the physical captivity of slavery, Sethe finds the impetus of that captivity chasing her and threatening to take her children to the place where breasts are raped and milk is stolen, a place where pain is thrust on the black body in a way she is unable to control. To ensure their freedom from such violations, she decides to kill them, to "drag them through the veil . . . where no one could hurt them" (163). Because Sethe's intended task is interrupted, the death of the body through the spilling of blood liberates only one child from the physical and psychological consequences of captivity, however, leaving Sethe and her daughter, Denver, victims of limited mobility and psychological deterioration. The liberatory intent of Sethe's act of love collapses beneath the weight of social mandates defining "good" mothering until the residue of conceptual violation, in this case a physical manifestation of guilt and shame, haunts them. Sethe's psychological suffering assumes a material presence as the liberated flesh of the child, her "crawling already" baby girl, whose throat she cut, returns in the form of a ghost.

Sethe's mother's milk, so necessary for the maintenance of self and others, is reconceptualized through this tragic story of liberation. Morrison describes both the breasts from which it flows and its acceptance by Sethe's surviving daughter, Denver: "Sethe was aiming a bloody nipple into the baby's mouth. Baby Suggs [Sethe's mother-in-law] slammed her fist on the table and shouted, 'Clean up! Clean yourself up!' They fought then. Like rivals over the heart of the loved, they fought. Each struggling for the nursing child. Baby Suggs lost when she slipped in a red puddle and fell. So Denver took her mother's milk right along with the blood of her sister" (152–53). In the eyes of Baby Suggs and others, the blood Sethe spills taints her role as mother, as the source of goods and goodness.

Baby Suggs cannot read beyond the body. For her, "loving the body" means protecting it from pain and racial hurt, touching it with gentle, nurturing care and preserving life within it at all costs. She does not make the leap from flesh as matter to flesh as spirit and metaphysical freedom. This, she expresses clearly in her sermon. "Here," she begins, "in this here place, we flesh; flesh that weeps, laughs; flesh that dances on bare feet in grass. Love it. Love it hard. Yonder they do not love your flesh. They despise it. They don't love your eyes; they'd just as soon pick em out. No more do they love the skin on your back. Yonder they flay it. O my people they do not love your hands. Those they only use, tie, bind, chop off and leave empty. Love your hands! Love them" (88).

Baby Suggs continues her list of sins against the flesh—all violent and all disrespectful of life. Because of her vision of body as flesh, she cannot see Sethe's "bloody nipple" as the ultimate gift of a supreme sacrifice. For her, it can never be the chalice of a Passover meal paying homage to a "passing" that promises the liberation of Denver's flesh—a commemorative "last supper" offered in a mixture of milk and blood, nurture and life. Instead, Baby Suggs reads a toddler's dead body as failed mothering, falls in that which death spilled, and misinterprets or, rather, misrecognizes a ritual of the spirit that nurtures and frees the flesh. She reads blackpain as woundedness, while Sethe claims a killing rage she hopes separates her and her children from present and future racial hurt.

Laura Doyle explains that Baby Suggs "gives place to 'flesh'" in her speech. According to Doyle, the enmeshing of body and "self-transformative speech" creates, for Baby Suggs, a sensibility and respect for materiality and living things (225). The place she creates for this flesh is an "intercorporeal place," a place of flesh-worship located "deep in the woods" (Doyle 224; *Beloved* 87). In other words, it is out of harm's way. Hidden deep in the physical spaces of a world that rejects the black body, its flesh, its history, and its meanings, Baby Suggs preaches self love as a personal and familial source of salvation and rescue from injury.

Sethe, on the other hand, sees the world's rejection, without exception, as one that wounds the black body while capitalizing on its pain and labor. For her, there is no safe place in that world—not even spaces located deep within individual hearts, which, for Sethe, are bound by and trapped inside that world. As a result, she harbors a love that is "too thick" for any of her beloved children to survive whole. Sethe's love has left her with "boys gone you don't know where. One girl dead, the other won't leave the yard" (*Beloved* 164, 165). Paul D describes Sethe through this "too thick" love as a *new* woman, one different from any woman he knows: "This here Sethe talked about love like any other woman; talked about baby clothes like any other woman, but what she meant could cleave the bone. This here Sethe," Paul D realizes, "talked about safety with a handsaw. This here new Sethe didn't know where the world stopped and she began" (164). Sethe certainly does not find safety in the woods (or heart) of a world set on serving black people daily doses of racial hurt. For her, the world around her (perhaps even consuming her) is one without refuge from racial hurt, a place where two assurances reside: "Love is or it ain't [and t]hin love ain't love at all" (164).

It is not until Baby Suggs's last days of life that she allows the fatal possibilities and experienced realities of these truths to overcome her. In that moment of realization, we are told, "Baby Suggs, holy, believed she had lied. There was no grace—imaginary or real—and no sunlit dance in a Clearing could change that. Her faith, her love, her imagination and her great big old heart began to collapse" (90). After witnessing Sethe sacrifice Beloved's life, Baby Suggs submitted to blackpain and racial hurt; she became complicit with them and "proved herself a liar. . . . 'Those white things have taken all I had or dreamed,'" she admits and allows the intercorporeal space she created for the "flesh" to collapse around her. Thereafter, she does not express love for hands, eyes, backs, or hearts. Instead, she "lay in the keeping-room bed roused once in a while by a craving for color and not for another thing" (89).

If we read the wounding and death of the body in *Beloved* in the same way as Baby Suggs does, we see the events occurring in the barn as infanticide, and we, too, are horrified. We, like Baby Suggs, are in danger of collapse beneath the overpowering weight of white power dominance that forced the hand of death. But, if we read the idea of flesh metaphysically, we understand Sethe's decision to kill—for she kills only that which holds the spirit of black subjectivity captive. She kills only the body. Beloved's death is a publicly displayed and tangible indicator of her body's position as the subject of wounding. Sethe's racial hurt is not so easily accessed.

As she leaves the site of this battle for liberty, only the blood covering her dress speaks of it. The narrator tells us, "The hot sun dried Sethe's dress, stiff, like rigor mortis" (152–53). This image of life held captive in the grip of death repeats and revises Sethe's earlier experiences of spiritual and physical wounding when her milk is stolen and her back is inscribed by Schoolteacher's whip (pen). It also attests to the psychological wounding she suffers while producing, or rather drawing forth, the red ink that writes her daughters' liberation. She must read this symbol of her pain against codes that would bind her to past experiences of racial hurt and a self-imposed captivity. Sethe fails at this task. Although she can write the story of liberation for her children publicly, she has not learned the secret to freeing herself of bondage privately.

Like the community who comes to gaze on her pain, Sethe cannot embrace, for herself, the liberatory impulses of her actions. The community reads her clothes through codes that deny the flesh and dismiss Sethe as a bad mother. For Sethe, the red that envelops her body colors not only her clothes but also her ability to reap the rewards of knowing and celebrating her own flesh. Secure in the knowledge that at least one of her daughters is free of slavery's chains, Sethe experiences a moment of introspective reflection and painful sublimation that others misinterpret. The text tells us, "She climbed into the cart, her profile knife-clean against a cheery blue sky. . . . Was her head a bit too high? Her back a little too straight? Probably. Otherwise . . . [the] sound [of singing] would have quickly been wrapped around her, like arms to hold and steady her on the way" (152). Sethe's submission to this silence and communal alienation acts as a barrier against her ability to move beyond the socially constructed story her blood-soaked garment tells.

It is only by acknowledging the separation of her flesh from the icons of captivity her body wears that Sethe is able to begin self-recovery. Only when she discovers the "Sethe" within can she arise and walk unfettered by yesterday's pain and today's concern for a community's scorn. Only then is she able to release the ghosts who hold her mind and body captive. Sethe achieves this moment of freedom with the help of the man she loves. Paul D gazes on her pain, understands her need for flesh, and encourages her toward it: "You your best thing, Sethe. You are" (273).

The absence of similar healing moments results in private and public wounding experiences for the captive female bodies in Gloria Naylor's *Linden Hills* (1985). Naylor creates a tale of bonds broken by a constructed body politics that pushes each of its primary players (male and female) into the arms of pain and absolute negation. From Evelyn Creton's private experience of bulimic emaciation to the bloody site of Laurel Dumont's public suicide, the devaluation and rejection of black women by black men exacerbates experiences of pain and alienation. Yet, even in this novel, the metatext of extreme body wounding functions as a salve that frees the flesh and releases the captive, especially the captive who reads beyond the horrors of its bloody and fiery ending.

Novels like *Linden Hills* force those living outside the text to see the blood that liberty spilled and to acknowledge their own connection to it. Like the viewer of a boxing match, readers are forced to see the body as body: limited, vulnerable, and dying. In this way, *Linden Hills* makes readers not only see but also feel the weight of that which continues to wound black bodies: historical silencing and absence, myths of mothering and mandatory sacrifice, dreams deferred (or, rather, dreams subordinated to masculine desire), colorism, and excessive materialism. Each of these is represented as a mode of captivity for black women in Linden Hills. Readers are often so overpowered by the hopelessness of the body's bondage and ultimate demise that they miss the freedom from captivity that a character's symbolic sacrifice by death provides. We read the body and are dismayed by its message when we should read the flesh and live the hope of its liberatory offering.

By wounding the posed and photographed body of Priscilla McGuire, for instance, Naylor sends a message of liberatory empowerment. We meet the deceased Priscilla through Willa Prescott Nedeed, whose husband has locked her in a basement with their dead son. As Willa turns the pages of Priscilla's private photograph album, she reads body wounding. Within each family photograph, Priscilla disappears beneath the figures of her husband and her son until she is lost in the bonding of masculinity that surrounds and overshadows her. The photo album reveals this when Willa notices that

> [Priscilla's] face was gone. The photo album trembled in [Willa's] cold hands as she realized there was no mistaking what she now saw: Priscilla McGuire ended at the neck—and without her features, she was only a flattened outline pressed beneath cellophane. The narrow chin, upturned nose, and deep fiery eyes were a beige blur between the two grown men on each side of her. The entire face, the size of a large thumbprint, had been removed. This had been done on purpose. There was no way this wasn't done on purpose. Cleaning fluid. Bleach. A drop of hot grease. Over and over, page after page, the smeared hole gaped out into the dim light . . . [Until s]he came to the last photograph. And scrawled across the empty hole in lilac-colored ink was the word *me*. (249, emphasis in original)

The pictures Willa contemplates are of a woman erased first by the domination of one man, her husband, who uses her body to duplicate himself in the form of a dark-skinned son and discards it thereafter. This son, who sees her as merely the vessel through which his body passed before finding life with his father, provides the second source of her domination and erasure from the photograph. The third vehicle of erasure she provides herself by writing over both men's fleshless codes and discourses about her and reinscribing her own. Through the destructive mechanism of her own hand, she enacts symbolically a body wounding that resists the discursive shadows and frees her flesh.

Although Pricilla writes over male-defined stories of absence and lack in lilac-colored ink, red fills this scene. It is framed by the image of blood spilled during Laurel Dumont's public suicide, and it is viewed through the eyes of a character who sees everything beneath a veil of blood. Willa's gaze is colored by a rage the narrator describes as "scratch[ing] at the scars in her mind." We are told that "she trembled as fresh blood seeped through the opening wounds. . . . Blood from the open scars dripped down behind her eyes" (204). Pricilla discovers the "me" inside and finds (metaphorically speaking) that her stash of ink is lilac, indicating a knowledge of self that is weak and not fully formed—but for Naylor, the ink is red. She fills the scene and our vision of it with blood that frees both our minds and her character, Willa, from captivity. Willa allows the bloody evidence of her psychological wounding and physical captivity to write over the fictions her husband inscribes until his definition of her as a flawed reproductive machine is silenced. For Willa, the body becomes "a mere shelter for the mating of unfathomable will to unfathomable possibility. And," we are told, "in that amber germ of truth she . . . conceived and reconceived" herself (288). This recognition and acceptance of the "me" inside creates within the text a space of stability and security where those (the reader included) who find themselves subject only to their own will and imagination can congregate.

As Willa escapes the basement where she has been held captive, her body is subordinate to an experience of liberation that renders her body's death by fire ineffective. The house fire, which she fails to escape, kills nothing of her eternal value, self-realization, or ethnic truth. These we, the readers of this bloody story, carry from the text. Naylor's red ink conjures a mode of transference that not only calls Willa into recognition of her own internal will and strength, but also calls the reader into a realization of life and renewal. If we read the flesh and not the corpse that housed it, we, like Willa, find the ability to free ourselves from gendered and racist forms of captivity. We discover a way to survive and to live.

Such a discovery is central to the struggles against pain and its ability to hold women captive. In Morrison's *The Bluest Eye* (1970), black women revise their relationship to pain so it functions as a source of pride and empowerment. The women Morrison presents wear conquered pain and illness as if they were badges. Trudier Harris claims such portrayals of black pain are created "against a backdrop of unwritten taboos and efforts to avoid stereotypes," but, in the process of avoiding one stereotype, others are supported and devised (*Saints* 11). In this way, black women writers accommodate perceptions that black people can endure more suffering, more wounding, than other human beings. At the same time, however, endurance that helps others survive pain, "with all its ambiguous dimensions, remains a metaphor for the possibility of autonomy, the possibility of a literature and a people writing and working against the odds to overcome those odds" (*Saints* 179).

Morrison's female characters allow age to mellow the impact of pain until it is nothing more than one more thing to ignore or endure. There is so much hurt in their lives, so much wounding, that their memories are coated in pain. Yet, they do not silence those memories. They give them voice and, by doing so, claim the power to define the boundaries of pain's influence in their lives and their living. In the epigraph to this chapter, Morrison's narrator tells us these women reminisce about their suffering until their voices "blended into a threnody of nostalgia about pain" (*Bluest* 109).

They have lived through the horrors of lynched and beaten fathers and sons, abusive husbands, physical illness, and childbirth—and survived. Thus, it is not so much the recollection of pain they savor and share as it is the memory of surviving it. They do not allow pain to render them or their lives hopeless. They approach pain in the same way Zora Neale Hurston approaches racial identity when she announces boldly, "I am not tragically colored. There is no great sorrow dammed up in my soul, nor lurking behind my eyes" ("How it Feels" 152). For Morrison's women and the people (male and female) they represent, this type of self-knowledge provides the best medicine, the best cure, for the aliments, prejudices, and racial hurt African Americans must face. It is a knowledge that synthesizes pain into a "purée of tragedy and humor" that sustains the self past the point of explosion and "beyond tears and terror" (Morrison, *Bluest* 110).

In *Saints, Sinners, Saviors* (2001), Trudier Harris outlines the social construction of black women as "balm bearers" and "towers of strength" in the U.S. cultural imagination. Her text reminds us that the stereotypical "strong black women," whose model real women attempt to follow, "ignore their own pains and troubles in favor of helping others" (9, 12). These women are expected to endure without complaint every pain, from childbirth or acute menstrual cramps, to the woundedness of a body, soul, and mind torn through years of exhaustion, abuse, and disappointment.

Although there is a tradition of endurance marking the lives of black women, rendering them nothing if not strong in the face of adversity, there is also a tradition of facing pain and exposing the destructive impulses of silent suffering. In 1978 Michele Wallace emerged as one of the first black women intellectuals to expose the crippling nature of mythic black female strength. That year, she published *Black Macho and the Myth of the Superwoman* and gave voice to woundedness as she validated a trend that black women writers of the 1970s, 1980s, and early 1990s followed—a trend exposing the lie of black women's invulnerability and inherent safety. Wallace writes:

> [I]magine, for a moment, that you had a little girl and circumstances dictated that she be released in a jungle for a period of time to get along the best way she could. Would you want her to think she was invulnerable to the sting of the snake, the claws of the panther? Would you like her to believe that she could go without sleep and food indefinitely and that she needed no shelter? Or would you want her to know something of her actual capabilities and human weaknesses, not enough to make her give up before she had begun, but just enough to make her want to protect herself? How long do you think she'd survive if you deceived her? And, more importantly, in what state would she survive? Imagine further that she believed her wounds were just another proof of her strength and invulnerability? (108)

Patricia Hill Collins develops this argument in her groundbreaking book *Black Feminist Thought* (1990). Collins agrees that the controlling image of black female strength distorts the picture black daughters receive as they prepare for the world's racial and gender hate. She also argues that this image is often used to dismiss the need for legal remedy, communal reassessment, and social transformation concerning the dangers black women face daily (115–18).

The work of writers like Toni Morrison, Gloria Naylor, Alice Walker, and others rise above stereotypical models of safety that demand incomparable strength and silent acceptance of racial or gendered hurt. Instead, black women writers help readers identify sites of danger masquerading as opportunities for demonstrating strength. Their texts expose the controlling image of the strong black woman as a potential wounding place. By privileging voice, this tradition of writing honors women's right to defy the nasty, complicated "underside" of silence.[3] Black women writers, during the period under survey in this study, like black men, present pain as a sacrifice for survival. For them, however, pain may also be an entrance to death that exposes uncompromised strength as a myth. At other times, pain for their characters is an indication that life continues within and through wounding moments, but only if one can envision the presence of pain as a measure or means of birth and rebirth. Both can be pain's outcome when resistance replaces myth and voice replaces silence.

The African American women's literature presented in this chapter insists that black women outside the texts remain whole by putting words to pains that have been silenced for centuries. With pens drenched in blood (a metaphor used here to represent the wounding experiences these writers bring into language), black women rewrite the stories existing beneath woundedness, beneath hurt, and beneath "killing rage." They write so others can find the ability to do more than survive. They write so other black women can survive *whole*.

6 | Expressing, Sharing, and Healing Black Pain

Pain is a personal experience—perhaps the most personal of all human experiences. It is not easily expressed or transferred; and, therefore, it is difficult to share. Because of this, pain can be an extremely alienating experience—one that distances the sufferer from others and renders him or her virtually unknowable, different. The only way this difference can be bridged is if pain becomes objectified. In this way, it is made available for sharing and for claiming. To obtain this status, however, it must achieve recognition through strategies and signs that provide it with an oral or visual symbolic form. In other words, to be shared, pain has to become pain of, for, or like something. It needs an interpretable signature (a recognizable, "iterable, imitable form") tethered to its origins that moves individual expression beyond an "inarticulate pre-language of 'cries and whispers' into the realm of shared objectification" and a world of language, image, and metaphor where the difficult to understand becomes easily readable (Derrida, *Limited* 20; Scarry 11).

Elaine Scarry maintains that the communicability of suffering, of pain, is more difficult than my abbreviated and appended summary of her ideas suggests—especially since her basic axiom rejects the possibility of articulating pain without imagining torture as its source (Glucklich 390). Furthermore, prolonged pain, according to Scarry, eludes language and destroys the victim's ability to communicate entirely. It unmakes its victim's world and renders the innermost being, or self, isolated and estranged from everyone including him—or herself. Although this is doubtlessly true within the framework of torture that Scarry describes, there are other ways pain can be communicated—other methods through which it becomes interpretable, even if the experience of pain is prolonged.

In "Sacred Pain and the Phenomenal Self," Ariel Glucklich maintains, "[P]ain is not only communicable but lies at the heart of the human ability to empathize and share. The symbolic and experiential efficacy of pain derives from the way it bridges 'raw' sensation with the highest qualities of human beings in a community of other human beings" (391). Prelanguage communications can provide individuals ostracized, alienated, and pained a "bridge" or pathway to coalition with others who may or may not suffer similarly. Pain's signature can be found within prelanguage structures whose origins make its oral traces appear, at first glance, to be inarticulate, "grotesque and funny," when they are, in fact, much more (Du Bois, *Souls* 138). With this focus, the discussions in this chapter consider public and private examples of shared black pain to identify signatures that communicate and provide access to meaning. Outlined within are several processes and consequences of sharing black pain—particularly the effect sharing has on the sociopolitical messages and healing potential of blackpain as metaphor.

Primal Recognition and Transference

In 1970 the psychoanalyst Arthur Janov noted profound healing in patients who experienced the release of "central and universal pains" (*Primal Scream* 11). He named this experience "the primal scream." Janov's understanding of *primal* connects feelings with meaning, the past with the present. The term originates with Freud, although Janov's use of it differs from Freud's. Before he developed his now-famous psychoanalytic methods, Freud developed *abreaction,* a therapeutic process that encouraged emotional catharsis as a way to achieve healing and wholeness. The process presented challenges Freud was unprepared to handle, and he abandoned it. Others, however, did not. The Freudian analyst Wilhelm Reich adopted and revived the cathartic model in the 1920s. Later, the originator of Gestalt therapy, Fritz Perls, was encouraging his clients to become more emotionally expressive as a means of healing and, by the 1960s, avant-garde theater communities moved the primal scream into the arena of shared healing experiences as they encouraged behaviors connecting the past to present emotional release (Turton, "Primal Integration").

Sam Turton, a practitioner of what is known currently as Primal Integration, claims that to be effective as a method for expelling pain or purging trauma, release must occur in "a safe situation" (n. pag.).[1] For many African Americans, this "situation" is found in the Black church. Through shared experiences of primal release, a fortress for coalition and nationalism is constructed, a fortress interpreted as impenetrable by those it shields.

Within this safe space black people share the release of black pain through an ancient prelanguage or primal code, fondly called the "shout." Born in the Southern Black church, the shout is encoded by immediate and remembered personal suffering. It is the most important—if not also the most valuable—means of rendering pain accessible and available for understanding, healing, and coalition building. For some, those who do not celebrate ecstatic spirituality and a few for whom church shouting was never an acceptable tradition, this language is mere emotionality—unnecessary and loud. For others it is, among other things, a way to exorcise or externalize black pain, giving it a form beyond the body, a form that is at once sharable, healing, and interpretable.[2] In the Black church, the shout is, among other things, pain's signature.

Even without the sufferer's conscious intention, the shout expresses, shares, and makes pain available for reinterpretation. In other words, through it, pain is externalized. The shout expels woundedness, moving it beyond conscious intent and beyond the individual suffering. Once externalized, a shout can cleanse, renew, and build individuals and others within the "safety" of a shared interpretive community. The shouter may not intend to cleanse anything. The shout he or she produces may be involuntary or reactionary, like saying "Ouch!" when one is kicked. Intent, real or assumed, is irrelevant.

Jacques Derrida asserts that "[i]n order to function, that is, to be readable, a signature must . . . be able to be detached from the present and singular intention of its production" (*Limited* 20). What is alluded to here is not the "empirical presence of a signatory," the *signature-form*, which is no more than the visible structure of a *signature-event* (Culler 126). The shout is the event itself.[3] Because it is a signature-event, the shout actually loses its power when written. Like a signatory (or autograph), the shriek written phonetically or otherwise is not the thing itself but the structure of the thing—if that. Like music, poetry, the sermon, and various other elements of the culture in which it is articulated, this signature-event is its most momentous when rendered orally.

In *The Souls of Black Folk* (1903), W. E. B. Du Bois attempts to penetrate the impenetrable by describing in language the experience of black pain's pre-language expression. His attempt exposes the contradictory nature of pain's "language of agency," a language within the symbolic contract of sign and metaphor that reproduces "the image of the weapon . . . [as well as] the image of the wound," making the image of pain, not the pain itself, available for sharing (Scarry 16). In other words, Du Bois articulates the structure of the signature, not the signature-event.

Although the language of cries and whispers is certainly not the only way experiences of pain are conveyed, it is an effective means for externalizing the burden of deeply felt wounds, ancient wounds that are always just beneath the surface of black people's lives. Like Ciel's "slight silver splinter" described in Gloria Naylor's *Women of Brewster Place,* the church shout is, in part, the remnant of historical soul wounding. The pain it expresses is not only political; it is historical, ahistorical, and transhistorical—fixed in the past, yet strangely and frighteningly immediate, mutable, and prolonged across time almost to the point of evolving into a normalized and sometimes counterfeit racial attribute. It is tethered to the depths of what it means to be Black in America. Constituted in this way, an individual shout is at once sharable and immediately accessible as an oral signature within a congregation of cries, murmurs, and shrieks.

Du Bois celebrates the shout as a cultural marker in *The Souls of Black Folk,* giving it (and the physical exuberance that often accompanies it) a name, "the Frenzy," and a place as documented social history. Of his visit to a Southern Black church, Du Bois writes:

> A kind of suppressed terror hung in the air and seemed to seize us—a pythian madness, a demonic possession, that lent terrible reality to song and word. . . . The people moaned and fluttered, and then the gaunt-cheeked brown woman beside me suddenly leaped straight into the air and shrieked like a lost soul, while round about came wail and groan and outcry, and a scene of human passion such as I had never conceived before . . . . [T]he Frenzy or "Shouting," when the Spirit of the Lord passed by, and seizing the devotee, made him mad with supernatural joy, was the last essential of Negro religion and the one

more devoutly believed in than all the rest. It varied in expression from the silent rapt countenance or the low murmur and moan to the mad abandon of physical fervor—the stamping, shrieking, and shouting . . . the weeping and laughing, the vision and the trance. (137–38)

In the first instance, Du Bois depicts "a kind of suppressed terror" and "pythian madness" that seize everyone—including himself. Word and song achieve a "terrible reality" as souls are "lost" to both demonic and Divine spirit possession, both joy and weeping. The contradictory and chilling nature of these descriptions exemplify the difficulties of sharing the "felt experiences" beyond the primal or core trajectories outlined in my opening comments. In so doing, they prove Scarry's claim that pain's language of agency is unpredictably instable, with its interpretation achieving a negative or sinister effect just as easily as a positive or moral one.

In Du Bois's descriptions the tether connecting the expression of pain as an event to its original source and primal impulses is weakened, but not broken. According to Derrida, "[i]n order for the tethering to the source to occur [and be sustained], what must be retained is the absolute singularity of a signature-event and a signature-form: the pure reproducibility of a pure event," the impossibility of a possibility (*Limited* 20). The cleft of impossibility evident in Du Bois's task exposes a threat implicit in the failure to reconnect or trace what he witnesses back to its primal or original source. The failure to refer pain's objectified attributes "to their original site in the human body," Scarry claims, "will always work to allow its appropriation and conflation with debased forms of power; conversely, the successful expression of pain will always work to expose and make impossible that appropriation and conflation" (13, 14).

Du Bois's juxtaposition of evil with good draws out the possibility of appropriating and using the shout's symbolic capital in opposing ways. This is perhaps why some African Americans characterize the shout as a positive form of communal sharing. For them, it validates and elevates spiritual awareness and cleanses the soul, while others interpret it only as noise made by a suffering, debased, uneducated, and inarticulate people. Issues of power and class that distinguish African American interpretive communities are implicated through these appropriations of symbolic capital. The divisions such appropriations create offer individuals in some communities a safe space and language for healing and camaraderie, while others find the shout a threat as well as a source of shame and social injury.

It is clear, however, that Du Bois easily recognizes and understands pain's objectified "language" as expressed by those around him. Appropriating that pain (although not in a way anyone would describe as debasing) to enunciate it through an alien discourse is a difficulty he does not overcome so easily. Instead, a fearful cast of binary oppositions encases the moment he describes in a spiral of meaning and supplementation.

Once Du Bois identifies pain's core, he is able to confine his descriptions of its prelanguage expression to a singular interpretative space and signature-event. Because Du Bois cannot actually reproduce the oral signature of the shout in his text, the spiral never ceases to exist, though now it is less frighteningly awesome in its supplemental effects. At that moment in the excerpt, his observations reveal the simultaneous presence of pain and pleasure, "the weeping and laughing" often associated with religion without the "hellbound" sense of shock and wonder presented initially. Instead a sense of recognition is communicated. As submission to and expression of the wound itself occurs, Du Bois describes the joy surrounding him as maddening, supernatural, and physical. The shout, or frenzy, is now "essential," "rapt," and conducive to the imperial wisdom of visions and trances. Du Bois's use of the word *passion* is profound, for it is through this word that the lucidity of a new signature-form is proposed and the site of the parishioners' primal trauma is confirmed.

The word *passion*, as it appears in Du Bois's text, mirrors the internal structure, contradictions, and sacrificial impulses of blackpain as a metaphor and unifying agent expressed in the "frenzy" and the shout. Its religious connotations demand that we acknowledge the relationship between church shouting and the primal or the core site of pain that this prelanguage discourse expresses. In *Summa Theologica*, St. Thomas Aquinas describes pain as a "passion of the soul." In this light, the "terror" Du Bois senses in the church results from exorcising pain's potential for "soul murder" through the shout.

Passion is also reminiscent of the painful death Christ suffered on the cross, known as the Passion of Jesus Christ, a passion narrative, or, in dramatic recreations of Christ's death and suffering, a passion play. Du Bois describes as a "human passion" what is being interpreted in this text as pain's presence and prelanguage expression in the Black church. In doing so, Du Bois limits the terms of its interpretation while conjuring an assortment of meanings that range from rituals of sacrifice, scapegoating, and salvation to notions of silently enduring pain and sharing sacred (or moral) pleasure. Each of these is

applicable to the "sentient distress" of the congregants (Scarry 15) as they release internalized, unnamed, and silently endured hurt.

The shout is woundedness expelled, sacrificed for the sake of healing,
wholeness, and communal unity. It is the pain of blackpain, embodied and
made available as a reminder of possible salvation for those whom racism
wounds daily. It is blackpain as a trope drawn against the hard edges of a situation gone wrong, a dream deferred, specular fear, and experiences of racially
motivated assault. And, ultimately, it is stress animated, stirred up, and heated
until potent and transferable.

In sum, the shout is a celebration and acknowledgment of God's grace, as
well as a deep, primal release of woundedness. It is a clearinghouse for abuses
experienced beyond the doors of the church, a prelanguage discourse signifying the release of abuses that often render black people scapegoats for the fears
and weaknesses of others. It offers moments of purging wherein the dreadful
weight of racism's domination and other hurtful experiences are neutralized—
if only for a brief time—allowing black people to detoxify from racist injustices
that spiritually, physically, and psychologically wound.[4] In the church, ances-
tral memory and comfort, communal coalition and ritual unite worshippers
who feel safe to communicate great pain. Through the shout, they release the
pain of racism's social, political, and economic wounding, giving it presence
and exposing its terror while also weakening its power over individual experiences of pleasure and Being.

Emotional Contagion and Intersubjective Bonds

In a 1998 article titled "Is the Pain Too Much to Watch?" the *Los Angeles Times*
feature writer Greg Braxton provides a secular example of how immediate and
remarkably "real" the experience of pain's signature-event or primal release
can be. His report also demonstrates how difficult it is for language to recap-
ture and restrict meanings associated with this method of sharing pain. Braxton begins his article as follows:

> The anguished scream pierced through the auditorium at the Magic Johnson
> Theatres in Baldwin Hills like a white-hot sword during a first-weekend showing
> last December of the slavery drama *Amistad*. In the lobby, the [black] woman,
> still trembling and crying, explained that she found the brutal depiction of the
> torture and cruelty [visited upon] the slaves too unnerving, and that she iden-

tified too closely with the incident. She was referring to a section of the film that focused on the Middle Passage, the journey made from Africa to the Caribbean by newly sold slaves. The scene showed bloody beatings and other atrocities in a graphic manner previously unseen in a mainstream Hollywood film. (8)

Words can never duplicate the depth of experience conveyed through this woman's primal scream. Neither can they reveal the transference of pain through time and space that causes her to identify "too closely with the incident"—at least not in the same way or with the same intensity as her prelanguage expression does. As the original response and release of an otherwise inexpressible and ancient hurt—a prelanguage discourse rooted in a history of struggle—the woman's shriek, like the church shout, is the signature-event announcing the arrival and recognition of tensions and umbilical links connecting collective memories of pain with private experiences of soul wounding.[5] Like scars stretched across the face of time, blackpain is recognizable by all who can read its impulses—no matter where it originates or what form recognition's primal expression takes.

David Morris mentions something similar to this when he talks about pain's ability to unite people across time. In a chapter he calls "Painful Pleasures: Beauty and Affliction," Morris discusses the surgeon and fiction writer Richard Selzer's work on the rhetoric and beauty of surgical wounding. Morris observes, "[T]he wound in Selzer's work at times contains the power to join people together, much like sentimental pain for Wordsworth." Selzer's analysis of Homer's *Ulysses* describes a wound as "the emblem of all the shared pain and despair, the disappointment and the exhilaration that are the measure of [Ulysses'] relationship" with Eurycleia, his nurse. It is because she recognizes the scar left by a wound Ulysses suffered during a boar hunt that Eurycleia is able to connect her past with his after twenty years of separation. The scar alone gives her the ability to identify him when others cannot. Morris writes that "the scar, like the pain it signifies, binds them together across the years" (*Culture* 221).

The excerpt from Braxton's article presents a timeless unity between past and present wounding experiences. It also exemplifies just how devastatingly "real" cinematic representations of black bodies in pain can be, especially when the world and individuality such cinematic moments symbolize and subsume are one's own. Blackpain links the woman in the Magic Johnson Theatres' auditorium to the characters she watches. And because she recognizes this link and claims it, she allows herself to share the wounds and pain the film calls forth. For her, the events witnessed become intimately immediate and unbearably "real." She is like Fishbelly, in Wright's *The Long Dream*, who "saw a dark, coagulated blot in a gaping hole between the thighs [of Chris's castrated corpse] and, with a defensive reflex . . . lowered his hand nervously to his groin" (77).

Intersubjective experiences such as Fishbelly's are dependent on the ability to see pain's victim "*bodily*, as a flesh-and-blood human being" (Beyer n. pag.). This is easy for Fishbelly, who knows the castration victim, Chris, as a friend. This knowledge gives him access to an intersubjective experience to which he responds with a self-protective gesture. *Amistad* (1997), however, offers no real foundation for "seeing" any black character beyond his or her role within a suffering communal body, because the captured Africans are not presented as fully human—as *Dasein*.[6]

The film does not reveal the characters' personal or individual dreams or present the impact of their capture on family and friends. The closest the film comes to revealing the personal and intimate side of the African captives' lives comes midway through the film in a flashback depicting the wife and child of Sengbe Pieh, or Cinque, the African protagonist in the film. Janet Maslin of the *New York Times* describes the scene as erupting "into lush color for a glimpse of Cinque's wife and child in their peaceful village," just before abruptly snatching the protagonist from the warmth of family.

For Maslin, the scene offers the viewer an opportunity for achieving full empathy and immediacy. However, the lack of eye contact or even a shared glance between Cinque and his family leaves the scene cold. "Viewers wishing to avoid waterworks," Maslin observes, "can only be grateful that Mr. [Steven] Spielberg denies the wife and child a backward glance." The backward glance would have brought the terror of the family's separation from the background onto center stage. Instead, only Cinque experiences the horror and shock of being dragged from his home. We are led to believe his wife and child walk away unharmed, even oblivious to the trauma their family has just suffered. This scene, although a welcome shift in tone, brings little to our understanding of Cinque as "fully human".[7] *Amistad*'s audience does not achieve an understanding of the lives destroyed or the families and dreams broken by the atrocities shown because none of the characters emerge as human beings. Instead, they are bodies—abused, discarded, disrespected, and lost.

There are at least two causes for this. First, the actors do not speak in a lan-

guage most members of the audience can understand. Professor Clifton Johnson of Tulane University translated portions of the script into the Mende di-
alect. The effect is not one of authenticity. Instead, it is alienating and cold.
Second, viewers learn no intimate details about the people the African actors
are supposed to represent. Instead, they remain alien, one-dimensional cari-
catures of history's silenced and invisible heroes.

Particularly notable is the process by which Cinque is made alien. Spielberg
sought and found an unknown actor and former model, Djimon Hounsou, to
play the role. The problem is not Hounsou's acting ability; the problem is his
alien status as a performer (at least to the majority of his audience at that
time). Because of it, the audience has no memory of him (or his cohorts), no
way to envision him as familiar. Instead of relating to the characters, we are
asked to focus on and contemplate events—not people, not lives. Furthermore, we are encouraged to relate to black bodies huddled before us as icons
of blackpain (not individuals)—this time representing the incredible horror
of middle passage and its consequences. Suffering makes the character's bodies visible and consumable, while their "alien" status renders their lives invisible. As a result, they are a barely comprehensible communal body, if not also
a subhuman one.

Additionally, as Michel Foucault claims in *Discipline and Punish*, such
bodies are representative of the sovereign's restrained power, and punishment
or the violence against these bodies is representative of power released, not of
justice or moral reasoning. The longer viewers witness images of the black
body in pain, the stronger its dehumanizing visual effects. Viewers become de-
sensitized to the human element within the visual offering of pain. As a result,
the human being presented as mere image gains interpretative value as alien,
undesirable, and even criminal. In other words, terror and absolute power
overshadow any focus on human pain or suffering as the black body is rendered equivalent to the sometimes criminal, but always alien, tortured body.[8]

The shift to absolute power in *Amistad* blocks viewers' access to an intersubjective understanding of the events and the people portrayed. Instead, it
transforms the movie theater into a torture room where an audience, seated in
darkness, is forced to witness extended images of blackpain, death, murder,
and wounding. Viewers witness the shocking indifference of slave traders
who chain living bodies together and hoist them into the sea. They sit dumb-
founded as a child is born amid death and feces. Images such as these further
transform human beings into bodies of pain and objects of spectacle.

Can we say with certainty that the woman in the Magic Johnson Theatres screams because she empathizes with the pain on display, or is she more likely to be in sympathy with the characters' plight? Perhaps she is responding to an experience of what psychoanalysts call *emotional contagion,* an involuntary emotional response to what would be, in this case, specular pain.[9] What is the woman's mode of access and association? What leads her to scream, and is that scream akin to the church shout, which, in the transference of blackpain among participants of an active interpretive community, is a sympathy-driven and motivational arm of coalition building? To answer these questions, the differences among emotional contagion, empathy, and sympathy need further clarification.

Lauren Wispe explains the differences between empathy and sympathy in terms of how we understand and relate to the sufferers' pain. She reminds us that understanding is the objective of empathy. In it identity is sustained, while sympathy reduces self-awareness. "In empathy," she explains, "one substitutes oneself for the other person; in sympathy one substitutes others for oneself. To know what something would be like for the other person is empathy. To know what it would be like to *be* that person is sympathy. In empathy one acts 'as if' one were the other person. . . . The object of empathy is understanding. The object of sympathy is the other person's well-being. In sum, empathy is a way of knowing; sympathy is a way of relating" (*Psychology* 5).[10]

Mamie Till Bradley, for instance, demonstrated sympathy when she saw the mutilated body of her son, Emmett Till, for the first time. "I didn't want that body," she recalls. "That couldn't be mine. But I stared at his feet and I could identify his ankles. I said, those are my ankles. Those are my knees" (Thomas, "Emmett's Legacy" 5).[11] Bradley's knowledge of her own body is conflated with the body she sees before her, and although she "didn't want that body," it becomes hers. This is sympathy: expressing sensibility to another person's suffering to the point of sharing it and eventually acting on behalf of that person to change the painful circumstances, causes of discomfort, or source of wounding. Bradley acts by allowing the world to witness the horror of racism. Her activism animates her sympathy. Like the woman in the theater, her experience is not intersubjective, however.

According to Edmund Husserl's theory of phenomenology, intersubjectivity is an "empathic experience; it occurs in the course of our conscious attribution of intentional acts to other subjects, in the course of which we put ourselves into the other one's shoes" (Beyer n. pag.). Intersubjectivity requires the imitational and involuntary experience of empathy—not sympathy, not emotional contagion (also called *emotional identification*). The woman's scream, although primal, affective, and humane, is involuntary—the direct result of emotional contagion.[12] There is neither complete understanding of the experiences she watches nor a relational or behavioral interaction between her and the captives she watches. There is only emotional recognition or "identification" via tropes that allow her to interpret what she sees as similar to her history, her past, her situation, and, by association, her body.

The woman's gaze activates meanings in which "the past, present, and future are synchronized into what is essentially a deconstructive configuration" (Holloway, *Moorings* 73). As a transhistorical activity, her gaze validates the signature-event, which is her scream, but does so within and beyond its original context. Of course, as Jonathan Culler reminds us, "Meaning is context-bound, but context is boundless" (123). Viewers expand the context to incorporate their varied experiences and knowledge. When the film shows bodies immobilized and hoisted overboard, one viewer, interpreting the trope through personal experiences, may see black youth handcuffed and shoved into police cars and prisons. The film's depiction of a child's birth amid the squalor of death, decay, and captivity may be recognized by another viewer as a child born amid the filth, death, and decay of an urban crack house.

For audience members who find it difficult to view the past as over, as done, it is more "realistic" to envision the tropic or symbolic economy of black pain as woefully present and real. The narrative capital of contemporary black bodies in pain translates into "the referential illusion of an organic real" that is disheartening in its similarity to a tragedy plucked out of time and displayed dramatically before us (Wiegman, *American Anatomies* 41). In this state of overrecognition, audience members may not experience intersubjectivity, but they can experience emotional contagion. As a result, the ability to enjoy what is being watched, realize civilizing guilt, or engage in scopophilic guilt is compromised, or worse, lost.

The desire to see is betrayed as black viewers become players and wounded bodies in the tragedy set before them. Having few heroes with deep melanin coloring their skin to celebrate and, more often than not, gaining neither profit nor power from the moviegoing experience, black people are left with little beyond a promise of pleasure that turns out to be a painful—and embarrassing—scopophilic gaze. This is important, because it is for the promise of pleasure and an "illusory sense of power" that we watch (Cripps 133).

It is not too much to assume that, as moviegoers, black viewers expect *Amistad* (or any other film about this slave-ship rebellion) to give body to an ego ideal that affirms self-pride and a history of slave-ship resistance that confirms what they, perhaps, "knew existed all along". Unaware (or not) that before evening's end they will become witnesses to twenty minutes of specular pain (with bodies unclothed and black male genitalia on display), audiences gather as if attending a carnival or some other carefree amusement. With popcorn and soda in hand, they hope to relax, enjoy, and maybe even gain some relief from a sense of powerlessness experienced in the world beyond the screen. But before they can claim pride in the Africans' ability to overcome their enslavers, viewers are bombarded with graphic footage of what could be considered a public mass execution. Viewers expecting the film to guide the gaze of others toward recognition of an empowering history are disappointed, "disciplined," and chastised as surveillance turns its gaze on their "ego ideal" and revises it. Instead of building a moment and safe place in which to share black pain and enter a process of healing, *Amistad* reminds audiences that the black body is always abused, already broken, and constantly pained.

Empathy, and of course profit, ignites interest in such cinematic projects as *Amistad*. The film is constructed as if its purpose is to help viewers understand the captives and the history of a people who, even today, are wounded by slavery's legacy. Because of this singular focus, *Amistad* does not have to deal with culpability in the past or the present. Therefore, it fails to challenge the ideological framework supporting the white nation and institutions that allowed slavery to exist in the first place.

It does offer blackpain, however, as a shared entertainment, which can also function as a vehicle for disciplinary and surveillance activities bordering on voyeurism. Through it, sharing occurs, but with a disaffected empathy that works "undercover" to maintain the status quo. The benefits of moving beyond the metaphor, sharing human woundedness (black pain) and its healing, then, must be found elsewhere—in the signature-event Du Bois calls "the frenzy" and shouting, for instance, or in the shared belief systems supporting conjurational spirituality. Such sharing encourages sympathetic engagement and sometimes helps those involved in the event of sharing to not only claim their own pain but also claim responsibility for healing the pain of others.

Conjurational Spirituality

Conjuration, herbal remedies, voodoo, and hoodoo (or *root-work*, as it is better known) are often tossed in the same sack and dismissed as outdated, false, or deceptive practices. Many think them useless in terms of providing real healing. Various Black folk cultures, however, acknowledge and value each of these as venues for healing both the mind and the body, especially when science and medicine fail to provide such healing, or when these institutions are suspected of being the source of harm. These beliefs are validated through Christianity, which is the most dominant African American religious belief system. The doctrines and practices of Christianity lend themselves easily to the philosophies and healing magic (or *soul power*) of conjurational spirituality.

In *Conjuring Culture* (1994), Theophus Smith describes the Bible as a "magical formulary or sourcebook," a talisman for "cures and curses" used by African American faith healers, root doctors, and diviners, or conjure performers, who practice a healing spirituality (6). "Is any among you sick?" the writer of James 5:14 asks. "Let him call for the elders of the church; and let them pray over him, anointing him with oil in the name of the Lord: And the prayer of faith shall save the sick, and the Lord shall raise him up" (James 5:14–15). The apostle's question and his answer provide entrance to a tradition of prayer and anointing known in Black folk culture as *a laying on of hands*. In this passage and others, the Bible proposes a ceremonial approach to healing similar to African and slave practices found in the work of root doctors, conjurers, and shamans. Each designates elders as healers; each claims to soothe pain and cure disease; and each relies, in part, on faith and spirituality for success.

Among African Americans, conjuration has functioned for two centuries as a means of engaging proactive instead of reactive responses to blackpain and black bodies in pain. For believers, the lines separating religion, magic, and science are thin. In fact, Smith draws only one primary difference between medical (considered compatible with Christianity) and magical (considered contrary to Christianity) conjuration. "What distinguishes magic from science as a cognitive and transformative system is its heightened, intensive reliance on ritual performance and mimetic (imitative) efficacy" (13). Other distinctions (particularly those delineating one as good, the other evil) often fail to limit the possibility of the two coexisting in the conjure performance of Black folk religion.

Still, the terms used when speaking of conjurational spiritually are very important. Conflating terms weakens and causes misunderstanding of them all. Smith comments, for instance, that "[a]n unqualified application of the term 'conjure' [in] its Latinate senses can obscure the pharmacopeic and medicinal elements that distinguish African American hoodoo from its related traditions such as voodoo cults and sorcery" (49). In the discussion to follow, the pharmacopoeic and magical elements of conjure are considered equally effective forms of bodily and psychological healing. They are often copartners with religion and faith in relieving the social, psychological, and physical effects of black pain.

The recognition of this partnership is certainly not new. During slavery, the "chief remaining institution [of African heritage] was the Priest or Medicine-man. He early appeared on the plantation and found his function as the healer of the sick, the interpreter of the Unknown, the comforter of the sorrowing, the supernatural avenger of wrong" (Du Bois, *Souls* 141). The historian Charles Joyner reports that on the Waccamaw rice plantations of South Carolina, conjurers were often called on for medical purposes. They adapted their knowledge of African pharmacopoeia to the semitropical low-country environment. Joyner adds that healers in the slave community he studied coupled herbal remedies with divination as a form of psychotherapy intended to secure comfort during times of great pain, illness, stress, and fear (148).[13]

As Joyner, Smith, and others have pointed out, herbal and faith healing are authentic therapeutic tools in Black folk culture. Popular cultural representations of these practices tend to replace conjurational spirituality with conjurational sensationalism, however. The image of the magical, mystical, and often evil black conjurer has been absorbed easily into film and literature. In almost each case, the medicinal work of the conjurer is capsized by sensationalism and sorcery—making even the healing practices of black people appear un-American and, therefore, tainted. We see ominous (even frightening) depictions of the conjurer in movies like the 1997 films *Midnight in the Garden of Good and Evil* and *The Devil's Advocate,* and the more recent *Pirates of the Caribbean: Dead Man's Chest* (2006). Short, serialized programs like the *Outer Limits,* shown on science fiction television stations, also offer brief moments wherein the stereotypical black root worker appears.

Although the images referred to feed the American desire for experiencing a certain degree of exotic otherness (from a safe distance), none consider the conjurer in her or his role as folk healer. The closest we get to this recognition in film is the magical root worker of *The Devil's Advocate* who silences the lawyer prosecuting him by stealing his voice. This magic helps the conjurer win the legal right to practice his religion's ritualistic animal sacrifice in the inner city while publicly humiliating the lawyer. The storyline functions as a caution against the mysterious powers developed by black practitioners of nontraditional religions. Both are seen as evil. Since someone insensitive to conjurational spirituality, a representative of the legal system, is silenced, the storyline offers an example of possible dangers magical conjuration poses for the white nation and its laws. The fears it seeks to arouse are very similar to those nursed by frightened slave masters who forbade slaves to engage in conjure or practice any religion without white supervision and approval (i.e., surveillance).

A more accurate picture of conjurational spirituality is drawn in African American literature wherein the faith healer is the trusted ally of wounded souls, a spiritual advisor, and the only true source of solace for black people whose bodies, spirits, and minds are in pain. *The Interesting Narrative of the Life of Olaudah Equiano or Gustavus Vassa, The African* (1789), for instance, explores the complex yet dynamic relationship of medicine, spirituality (or religion), and magic in African folk culture. According to Equiano, the narrative's author, tribal healers in his native land were spiritualists and priests whose magic healed wounds and other physical complaints. Like early European physicians, "[t]hey practiced bleeding by cupping, and were very successful in healing wounds and expelling poisons" (43).

We find the healer whose magic transforms death into life through a laying on of hands in both *Women of Brewster Place* (as seen with Mattie Michael) and in Gayl Jones's 1998 novel *The Healing* (where a traveler named Harlan is rumored to have healed herself of a knife wound immediately after receiving it). Harlan is so powerful her touch can heal both psychological and physical wounds. Naylor's *Mama Day* (1988) presents the cultural magic of, and communal need for, conjurational spirituality through her characters' interactions with Miss Miranda (also called Mama Day), a midwife and conjurer whose impressive "powers" can heal or destroy as she desires.

Miranda is a root worker who does "good magic," but when she learns that another conjure woman named Ruby has "fixed" her grandniece, Cocoa, and made her ill (by placing worms inside her), Miranda reluctantly employs her powers to destroy the woman's home. She calls out to Ruby three times and receives no answer (although Ruby is in the house); then, using a cane as an instrument of delivery, Miranda begins her magic:

> She don't say another word as she brings that cane shoulder level and slams it into the left side of the house. The wood on wood sounds like thunder. The silvery powder is thrown into the bushes. She strikes the house in the back. Powder. She strikes it on the left. Powder. She brings the cane over her head and strikes it so hard against the front door, the window panes rattle. Miranda stands there, out of breath, with little beads of sweat on her temples. . . . The door don't open when she leaves, and the winds don't stir the circle of silvery powder. . . . Miranda climbs the verandah steps and enters the front door of the other place. She closes it securely behind her. The lightning is flashing in the clouds. She's asleep when the clouds get lower and the lightning nears the earth. . . . It hits Ruby's twice, and the second time the house explodes. (270, 273)

Mama Day's magic is simple; her revenge, final. This is the first step toward Cocoa's healing. The second step Miranda provides through her touch. Cocoa tells the story: "When her hand passed over a place where they [the worms] were burrowing, they would remain still until she went on to another part of my body. And by the time they had built up momentum again, she was back there stroking" (290). Mama Day sings a gospel melody as she works her healing magic into Cocoa's body through a laying on of hands. But "her one hand against so many of them" is not enough (290). She needs the hands of Cocoa's husband, George. What she demands, however, is his life.

George does not believe in the cure, and because he is "disbelieving," he decides not to participate in Cocoa's healing until he is "beaten down to believe" (299). Still, Naylor leads us to understand, George's death is a necessary part of Cocoa's healing. He dies of a heart attack after trying to secure an object (he does not know what) from a hen's nest. Once inside the chicken coup and after a furious battle with a red hen, George reaches in the nest and discovers there is nothing there besides his empty hand. Wounded from his fight with the hen, he returns to Cocoa and dies as his bloody hand slides down her shoulder. After that touch, she begins to heal.

A large part of the power of conjuration to heal rests in the "patient's" ability to believe in it, want it, and follow simple instructions. Dr. Buzzard, a pseudo-healer in Naylor's text, thinks seriously about this after talking to George about the power of disbelief. Only then does Buzzard (who admits to being a fraud) think about a man he was unable to heal, "the single one who [false conjure] ain't worked for." Buzzard comments, "Ya see, I had given him something that he just couldn't believe in—and him disbelieving, whether I'd offered him a miracle or not, guaranteed it to fail" (292).

Like Dr. Buzzard and like Minnie Ransom, the healer in Toni Cade Bambara's *The Salt Eaters* (1980) who asks Velma Henry, "Are you sure, sweetheart, that you want to be well?" (Bambara 3), Mama Day is able to heal only if her patient wants to be healed and can believe or find hope in her and the cure she offers. Trudier Harris describes women like Mama Day and Minnie Ransom as "extranatural," able to "transcend temporality." They are women "whose strength is cast in the more than human" (*Saints* 79). Even so, Harris writes that "what people and characters around them believe about conjure women—and I include healers in this group—is as important an indicator of their power as what the women are actually able to accomplish" (*Saints* 80).

After the character Bernice, in *Mama Day*, is healed from ovarian cysts, for example, Miranda tries to ease her wait on pregnancy. She uses a placebo of "magical" pumpkin seeds dyed in saffron water, squash, and dewberry juice (which Bernice is to plant during menstruation) to help her patient find hope. When another character expresses doubts about the usefulness of such a deception, Miranda informs her: "The mind is a funny thing . . . and a powerful thing at that. Bernice is gonna believe [the seeds] are what I tell her they are—magic seeds. And the only magic is that what she believes they are, they're gonna become" (96).

Not only is the desire for healing a necessity in conjurational cures, but community support is also important. Healing is not a solitary venture in African American communities; it involves the psychological support and physical touch of family and friends. Toni Morrison's *The Bluest Eye* presents healing as a communal rite with the conjurer at its core. The narrator explains that friends visit the woman they call Aunt Jimmy for five days before they call for the conjure woman. Some bring herbal remedies, some lay hands on her (rubbing her in liniment), while others read the Bible and give advice for home remedies that were "prolific, if contradictory" (107–8). When none of their remedies help the ailing woman, they send for M'Dear, a conjurer and healer—"a savior in the extranatural tradition"—whom the text describes as a "decisive diagnostician" (Harris, *Saints* 79; Morrison 108).

Morrison makes it clear that this healer has the support of the religious community by making her enter the scene with the local preacher whom she

"looms" above—an indication of her supreme powers over conventional medicine. M'Dear's visit is short and her diagnosis given without Hollywood dra-
matics or unnecessary flamboyance. She uses her hands to measure, test, and
survey the strength and health of the women's body. She strokes Aunt Jimmy's
hair, her hand, her fingernails, and face. She even listens to Aunt Jimmy's stomach and examines her stool. After instructing the women gathered around the
sick bed to "[b]ury the slop jar and everything in it," she says to Aunt Jimmy,
"You done caught cold in your womb. Drink pot liquor and nothing else" (108).

M'Dear examines Aunt Jimmy with confidence and professionalism. Although it appears she uses magic and intuition to reach her diagnosis, her
remedy is natural. It provides Aunt Jimmy with highly concentrated nutrients
and vitamins in a form (liquid) that is easily absorbed and distributed throughout her body. It does not matter if the "cold" in Aunt Jimmy's womb is malnu-
trition, a slight stomach irritation, or some other illness, the remedy given
works as a pure and natural source of healing. Her instruction to the community of women to bury the slop jar is also natural (keeping the foul-smelling
bodily excrement under the patient's bed is not only unsanitary, it promotes
illness and the growth of bacteria).

Trusting M'Dear's diagnosis, the community of women provides Aunt
Jimmy various kinds of "pot liquor," and as they expect, she begins to recover
from her illness—that is, until she eats a piece of peach cobbler one of those
well-meaning friends serves her. Aunt Jimmy believes in her cure, and she has
the support of family and friends who also believe in it. But when she fails to
follow the healer's instructions, she dies "of peach cobbler" (107).

There is an element of respect and awe associated with the conjurer and conjurational spirituality that Morrison's story does little to diminish (nor should
it). By providing a humorous cause of death, however, Morrison's story of Aunt
Jimmy reflects real-world scenarios in which laughter is expected to weaken
the impact of a painful situation. It is not easy to respond to wounding and
trauma with laughter; and sometimes, it is equally hard to respond to racial
hurt with tears. It is much easier to feel, contemplate, or react to each with
anger, fear, and resentment.

Hoodoo and faith continue to be viable resources for Black folk culture in
need of healing venues beyond traditional institutions and structures. Humor,
however, crosses boundaries that extend beyond the black community. More

than primal release, emotional contagion, or conjure, humor has a stronghold on beliefs about how to soothe devastating pain and racial hurt. However, it continues to be a major player in the game of cover-up and denial all Americans, regardless of race or ethnicity, play when trying to resolve the social and personal impact of blackpain.

Laughing 'Til It Hurts

My grandmother dismissed racial hurt with a condescending smile. When many would have reacted with anger or simply relieved their pain with tears, my grandmother raised her brows, lifted her shoulders, and, pressing her lips together in what was either a smile or a smirk (I never knew which), she dismissed the offenders and the offense from serious consideration. She acknowledged their racism, disrespect, and rudeness by ignoring it and them. I thought this meant the attempted assault was beneath her—undeserving of a verbal response. Yet, during one of these moments, I asked her how she could remain so calm when the hatred and disrespect I witnessed hurt me so deeply. "Sometimes child," she said, "you have to laugh when you feel like crying."

Others have noted and expressed similar sentiments. According to the psychologists William H. Grier and Price M. Cobbs, "[A]ll suffering people turn in their sorrow to laugh at themselves; they laugh to keep from crying" (95). From laughter's blueslike transcendence comes renewed mental courage, reclaimed physical strength, and spiritual rebirth. It is therapeutic and has been considered so since the Middle Ages.[14] And, although humor is a powerful remedy for pain, at the center of its effectiveness is the potential for further injury.

Laughter that takes its "punch line" from moments of racial wounding, for instance, works within systems of value and acculturation that maintain white-nation domination. As such, it can promote more pain and silence more voices than it frees. The comedic use of the word *nigger* offers an example. Richard Pryor used this word frequently during the height of his comic career. And although thunderous laughter followed when he used it, Pryor admits there was nothing funny about it (Pryor and Gold 175). After years of making "fun" of himself and the people he identified with the word, Pryor denounced it as "wretched." Its history is too thick with blood and black bodies murdered, mutilated, and despised to invoke painless comical reflection.[15] At most, it is a word demanding listeners to *laugh to keep from crying*.

Repetition cannot empty the n-word of its history, especially when each time it is spoken or written, meaning proliferates in spirals around it, and instantly, we are aware of that history, its relationship to slavery, lynching, disfranchisement, denunciation—a history of pain, struggle, and victories won at tremendous cost. In fact, the word's power as an agent of bonding depends on that history for meaning just as much as the word-as-insult does. Regardless of context or intent, it is always a word distilled from fear and hate for the purpose of controlling, maintaining, and prescribing hierarchical relationships and systems of exclusion. No matter how much black people claim an unproblematic transition from hurtful to healthy (and often ritualistic) nominative possession, the pain of derogatory name-calling endures.[16]

Why? Because it is impossible to purge racial hurt from this word or any other word whose trajectory of meaning, distinction, or power is irretrievably linked to racist origins. *Nigger* is such a word. According to Randall Kennedy, African Americans use the term to remain mindful of social realities, or (in other words) "to keep it real." Some use it to "rope off turf" for profit in the music industry and in comedy. Others recognize it as a means of gaining empowerment and defying racial subordination and pain while distinguishing themselves from (the culturally self-ostracized) assimilated "Negro" (47–49). It would be wonderful if it were possible to achieve these meanings without calling forth memories of degradation and pain. But it is not. In each case, meaning can occur only if the word's relationship with a history of subordination and murder is maintained and monitored—kept just beneath the surface, but kept just the same. When used by black comedians or in discourses of humorous, ceremonial play (such as the dozens), the word is a form of symbolic violence.

I find this same kind of symbolic violence is often at the center of the black comedic presence in popular culture, particularly when we look at men like Bert Williams and Sammy Davis Jr. These were men whose talent during their lifetime was broadly accepted by white-nation advocates while their bodies and racial heritage were not. Both men wore masks of inert, silent acceptance: Davis as the center of poorly disguised racial jokes delivered to audiences by his "rat pack" buddies and Bert Williams as one who donned burnt cork and performed for white crowds who would not let him sleep in their hotels or dine in their restaurants.

Williams's racial hurt at having to literally mask his beautiful face and hands beneath blackface makeup and gloves was made acutely obvious after his death when his wife refused to let his Mason brothers place gloves on his hands. She wanted them to be seen in death since he was forced to cover them in life—a symbolic gesture for sure, but one offering reflection on a lifetime of hidden beauty and desire. Much later, evidence of his pain, as well as the pain and embarrassment his performances caused other black people, was revived through a performance given in his honor by Ben Vereen at the 1981 Reagan Presidential Inaugural Gala. Intended as a tribute to a great comedian, Vereen's performance was edited for television in a manner that created a scandal and a tremendous amount of racial hurt.

The historical material that gave context, seriousness, and tribute to the performance was deleted from the televised version, leaving nothing but an abstract image of blackpain for the audience's contemplation. "The character who appeared wore baggy clothes and blackface makeup, and shuffled about the stage. His speech and song seemed slow, and his grammar woefully inadequate" (Woll xii–xiii). Although this was an accurate representation of Williams's performances, without the humanizing historical context Vereen intended it to have, the performance was a painful mockery of black people. Presented before a Republican presidential administration whom many feared would have very little sensitivity to African Americans' social, economic, and political needs, it functioned more like a warning than an honor. The performance was not funny; it was not dignified; and, it did not soothe the memory of blackpain. Instead, it *was* blackpain.

Just as Williams's wife wanted to reveal the man beneath the mask by unveiling his hands, Vereen wanted to reveal the man behind the performance by telling his story. This, however, he was not allowed to do, and Bert Williams remained disguised beneath blackface (as was Vereen). Vereen's original act offered America a pristine picture of the pain Williams suffered, and although Vereen (like Williams) made America laugh, he was never able to laugh about the inaugural performance. Instead, he followed Williams's path by receiving rejection and anger from African Americans who did not want to look too closely at the past—especially not when presented through the "tears of a clown." It seems the white nation, however, loved it and rewarded Vereen's comic verve with a stint on Broadway, just as Williams was rewarded a place in Broadway's Ziegfeld Follies.

Black intellectuals and critics in the early twentieth century also felt shame and embarrassment when Bert Williams and George Walker presented the musical *In Dahomey* to New York and London theatre patrons. One professor of business, Albert Ross, chided the pair of comedians, charging that they "held the old plantation Negro, the ludicrous darkey, and the scheming grafter up to entertain people . . . [when they should write about men like] Locke, the Negro Rhodes scholar at Oxford" (Woll 40). Williams and Walker, however, reminded the professor that their livelihood came from audiences that expected the type of comedy they provided. To give the audience otherwise would end their careers and the careers of those black actors, actresses, stagehands, writers, and creative artists they employed. The paradox of their situation is two-pronged: complicity was the sacrifice they made to shelter their craft, while symbolic violence was the bill they paid for the healing promise of laughter.[17]

Unfortunately, this promise most often does not secure healing for black audiences but accomplishes just the opposite. Moreover, it allows nonblack subjects an opportunity to experience the positive and healing effects of laughter, while black people, "laughing when they feel like crying," remain distanced from the same type of healing pleasures.

Such pleasure is considered by many to be a cure for racism, proof of American equality and tolerance. This became painfully clear to me when one of my white male students expressed his desire for a voyeuristic and "entertaining" relationship with those he considered inferior. As our class discussed American race and gender consciousness, this student raised his hand and said with unbelievable innocence, confidence, and self-assurance, "Do you know what I think they [meaning minorities and all women] should do?" and, after a pause answered, "Make us [white patriarchy] laugh." For the sake of clarity he added, "Like Eddie Murphy." This student's interpretation of black people's role in comedy (and in society) does not concern itself with healing black pain or diminishing its symbolic capital. For him, comedy is not available for Black consumption but for a white audience in need of a temporary and harmless source of entertainment and relief.[18]

For the most part, laughter generated from racist jokes and racial humor wounds the wounded. It may help the injured "limp through" the pain—as Richard Wright describes it (*Black Boy* 84). It may even be the elixir that makes racism "go down easier," but it is not the cure or solution for black pain—not even when shared as an intragroup code (or game of verbal play). Such laughter is always double-edged and may even be the source, for some, of spiritual wounding and soul murder.

We find examples of this throughout the work of Zora Neale Hurston in which characters share laughter to cure the wounded individual and communal spirit of both gender and racial hurts. In *Their Eyes Were Watching*

God, front-porch humor (or signifying games) provides spaces where black people can laugh at themselves without the "danger," the vulnerability of an outsider's attack. Unfortunately, this does not address the pain inflicted by those inside the circle of racial security whose humorous or signifying comedy is not meant to wound or kill, but often does. The most memorable example of this in Hurston's novel occurs when Joe Starks and his wife Janie verbally fence:

> "Don't stand dere rollin' yo' pop eyes at me wid yo' rump hangin' nearly to you knees!" [Joe says.]
>
> A big laugh started off in the store but people got to thinking and stopped. It was funny if you looked at it right quick, but it got pitiful if you thought about it awhile. It was like somebody snatched off part of a woman's clothes while she wasn't looking and the streets were crowded . . .
>
> "Naw, Ah ain't no young gal no mo' but den Ah ain't no old woman neither. Ah reckon Ah looks mah age too. But Ah'm uh woman every inch of me, and Ah know it. Dat's uh whole lot more'n *you* kin say. You big-bellies round here and put out a lot of brag, but 'tain't nothin' to it but y' big voice. Hump! Talkin' 'bout me lookin' old! When you pull down yo' britches, you look lak de change uh life.". . .
>
> "Ah ruther be shot with tacks than tuh hear dat 'bout mahself," Lige Moss commiserated.
>
> Then Joe Starks realized all the meanings and his vanity bled like a flood. Janie had robbed him of his illusion of irresistible maleness that all men cherish which was terrible. The thing that Saul's daughter had done to David. But Janie had done worse, she had cast down his empty armor before men and they had laughed, would keep on laughing. (122–23)

This is a signifying game gone bad. After that evening, the defeated Joe Starks wanes, never to recover. Janie's words, funny enough to wound well beyond that evening, hurt him far more than being "shot with tacks." One might say he got what he deserved, since he did "start it." For most of his relationship with Janie, Joe makes her the butt of his jokes in order to silence and weaken her. When she finally speaks, her words invite the porch talkers to gawk at her husband's genitals just as his words invited them to gaze at her body.

"You heard her, you ain't blind," Walter says to Joe. His statement draws a relationship between hearing and seeing and solidifies the voyeuristic nature of both their insults. They also peel back the mask of Joe's omnipotence. Thus weakened, he suffers a wounded spirit and becomes a victim of soul murder.

Janie's "funny" insult helps her feel better. For her, it provides access to an emotional truth that vindicates her and saves her from embarrassment. Unfortunately, it kills Joe.

Laughter's two-edged sword rarely kills, although the individual who becomes the "butt" of any joke—particularly a racial joke—may realize the emotional truths beneath the laughter and be wounded by them. When racial or gender stereotypes and blackpain become the central features of laughter, someone is sure to be broken or embarrassed by the experience. Yes, laughter heals. We must be able to laugh at ourselves and the multitude of difficulties we face daily. Doing so keeps us sane—or so we are told. In this regard, the benefits of laughter are not in question. It is how and whom laughter heals that is of concern here. Dodging the soul murder of painful rhetoric to secure laughter's healing is difficult when one is the subject of defaming jokes. One way through the potential racial hurt produced by blackpain's presence in comedy is to recognize the oppositional messages and emotional truths racialized humor might express covertly.

For an examination of this theory, I return to Bert Williams, who was an expert at cloaking the emotional truths of race and racism in his comedy. Like many comedians who followed him (Jackie "Moms" Mabley among them), he offered oppositional social analysis as a pathway though the racial hurt and blackpain he presented as the fodder of surface humor. I offer three examples for consideration:

Joke One
The colored maid came to the lady of the house and asked, "Please mam, Miss Alice, kin I git de aft' noon off a week frum nex' Wensdy?" Then, noticing an undecided look on the lady's face, she added hastily, "I wants to go to my financees fun'al." / "Your fiance's funeral" exclaimed the lady. "Why Lulu, you don't even know that he is going to die, let alone the exact day of his funeral. That is one thing we can't any of us be sure about—when we are going to die." / "Yassum," said the maid, and then with a triumphant note in her voice, "But I sho is sho 'bout him, Miss Alice, 'kase he's qwine to de 'lectric cheer." ("Bert Williams Joke Books," Book I, 85)

Joke Two
The Reason: Spruce Bigby was very bald. Lafe Brackston trying to "kid" him, asked, "Spruce, how'd you lose all yo' hair?" / "Twuz too nappy, like your'n," said Spruce, "an' I pulled it out." ("Bert Williams Joke Books," Book I, 87)

Joke Three

Somebody's done sed, dat de uglies' kind a trades has dare moments uv pleasure an' I beleeves it; 'cause ef I wuz a hangman or grave digger, I could git some sho nuff injoyment out a workin' fuh certain folks I know. ("Philosophacs and Philosophibs according to Spruce Bigby," "Bert Williams Joke Books," Book I, 91)

Death, pain, and more death are the subjects of these jokes, and in each case, there is a hint, if not a blatant reference, to racism and racial hurt. The first joke's competition between mistress and maid demonstrates that even when black people challenge white people, even when they win, there is a price to pay. In this joke, the price is death. Such was the case with Sam Hose, who was burned alive in 1899. The offense that ended with his death began as a demand to be heard, respected, and paid by his white employer. Du Bois "intuited that Hose was probably guilty at worst of committing an act of violence against a white in the course of defending his right to disagree" (Dray 7).

The second joke reveals the extent of black people's sensitivity to American beauty standards—not even extreme pain can curtail its influence. The joke suggests the only way to overcome the "ugliness" of black bodies constructed in America as wounded, unnatural, inhuman, and unattractive is to uproot and destroy the object of offense. This, in many ways, is what blackpain and racism does to black people. It separates a people from their "roots," and, having them in a weakened state, attempts to destroy them (through lynching, poor medical care, and other racial hurts). Likewise, blackpain separates a people from their "root" identities and destroys the preexisting image or reality only to replace it with one more useful to white-nation building and its advocates.

The third joke can be read any number of ways, including as an "inside joke" spoken for the benefit of Blacks attending Williams's comedy performances or for Williams himself. It speaks to the killing rage of those who may have wanted to "bury" the people who hated them and caused them so much pain—to act as "hangman" to people who have acted as the lynch-men (and lynch-women) of so many others. The opportunity to articulate such emotional truths humorously offers a certain amount of satisfaction—if only for a moment.

When racial or gender stereotypes and blackpain become the central features of laughter, someone is sure to be broken or embarrassed by the experience. Yes. Laughter heals. That is not in question. It is how and whom it heals that is of concern here. Dodging the soul murder of painful rhetoric to secure laughter's healing qualities is difficult. No one emerges from an encounter with blackpain cleanly; no one escapes its call for opposition, compromise, or complicity without making a choice.

Although there are many ways to heal from such encounters, no method is fail proof. One may shout, talk, consult the conjurer's pouch, or laugh to avoid crying, yet remain wounded and in spiritual jeopardy. Providing that blackpain persists in its operations as a tool of domination, exclusion, and control, the need for healing from racial hurt will recur for not only black people but for everyone else who experiences painfully its articulation of power.

Conclusion
Three Steps beyond Horror

The history of black bodies in pain and their abstraction in American popular culture and institutional practice is broad—so broad, in fact, that it is nearly impossible to narrow a discussion of it without minimizing something "too important not to mention," distorting something too emotionally shattering to present unveiled, or sensationalizing something too politically charged to tame. Consequently, much has been left out of this study. Absent, for instance, are considerations of Black-on-Black gang violence, child abuse, sex, capital punishment, medical practices, sports, and other subjects either deemed beyond the scope of this study or mentioned only in brief. Many very pertinent topics are simply too broad to cover adequately in this study. The discussion of laughter presented in the last chapter, for instance, merely peeks at comedy's relationship to blackpain. A thorough study would require an entire volume. For this reason, I offer my contemplations of it as a point of departure for a more in-depth review.

Although the discussions presented herein do not cover all (and should not), they faithfully offer relief from blackpain by examining, interpreting, and, thereby, demystifying it as a metaphor, as symbolic capital, and as disciplinary action used to benefit white-nation politics and systems of exclusion. Reverend

Taylor in Richard Wright's "Fire and Cloud" suggests unity as another method of securing relief from the racial assaults and disciplinary action of blackpain. "Ah *know* now!" he claims. "Ah done seen the sign! Wes gotta git together. . . . [I]ts [time] fer us t ack" (404). By reflecting on his words, I do not assume the solutions to the problems raised in this study are easy, quick, or trouble free. Taylor does not ask, as Rodney King did, "Can't we all just get along?" And neither does he suggest that violent retaliation is an answer. Instead, he calls for communities and individuals to redefine responsibility and act on it to challenge racism's influence on Black life. The lack of such action, as this study has demonstrated, *is* complicity.

Linda Williams suggests something similar as she insists that studies such as hers (and, by extension, this one) might issue a call for responsibility that demands cultural consumers recognize and analyze the "signs of racial virtue and villainy" when confronted with them (*Playing* 298). Her solutions can be a means of disrupting the racial marking and the symbolic violence of blackpain in literature, film, and everyday life. Williams writes: "Faced with the powerful influence of the melodrama of black and white, and with its often regressive influence in American culture, perhaps the best thing we can do is to name and recognize melodrama when we see it" (309). Assuming this type of responsibility, in relation to the arguments I have presented in this text, means examining the heart of white-nation sociodicy without end and exposing the potential for black and white America's denigration present within it.

"Pop" psychology would have us believe that writing is a method for meeting this responsibility. Writing, we are told, frees the mind from painful memories and wounding assaults and can effectively bring others to action. While researching and writing *African Americans and the Culture of Pain*, however, I found that this is not all writing accomplishes. Frederick Douglass's life as a writer is an example of another "truth," one I cannot resist sharing as I conclude this study.

Douglass's subject position as an "eyewitness" to slavery's cruelty prevented him from attaining the "full humanity and universal subjectivity" the mythology of American citizenship requires (DeLombard 275). According to Jeannine DeLombard's essay "'Eye Witness to the Cruelty,'" Douglass could never separate himself from the rhetoric and social memory of the black collective his literary efforts come to represent (246–47). His status as an icon of abolitionist rhetoric locked the free Douglass within a cultural text that defined him as subordinate and pained. Even after writing and distributing his narrative, both Douglass and his body continued to function as popular icons of a suffering, non-American, "Othered" people.

I reflect on the iconic paradox Douglass faced now as I remember my own response to the film I discussed in the opening pages of this study. Even after writing the first draft of *African Americans and the Culture of Pain*, I was not free from the impact of blackpain's racial hurt. Not until I realized my negotiated readings of the social texts I encountered while watching *Jasper, Texas* and abandoned that approach to understanding did I even come close to being symbolically "pain free." That goal, I discovered, cannot be achieved without moving "three steps beyond horror." This phrase describes the protocol used in this study for interpreting blackpain as an image and as an essential text within American mythologies of identity and safety.

The first of the three steps demands that we discover oppositional readings of blackpain, both verbal and visual, that expose its soul-murdering potential. Dominant, or hegemonic, readings offer blind acceptance of white-nation iconography and textual codes. They provide access to an inheritance promised only to nonblack American citizens and those would-be citizens who accept a mythology relegating black bodies as sites for discarded and unwanted identities and experiences. For them, a pain-free existence is possible, even probable, in America—or so the myth goes. The readings that emerged from my original impression of *Jasper, Texas* are not dominant readings, however. That is, at least not completely, since they only partially accepted the codes, viewing these codes as an aberration of general rules. My initial reading acknowledged the abstraction my body would become within that paradigm but failed to denounce it. I was a negotiating reader; I negotiated my way beyond truth by denying the symbolic messages and racial hurt I first recognized. In an instant, the negotiating reader rejects opposition and refuses to challenge dominant (and demeaning) racial codes. Black "negotiators," as we might identify them, accept the abstraction and therein wound themselves. In other words, they engage in symbolic violence rather than challenge the signifying structures relegating their bodies to a painful abstraction.

I argue throughout this study that oppositional readings are the only readings black people can employ if they are to gain any semblance of a pain-free and empowered relationship to blackpain. According to the cultural critic and scholar Stuart Hall, oppositional readings are produced by individuals whose social positions are in direct conflict with the preferred or dominant reading of a text and are, therefore, the most radical and culturally transformative

("Encoding" 128–34). Blackpain is a marker and metaphor of exclusion and denial existing in direct conflict with black people who live, love, suffer, laugh, and die as human beings always do. In fact, blackpain does not speak of a people but of a purpose and a plan that undermines, if not also destroys, awareness of the human African American presence in popular culture and in real life. For this reason, I use *black pain* to identify *whose* pain (that of black people), while restricting the use of *blackpain* to the world of metaphor and racial hurt.

The second step beyond horror, then, acknowledges hurt as a primary focus of meaningful interpretation and analysis. My experience of *Jasper, Texas* was similar to how Chester Himes describes a brutal beating in the *Quality of Hurt:* there was "too much pain and not enough hurt." My focus on pain was a distraction that weakened my search for meaning. It compromised my ability to put into language my rage and fear at racial hurt. My empathy for the pain I was witnessing debilitated me intellectually, and I ran. To achieve an oppositional reading of the scene, I needed to find the site and source of my own racial hurt and develop my responses around it. If pain remains the central focus, mobility is crushed, action is compromised, and meaning is never delivered. Ciel, in Gloria Naylor's *Women of Brewster Place*, makes pain her focus and inflames her experience of injury, which has been caused by her daughter's death (among other neglects and abuses). Unlike the invisible man (in Ellison's novel), Carl Brashear (in *Men of Honor*), Mann (in *Rosewood*), and the "boy" (in Richard Wright's "Going to Meet the Man"), she does not contain pain but lets it consume her instead. She does not take that third step beyond horror until Mattie pulls her back from pain's relentless onslaught. That is when she releases weakness and survives, safely.

With the third step, we not only release weakness, we decide how we will respond to hurt. We contemplate how to move through it safely while remaining cognizant of the difference between it and pain. In this step, we silence the pain and give voice to the wounds, or racial hurt, blackpain carves within us. And, eventually, we discover the strength of resistance. This step is perhaps the toughest to take because it requires us to redefine our relationship to and responsibility for blackpain. It gives us choices, but only two: complicity or silent mobility. By this, I mean we either choose to do additional harm through the symbolic violence of silent acceptance and escape, or we silence the roar of too much pain while mobilizing the strength to take action against our body's real enemy. That enemy is not pain but racial hurt, and its source is racism.

My experience proved to me that black witnesses of black pain cannot simply "watch from the trees"—even in retrospect—without becoming linked to the images of wounding and mutilation on display. Such a witness, this text claims, experiences his or her own body's symbolic value in negative and personally silencing ways. It is difficult to face the abstraction I call blackpain, to acknowledge its negative symbolic value and accept responsibility for its cultural revision through oppositional analysis without navigating successfully the temptation of inert silence and complicity.

A passage in W. E. B. Du Bois's *Dusk of Dawn* is emblematic of the silencing inferred here. When faced with the difficult decision of plotting a course through blackpain or avoiding it altogether (and, thereby, being complicit with it), Du Bois began to "turn away" from his life's work, a move that threatened to impoverish us all. He explains the temptation of silent complicity he faced in a passage documenting his response to accusations that Sam Hose had killed his white employer. "I wrote out a careful and reasoned statement concerning the evident facts and started down to the *Atlanta Constitution* office," Du Bois explains. "I did not get there. On the way news met me: Sam Hose had been lynched, and they said that his knuckles were on exhibition at a grocery store farther down on Mitchell Street, along which I was walking. . . . I turned back to the University. I began to turn aside from my work" (58, 67).

The historian Thomas Holt argues that Du Bois's moment of *turning aside* is the choice we make each time we do not accept responsibility for recognizing and analyzing experiences of everyday racial marking and assault. I made this choice as I witnessed the televised simulation of James Byrd's murder and ran from the family room of my home in tears. Unlike Du Bois, who did not "turn aside" but returned to a lifetime of social assessment and activism, the majority of us accept blackpain as natural and commonplace. We ignore it, or, in our roles as cultural critics and consumers, we treat it as if it "were somehow outside normal historical and social processes, as if 'trans-historical,' or epiphenomenal" (Holt 3–4). To do this is to be complicit with racist social dogma. We are all (regardless of race) bamboozled, silenced, and, ultimately, marked through inert responses and everyday withdrawal.

In the end, I have not "turned aside." *African Americans and the Culture of Pain* is my refusal to withdraw from the impact and meaning of the wounded and mutilated black bodies ever present in American popular culture and sociopolitical history. By researching and writing this text, I learned that to claim or give voice to pain is detrimental to personal agency. In fact, unless presented in opposition to white-nation domination, any sustained public discourse on the experience of black pain deflects from the more crucial and lasting concern of racial hurt. Black cultural productions, whether presented by men or women, offer more than the expression of pain—the "Ouch!" of black pain. They offer an examination of (gender and racial) hurt, its social functions, and how to survive it safely.

Black male writers and filmmakers, at least those reviewed in this text, give voice to the wound while allowing pain to speak of loss and empowerment. They do not focus on the void or on what is lost but on the move beyond that void, which teaches others, as well as themselves, how to survive racial hurt safely. For their protagonists and communities, pain is evidence of weakness leaving the body. Being and remaining a man is much more important than how pain feels or the length of time one endures it. Being and manliness are defined by how one fills the void weakness leaves behind as it is expelled.

Black women emphasize the site of wounding, calling it out for examination and validation. Their texts seem to demand that we look at hurt in places and in ways that have been forbidden: "Here! Right here is where the wounding occurred and this is how it happened!" Their texts also seem to say, "Look at how it happened, and survive it." As Toni Morrison reminds us, these are not stories to "pass on" (*Beloved* 275). The stories black women tell are tales to hold, to touch, and grow beyond.

This study has demonstrated that black writers and filmmakers (those like John Singleton and George Tillman) do not focus on pain—not while racial hurt threatens a more profoundly devastating end. For them, pain is physical, mental, and spiritual suffering. It may even bring one to physical disfigurement, mental illness, and death, but it is not the central point. That honor is reserved for hurt. Hurt is a compromised will, a soul wounded and in danger of being present "in the world" but not a present *Being* "of the world." While pain *is* and must be endured, it does not matter. Hurt, particularly racial and gender hurt, matters and must be challenged, exposed, and transformed if black people are to survive.

As deliberate and meaningful as this message may be, survival is not enough. Satisfying killing rage with stories of emotional truths or offering empathetic understandings of racial hurt is not enough, and neither is sharing healing moments through a church shout, conjurational spirituality, and laughter. Each of these strategies has been acknowledged in this text, but ultimately, it takes more to overcome the legacies of blackpain. It takes courage and the will to "turn it out!" By this, I mean exposing its partnership with systemic racism and ethnic bias.

The two-dimensional characterization and representation of African American pain presented most often in popular culture compromises the intelligence, will, and courage of black people, leaving nothing but bodies in pain to represent African American lives and history. Unfortunately, audiences easily ignore the dehumanizing and undeserved torment racism inflicts on these bodies. Instead of acknowledging the potential for denigrating Black life such entertainment possesses, we follow Hollywood's mandate to become voyeuristic consumers of white-nation rhetoric, consuming ugly images and grisly offerings of blackpain as if doing so were essential to our very existence. And, for some, it may very well be essential. Black bodies in pain provide white bodies an "imagined home" safe from racial wounding and the everyday racial markings of blackpain (Rogin 13). It is not the home equality would imagine and not a place where black people are allowed entrance. Yet, many knock on the door—unable to believe the myth of America's pain-free citizenry does not include everyone. Some are allowed inside, but none of these black "outsiders within" are ever pain free.

Black bodies, regardless of class or social status, are living memorials to black suffering and trauma. The symbolic capital and continual presence of blackpain in the American cultural imagination renders these bodies memorials of a hateful past. As an unchallenged metaphor and cultural image, blackpain signifies all black bodies without respect to persons. Instead of seeing a need for change, readers of blackpain who accept negotiated or dominant interpretations of black bodies are encouraged to either laugh at black people's lives and dismiss them or be repulsed by them and forget them—to "turn away." In both cases, viewers whose lives and racial associations are much different from those depicted enter a vicarious experience of the "Other's" world as absurd and pained.

This is where the idea of "turning it out" becomes most pertinent. As long as images of black mutilation and racial assault go uncontested, as long as there are few oppositional readers charging "Foul!" blackpain will continue to cripple or compromise Black lives daily. This book is my way of "turning it out." In it, I expose the legacies and messages of blackpain's symbolic capital that caused my distress as I watched *Jasper, Texas* that Sunday night in June 2003. My negotiated experience of blackpain uncovered raw, newly exposed avenues of meaning that surfaced in an instant and were just as quickly misrecognized, forgotten, and denied. The tears I misread that night as pity for a man I knew would be dragged to his death behind a pickup truck I now understand as tears shed for the communal body he and his body represent. They were tears shed for others as well as for myself: black people who share the racial hurt demanded by social contracts defining blackpain's symbolic capital, and others (of all races) who feel powerless as agents of change.

If we ever hope to discover the "home" Toni Morrison envisions as "a new space . . . safety without walls . . . difference that is prized but unprivileged," we must admit we have not yet recovered from our past ("Home" 12). America is not fully healed. Black people are becoming increasingly less visible as Beings and more present as abstract notions and stereotypes. Although we have come close to healing, we still have open sores, injuries bleeding from ongoing assaults of racism and prejudice, blatant and inadvertent stereotyping, defensiveness, denial, and racial hurt. We must turn it OUT!

But how? What exactly does that mean? What are we being asked to do? In *Codes of Conduct* (1995), Karla Holloway equates "turning it out" with "acting colored," by which she implies bringing notice to race-wounding events as they occur, wherever they occur. "Turning it out" requires rejection of social scripts that do not empower, scripts that allow some to wound or inflict pain while others stand by watching. It demands the rejection of cultural mandates that require individuals to experience acts of racist violence and disrespect in inert silence. In the end, it requires removing whatever prevents healing and simple acts of human kindness. Holloway writes, "In one sense, turning it out or acting colored means that we give up trying to respond to a situation as if both we and they [the offending party] are operating with the same codes of conduct" (29–31). Otherwise, we give up power and deny the symbolic violence our choice produces. In other words, when we do not "turn it out," we become complicit with racism and racial hurt.

Lorene Cary notes in *Black Ice* (1991) that "[t]urning out [i]s not a matter of style; cold indignation work[s] as well as hot fury. Turning out ha[s] to do with will. . . . [We must come to regard it as] a metaphor for black power and black duty" (58). I agree. It is a matter of will—or better, it is a matter of transforming unfortunate circumstances and stopping racist behaviors through soul power. "Turning out" the social, psychological, and emotional damages caused by the continual presence of blackpain in American popular culture and our everyday lives, then, means exercising the right to stand up and stand out for those things that bring wealth to our spirits (national and personal), because we expect such wealth, deserve it, and are determined to receive it.

Notes

Introduction

1. James Byrd's children are Jamie, Ross, and Renee. His parents are James Byrd Sr. and Stella Byrd. Both still live in Jasper County, Texas. The family connections between James Byrd Jr. and the film's director, Jeff Byrd, were not made clear in the materials I discovered.

2. Based on arguments set forth in *Blackface, White Noise* (1996), Michael Rogin might describe what happens to Byrd's body in terms of "the surplus symbolic value of blacks, the power to make African Americans represent something besides themselves" (14).

3. The television movie version of Laci Peterson's story, *The Perfect Husband* (2004), directed by Roger Young and written by Dave Erickson, addresses the story of Laci's husband, Scott Peterson, and his dilemma under suspicion for her murder.

4. The *Dateline* story presents Peterson within the boundaries of journalism's code of ethics. The oldest professional journalism society, the Society of Professional Journalists, instructs ethical journalists to "treat sources, subjects and colleagues as human beings deserving of respect." This code of ethics followed by members of the organization's 250 chapters asks that journalists "minimize harm" and "be sensitive when seeking or using interviews or photographs of those affected by tragedy or grief." The pictures of Peterson remain whole, demonstrating sensitivity to the effects of the tragedy on her family and others who watch. Perhaps the appearance of Byrd's story on premium cable television mitigates the importance of such gentle concern. Also, audiences (both inside and outside the United States) tend to accept male bodily mutilation more readily than the mutilation of women's bodies. The destruction of pregnant women's bodies speaks fiercely as a reminder of how vulnerable our ideals and social constructs really are. Such visual imagery would suggest the destruction of wholesomeness, familial nurturing, and, ultimately, of our species. See Society of Professional Journalists, "Code of Ethics."

5. Peterson was born Laci Denise Rocha. Rocha is a Hispanic name.

6. For more information about these murders and the divergent public interests they garnered, see "Evelyn Hernandez and Laci Peterson" by Remember Evelyn Hernandez. Also, see stories about LaToyia Figueroa, a black Hispanic woman murdered in July 2005. The sparse media coverage of her disappearance raised questions about racial bias in news reporting and community concern for the treatment and disappearance of women of non-Anglo, nonwhite

ethnicity and racial identities. See Monica Lewis, "Pregnant Black Woman Missing" and "Police: Remains of LaToyia Figueroa Found."

7. There have been at least two documentaries (*Journey to a Hate Free Millennium* [1999] and *Two Towns of Jasper* [2002]), two books (Dina Temple-Raston's *A Death in Texas* [2002] and Joyce King's *Hate Crime* [2002]), and a song about this murder and its effects on the town and the nation. The lyrics and music of the song "Jasper, Texas" by Ron Orlando and Mystery Train express more compassion than the film. Liz Latham produced a short (twelve minutes long) film for the James Byrd Foundation for Racial Healing titled *Remember His Name*. She is currently producing the documentary *God's Perfect Hate*, which spotlights Byrd's story. Byrd's mother, Stella Byrd, tells her story in *Hope in the Midst of Despair: A Grieving Mother Speaks* (2003).

8. In this study, *racism* refers to "an organized system, rooted in an ideology of inferiority that categorizes, ranks, and differentially allocates societal resources to human population groups" (Williams and Rucker, "Understanding" 75). I am most interested, however, in its effects when coupled with individual and group prejudice—particularly violent manifestations of prejudice.

9. For a more in-depth look at the medical issues raised in this chapter, please see Harriet A. Washington's *Medical Apartheid* (2006). Washington traces the "[d]angerous, involuntary, and nontherapeutic experimentation upon African Americans" from the eighteenth century to the present. It seems in matters of medical service, treatment, diagnosis, and follow-up, minorities are still getting a "raw deal." Statistics and findings about the medical treatment of blacks compared to whites are startling: "[B]lacks are less likely to be offered an operation to save [a] limb . . . Infant mortality rate is 2.5 times higher for blacks . . . blacks are 34 percent more likely to die from heart disease . . . blacks are 50 percent less likely to get heart bypass surgery . . . blacks are 25 percent less likely to get pain medication" ("Health Care's Racial Divide").

Bias exists in African American and Hispanic communities in regard to pharmaceutical services. A recent study "investigat[ing] the availability of prescribed opioids in New York City" found only 25 percent of the pharmacies in predominantly nonwhite neighborhoods had enough opioid-derived analgesics to treat patients with severe pain. Compared to the 72 percent of pharmacies stocking sufficient supplies in predominantly white neighborhoods (at least 80 percent white), this is quite distressing—especially since the reasons for the low stock are grounded in racism, stereotypes, and fear (see Morrison et al., "'We Don't Carry That'" 1023). According to a 2002 National Medical Association study, "Racial profiling [such as this] is more prominent in urban-area pharmacies. These pharmacies may refuse to stock certain opioids for reasons such as low demand, potential for fraud, fear of being robbed, or a belief that certain prescriptions are diverted for illegal use" ("Pain Is Undertreated," 1).

10. I am not in any way implying Morris is a racist. I am merely pointing out the near absence of black people and their pain in his book. Morris's handling of black pain is a weak link in an otherwise brilliant discussion of the culture of pain. Much like the Southern culture he condemns, Morris, perhaps unintentionally, relegates black pain to a world where it has no symbolic existence or consequence.

11. Since the novel and tragic drama are the most successful venues for shaping a "Western knowledge of suffering" and pain (see Morris, "About Suffering" 36), I concentrate primarily on

novels and film, which I believe are the most widely used vehicles for dramatic storytelling in our present age.

12. Not even institutions of higher learning are exempt from stereotypical body reading. Note, for instance, this story Karla F. C. Holloway tells in *Codes of Conduct* (1995): "I recall an early teaching experience in Michigan, when I was teaching a composition class made up of students from various majors across the university. That section had a large number of nursing students enrolled. One night they brought me their medical textbook and shared with me the chapter on patient care and intervention in emergency room medicine. The book stated quite explicitly that if your emergency room patient was a black woman, medical personnel could expect her to be overweight, wearing a wig . . . screaming and hysterical beyond a 'reasonable' measure of her pain and discomfort and very likely to be suffering from pelvic inflammatory disease. This diagnosis, regimen for care and prediction of patient behavior would be based only on the patient's gender and ethnicity!" (31–32)

Hillel W. Cohen and Mary E. Northridge attribute the impact of racism in the lives of African Americans with directly influencing "the depth of suffering and pain" black people experience. Cohen and Northridge believe "long established and growing health disparities are rooted in fundamental social structure inequalities which are inextricably bound up with racism that continues to pervade U.S. society." In short, racism and its stereotypes cause pain (Cohen and Northridge, 841).

13. I place the word *American* in quotation marks here to distinguish citizens of the United States from others living on the American continents (i.e., Brazilians, Canadians).

14. Using a more personal paradigm, Toni Morrison describes how phenotypic markers arrange the hierarchy of Americanization and how one of those markers, blackness, establishes itself in language: "When [immigrants] got off the boat, the second word they learned was 'nigger.' Ask them—I grew up with them. I remember in the fifth grade a smart little boy who had just arrived and didn't speak any English. He sat next to me. I read well, and I taught him to read just by doing it. I remember the moment he found out that I was black—a nigger. It took him six months; he was told. And that's the moment when he belonged, that was his entrance. Every immigrant knew he would not come as the very bottom. He had to come above at least one group—and that was us" (qtd. in Amgelo 21).

15. Shelby Steele claims, "In America, to know that one is not black is to feel an extra grace, a little boost of impunity" (4).

16. Lopez married the Latin singer and performer Marc Anthony in 2004 after two failed marriages to nonblack men (a thirteen-month marriage to Ojani Noa and a ten-month marriage to Chris Judd). With the March 2007 release of *Como Ama una Mujer*, Lopez revised both her sound and her image. The album is her first all-Spanish release. Pictured on the cover is a dark-complexioned, dark-haired Lopez.

17. Stuart Hall and Paddy Whannel establish the function and interpretive value of visual images by comparing them with the verbal images produced in literature. They suggest that meaning is conveyed through the image in film and not through plot and dialogue, as is the case in literature. "The kind of attention we must pay to . . . visual qualities is the equivalent of the attention we give to the verbal images, rhythms and so on, in our reading" (44).

18. As a term and as a concept, *blackpain* fuses the social constructions of race with the sym-bolic value of suffering. The word's semiotic construction emphasizes the bond of body and ex-

perience created within an order of "Otherness" that supersedes individuality to replace "Being" with alternative structures and meanings. Blackpain is a supplement to Black Being. As a supplement it "adds only to replace. It intervenes or insinuates itself in-the-place-of; if it fills, it is as if one fills a void. If it represents and makes an image, it is by the anterior default of a presence" (Derrida, *Of Grammatology* 145). Just as "art, *technè*, image, representation, convention, etc. come as supplements to nature," according to Derrida, so does blackpain serve as a supplement to Black "Being" in much of American pop culture and literature (*Of Grammatology*, 144–45).

19. This argument supports Orlando Patterson's explanations in *Slavery and Social Death* of how master communities relate to and depend on the social death of slaves. Patterson explains that slaves, being "the dead who still live," experienced liminality. They were marginal people, and the "marginal person," Patterson contends, "while a threat to the moral and social order, was often also essential for its survival. In cultural terms the very anomaly of the slave emphasized what was most important and stable, what was least anomalous in the local culture of the non-slave population" (45–46).

20. Roman Jakobson uses an interesting cinematic analogy to explain the easily mistaken difference between metonymy, which develops a continuous relationship from whole to part, and synecdoche, wherein a part signifies the whole. He equates synecdoche with "close-ups" and metonymy with "set-ups." The metaphor, which develops a discontinuous relationship between two wholes, he aligns with a filmic "'montage' with its 'lap dissolves'" (1114). To emphasize the primacy of black bodies in pain as an abstraction, I violate the boundaries of these definitions by collapsing each into a discussion of metaphor in this text.

21. Like Ho and Marshall, I want the phrase to remind us of the impact white racial bias, prejudice, and racism have on the lives and treatment of black people both today and historically. I want it to remind readers of the eighty-percent-black inmate population condemned to Sing-Sing's death house in 1960–63. We should recall "[w]hite male Los Angeles police officers beating Rodney King, Pete Wilson's rallying cry of 'Save Our State,' Tom Ridge's signature on the death warrant of Mumia Abu-Jamal, the six white male Greenwich, Connecticut, high school students coding 'kill all niggers' in their high school yearbook" (212). The phrase should help us remember only race mattered (not gender, class, or national origin) when Riverside, California, police shot a nineteen-year-old African American woman, Tyisha Shenee Miller, twenty-seven times as she sat in her disabled car. Neither did anything beyond race matter when nineteen of forty-one bullets fired by white New York City police officers penetrated the body of an unarmed black West African immigrant, twenty-two-year-old Amadou Diallo, killing him. *White nation* should not only help us remember these murders, it should also help us analyze why Ennis Cosby's murderer, the Ukrainian immigrant Mikhail Markhasev, bragged to friends, "I shot a nigger. It's all over the news" (Cosby 15a).

22. Pierre Bourdieu describes symbolic capital as existing within a self-perpetuating social economy as currency or credit that provides social agents access to property they agree is valued within a particular field of practice (*Pascalian Meditations* 166). This symbolic economy works only if the agents involved are successful in keeping hidden the operations of economic or social exchange systems that assign worth (Bourdieu, *The Logic of Practice* 112–13). Throughout this text I expose a few of those hidden systems of exchange.

23. Richard Dyer describes the processes of naturalization referred to here as the way social

agents who are white "colonize the definition of normal" (45). In the introduction to *"Race," Writing, and Difference* (1985), Henry Louis Gates comments that the naturalization of race is achieved through its inscription in discourse: "Western writers . . . have sought to make literal these rhetorical figures of 'race,' to make them natural, absolute, essential. In doing so, they have *inscribed* these differences as fixed and finite categories which they merely report or draw upon for authority" (6). Writing within a British context, the sociologist Paul Gilroy comments on naturalization processes that produce cultural nationalism and images of citizenship that exclude blackness from the category of "the people." This "new racism," as he calls it in *The Black Atlantic* (1993), grows out of recent historical moments like that involving Salman Rushdie's book *The Satanic Verses*, which "aligned 'race' closely with the idea of national belonging" (10). See also Gilroy's *"There Ain't No Black in the Union Jack."*

1. Overt and Symbolic Violence

1. The historian W. Fitzhugh Brundage describes Sam Hose as an unimposing figure who was nothing like the mad black rapist newspaper accounts presented of him. For them, Hose was blackpain—the "burly black brute" who threatened all of white patriarchy—but in fact, he was a "bright and capable man" who "seemed bashful and reserved around whites." Brundage reports the events leading to Hose's death as follows: "Early in April of 1899, Hose asked his employer to allow him to return to his home to visit his ill mother. He also asked Cranford [his boss] for money. The planter refused to advance him any money, and the two men exchanged harsh words. On the following afternoon, while Hose chopped wood at Cranford's home, his employer resumed the previous day's argument. The planter grew increasingly angry, drew his pistol, and threatened to kill Hose. In self-defense, the black man hurled his axe, which struck Cranford in the head and killed him instantly. Terror-stricken, Hose fled and began to make his way to his mother's home" (82–83).

2. I repeat this story in detail to emphasize how the enthralling presence of pain lingers, even more than a century after an assault occurs, drawing us into its horror while also repelling us.

3. The comments are from the September 2004 proofreading notes of Sarah Brusky, University of Florida graduate student.

4. Ironically, white participants in lynching meant to dishonor blacks, not themselves. According to Brundage, lynching was a method of discouraging violence against whites by causing blacks shame and disgrace. Brundage comments that lynchings consisted of much more than mere acts of vengeance. "They also dramatized as few other rituals could the domination of whites and the degradation and dishonor of blacks" (80). Later in this text I discuss how black victims of lynching subverted these attempts at degradation and dishonor.

5. Although there was usually great anticipation and excitement surrounding mob lynching, Brundage charges that not everyone was there for a "good time." We should not minimize the social and political symbolism (and justifications) of Hose's lynching and those of other blacks who faced similar charges of murdering a white man and raping a white woman. Such lynching avenged the desecration of a white patriarchal ideal. Brundage comments, "The lynching of the black murderer became a bloody drama in which the white community assumed the protection of the widow and fatherless family while at the same time it affirmed the tragic future and vulnerability that the family faced" (74). Brundage reminds us that causes for lynching that fall shy of desecrating the white patriarchal family "often failed to arouse a massive

communal response . . . whites did not interpret every attack by a black as an egregious assault on racial order" (75).

Unfortunately, an embarrassing number of lynching incidents in U.S. history appear to be without any justification beyond expressions of power and racial hate. The men who murdered James Byrd (John William King, Shawn Berry, and Lawrence Brewer), for instance, were reportedly members of a white supremacist gang who, not unlike the KKK and other organizations before them, hoped the grisly murder of a black man (what King called "taking a black out") would bring them respect and credibility among their peers. During John King's trial, a prison inmate, William Hoover, testified that King understood all too well the importance of executions to white supremacist organizations—particularly the execution of a black person (see Michael Graczy, "Murder Defendant").

6. The story of the slave ship *Amistad* and the West African captives who took control of it is documented in books, a film, and an opera. The opera, which premiered November 30, 1997, featured two "disempowered" black divinities: the Trickster God and the Goddess of the Waters (*Amistad,* dir. George C. Wolfe. Lyric Opera, New York). The opera reviewer Paul Griffiths commented, "[T]he composer, Anthony Davis, and his librettist cousin, Thulani Davis, have . . . gone some way toward rewriting an exemplary instance of liberalism as an African folk tale. . . . The Goddess of the Waters appears only for one big aria. . . . The Trickster God begins the opera with a long solo in which he insists that he is the tale teller, but then narrative authority is taken out of his hands and dropped" (E1). Griffiths further notes that no one in the opera emerges as a character of depth or with individuality: "The director, George C. Wolfe, and the set designer, Riccardo Hernandez, offer spectacle as some recompense for the lack of drama" (E1).

7. Building on the philosophy presented in Martin Heidegger's *Being and Time* (1968), Thomas C. Holt contends that one comes to know and realize oneself through everyday encounters with existence and "through one's consciousness of one's own mortality and selfhood" (9). Considering the juxtaposition of Laci Peterson's media persona as the girl next door with the representation of James Byrd's mutilated body and the continual repetition of similar images (discussed later in this study), mortality and violent death can become (and, actually, have become), for African Americans, naturalized as an anticipated and commonplace *threat.*

8. Paul Gilroy reads Burke's story as signaling the "doorway" of traditions through which "ethnic and racialized attributes would finally give way to the dislocating dazzle of 'whiteness'" (*Black Atlantic* 9). This dazzle cloaks the horrors of harm associated with nonblack bodies, marking out, for instance, the specifics of the real Laci Peterson's murder while highlighting and sustaining the image of *Laci,* the girl next door.

9. The French sociologist and neo-Marxist Pierre Bourdieu describes fields of conflict as sites where history is created and transformed through the constant struggle of positions, stances, and dispositions in conflict (see *An Invitation to Reflexive Sociology* 102).

10. Members of the New Black Panther Party and the KKK made appearances in Jasper during the trial. The Black Panthers, carrying weapons, made speeches and encouraged Jasper residents to engage in armed self-defense. Their efforts and the efforts of the Klan to promote what they described as "white power" were deflected after a single day, however, by communal unity as preached by clergy like Jasper's Reverend Kenneth Lyons.

11. The "founding fathers" created the nation's Constitution within a dual field of political

and economic concerns that included race silently, but distinctly. Black bodies, existing at the intersection of these concerns, achieved value based on a racially bound and organized subfield of power (i.e., slavery). The North wanted to weaken the South's voting power by lessening the "worth" of a particular group living in the South, while the South wanted to strengthen their representation and power by playing the same game of value and worth—only differently. While Northerners did not want to "count" slaves as part of the southern population, the South wanted to count them fully and thereby gain additional governmental representation and decision-making power. The compromise made by each side was included in the nation's Constitution as follows: "Representatives and direct taxes shall be apportioned among the several States which may be included within this Union according to their respective numbers, which shall be determined by adding to the whole number of free persons, including those bound to service for a term of years, and excluding Indians not taxed, three fifths of all other persons" (U.S. Constitution Art. 1, sec. 2.3). Interpretations of how and to whom the compromise acted as a benefit abound. Some historians argue the South benefited through higher numbers in governmental representation, while others view that representation as reduced by the compromise. Either way, one thing remains: the language of the compromise devalues black bodies.

12. Bourdieu notes that the hierarchy of "worth and worthiness" documented through symbolic capital is not equivalent to hierarchies of "wealth and powers." Almost in direct contradiction to this sentiment, he acknowledges "the Black in the ghetto" as oppositional to the "State nobility." His paradigm of legitimating processes and race, however, differs from the one presented here only in its somewhat narrow focus on economic capital and its relationship to justifying hierarchies of worth (*Pascalian Meditations* 242).

13. Laci's whiteness is exaggerated, illusory, and purposefully soothing. Her ethnicity is hidden beneath the awesome glare of this whiteness. The girl-next-door construction is thereby made pleasurably pain free, accessible, and justifiable. Meanwhile, a program like *Jasper, Texas* brings sharply into view the function of black pain as a "costly" yet necessary and dangerous commodity. One may even read its on-screen presentation as an ironic demonstration of black pain's existence as a pleasurable and costly commodity to be enjoyed only by those privileged enough to engage such pleasures from the "safety" and distance premium cable television provides. Additionally, "pay" TV allows a more dramatic and obscene presentation of pain and mutilation than major network television, which is restricted by its own description as "family-oriented television."

14. In "Living the Legacy: Pain, Desire, and Narrative Time in Gayl Jones's *Corregidora*," Maryemma Graham discusses the effect of black America's internal awareness of pain. She describes Ursa's experience of history as "ill-will, a pain," and as torture. What I describe here as memorializing pain in the black body, she considers an "invasion of history." To see the "presence of historical legacy as rather torture than tradition," Graham comments, "is to acknowledge the way in which history is experienced by its survivors precisely as a pained, sustained present" (450–51).

15. The most poignant appearance of a black character in this film is when a nameless black man visits the town just to torment a white man with a tale of black pain (a lynching, which the victim survived, though he lost his scrotum and was drenched in blood "to the waist"). This visitor is a large man who conducts his interrogation alone while threatening a similar retaliation of blood, loss, and pain if the white man (bound to a chair) does not name those responsible for

killing three civil rights workers. Once this man secures the desired information, he leaves town (and the film), never, we assume, to return. He is a false threat, and his appearance as a lone black avenger is a "setup." He has no real power or intention to act on his threats. His interrogation works because the racist whom he threatens sees only the murdering presence of a "burly black brute." The audience, however, understands there is no real threat or danger—if not before the scene ends, we know it as the black man, after shaking hands in partnership with the white FBI agents, leaves town.

16. Susan Sontag's *Illness as Metaphor* (1978) provides one example of symbolic violence. Her reflexive critique of violent semantic influences in socially and politically appropriated medical discourse transformed the medical field. Sontag maintains that negative metaphors of illness are harmful to those who suffer the affiliated disease, especially when society and the state employ those metaphors to define evil or to describe threats to national populations and national security. Metaphors in which crime might be described as "spreading like a cancer," for instance, are for her not only harmful to the public's ability to envision social healing but also devastating to the healing process of those experiencing the disease. Disease metaphors, she explains, tag the sufferer as a death-row citizen or resident "in the Kingdom of the ill" (2).

17. Early studies by white psychologists viewed black subjectivity and black people's woundedness as pathological and determined by slavery's legacy. "These [studies] constructed the Negro as a psychologically tormented individual whose entire identity was dictated by white racism" (Mama, *Beyond the Masks* 47). The black psychologists Kenneth and Mamie Clark (famous for their 1940s experiments on race using black children and dolls) considered black subjectivity constituted by a negative self-concept. Similar studies (including the psychology of *nigrescence*, which aligned with the positive self-image and subjective politics of the Black Power Movement) defined the black psyche consistently through or against a lens of white racism. In fact, Amina Mama commented in 1995 that there exists no acknowledgment of black "experience apart from that of racism . . . The nuances and intricate set of social etiquette and behavior, of betrayal and collusion, of inversion and resistance that constitute racism as a social process are barely touched upon" (48). Unlike the studies Amina Mama analyzes, I do not assume a monolithic black experience. I examine the "nuances," such as collusion and social etiquette, for instance, as distinct features of symbolic violence discussed throughout this study. See chapter 4 for a thorough discussion of these "nuances."

18. Freud labeled the quest to avoid pain the "pleasure principle" and defined it as a desire for satisfaction controlled only by the ethical strength of the ego and its submission to the "reality principle." His theories present the ego as a moral gauge through which individuals "reality-test" and weigh the prospects of pleasure and pain before acting. This "psychical activity draws back from any event which might arouse unpleasure" ("Formulations," 302). Freud outlines his two principles and theories on the death drive and pain in several texts, notably *The Interpretation of Dreams* (1900), "Formations on the Two Principles of Mental Functioning" (1911), and *Beyond the Pleasure Principle* (1920).

2. Racial Hurt and Soul Murder

1. Cathy Caruth comments that the truth trauma has to tell is "intricately bound up with its refusal of historical boundaries; that its truth is bound up with its crisis of truth" ("Trauma and Experience," 8). It is this crisis of truth that I suggest is perpetuated by a focus on pain. Pain may

be an avenue to truth, but it is not truth. Hurt (racial and gendered) is truth—at least for the purposes of this study. Hurt is the substance and cause of soul murder and the only pathway to short-circuiting pain's refusal to stay within historical boundaries. Blackpain presented as memorial time recalls endlessly a history of hurt that leads to the continual wounding and rewounding of Black lives and spirits. Revealing racial hurt promotes survival whole. In this context, wholeness means survival absent of the image or stigma of blackpain as memorial time—as a symptom of harm that quenches desire, will, and Being beneath the weight and symbolic pressure of "too much pain."

2. Robert Jay Lifton claims, "Focusing on survival, rather than on trauma, puts the death back into the traumatic experience" (Caruth, "An Interview with Robert Jay Lifton" 128). Survival, he contends, suggests an encounter with death. This is essential when speaking of a safe transition out of trauma, particularly the trauma of racial hurt and the pain associated with it in this country. Each encounter with racial hurt is a death encounter. I interpret both Alice Walker's concept of "survival whole" and my reference to surviving racial hurt "safely" as indicating a "death encounter" overcome; they both imply life.

3. The 1997 film *Miss Evers' Boys*, directed by Joseph Sargent and starring Alfre Woodard, depicts its title character as a collaborator with a medical system inflicting extreme racial hurt, mental and physical debilitation, and pain and death. The film, based on the "Tuskegee Study of Untreated Syphilis in the Negro Male," tells a story of human experimentation and institutionalized racism. From 1932, when the experiment began, to 1972, doctors denied a selected group of black men in Macon County, Alabama, access to penicillin, a known cure for syphilis. There were six hundred men involved in the government-sanctioned study. Of these subjects, 201 were infection free, while 399 tested positive for the disease. According to Brogna Brunner, "By the end of the experiment, 28 of the men had died directly of syphilis, 100 were dead of related complications, 40 of their wives had been infected, and 19 of their children had been born with congenital syphilis" ("Tuskegee Syphilis Experiment").

For forty years, Eunice Rivers, like the character representing her in the film, accepted guilt and self-blame for this tragedy. She was silently complicit with a system that did not acknowledge its responsibility until most of the men were dead. In 1997 the U.S. government took full and unconditional responsibility for the "deeply, profoundly, morally wrong" treatment the men received (Clinton, quoted in Hunter-Gault, "Apology 65 Years Late"). President Bill Clinton gave his formal apology on May 16, 1997, before the seven surviving members of the study in the East Room of the White House. A transcript of his speech is available online through the National Archives. See Bill Clinton, "Remarks."

4. Orlando Patterson uses the phrase *social death* to infer a loss of social recognition and human resemblance of subordinates (i.e., slaves) as mandated and controlled in cultural representations and symbolic images created by masters. For Patterson, social death is a living death in which the slave is depicted as the enemy of the state—an outsider or defeated enemy who has never achieved social presence—or as an insider who has fallen and, as a result, lost social presence. Neither "belongs" within the dominant sphere of influence and authority and neither is considered a "living" Being within that sphere.

5. In his studies of trauma, Henry Krystal comments that this "death" can lead to an "automatonlike behavior," which he claims is a survival technique adopted of necessity by individuals, like Sofia, who find themselves "in situations of subjugation, such as prison and con-

centration camps" (81). In these cases, the individual is unable to act defensively or aggressively owing to a certain amount of involuntary "freezing" suffered under painful stress. This paralysis, also called a "catatonic reaction" or traumatic immobilization, leads to automatic obedience. See also Max M. Stern, "Anxiety, Trauma, and Shock"; and Robert Jay Lifton, *Death in Life*.

6. The film version of *The Color Purple* is a little more pointed and humorous in its description of Sofia's found voice. "The dead have arisen," Albert's father declares.

7. Patricia Hill Collins suggests, "Commodification of the blues and its transformation into marketable crossover music has virtually stripped it of its close ties to the African-American oral tradition" (*Black Feminist Thought* 102).

8. The volume contains photography from an exhibition called *Witness*, which first appeared at the Roth Horowitz Gallery in New York City. Later it was displayed at the Andy Warhol Museum in Pittsburgh, Pennsylvania, in 2001 and, ultimately, at the Martin Luther King Jr. National Historic Site and Emory University during 2002–3. Emory now serves as its permanent home. A Web site linked to the exhibit can be found at www.withoutsanctuary.com. James Allen and John Littlefield coauthored the coffee table book of lynching photos titled *Without Sanctuary*.

9. During a 2001 "master's tea" lecture at Yale University, the filmmaker Spike Lee coined the phrase "Super-duper magical negro" to describe John Coffey and other black characters in recent films who are endowed with magical powers (S. Gonzalez, n. pag.). A year earlier, the *New York Times* columnist Christopher John Farley included *The Green Mile* and *The Legend of Bagger Vance* (dir. Robert Redford, 2000) in what he labeled the "Magical African American Friends" (MAAF) category of recent filmmaking (14). The Villanova University English professor and cultural critic Heather J. Hicks agrees. In "Hoodoo Economics," she argues that films like *The Green Mile, Unbreakable* (dir. M. Night Shyamalan, 2000), and *Family Man* (dir. Brett Ratner, 2000) depict MAAF who negotiate the social relations of gender and work. Hicks comments that each of these films create the "fantasy of a black man stepping in magically to bolster the crumbling fiction of autonomous masculinity" (40, 52).

3. Personal Protests and War

1. In the next chapter, I discuss the dangers of such complicity and inert silence as practiced within African American folk culture. My discussion parts with Laub's arguments but only in terms of where he couches danger ("Truth and Testimony"). Laub describes individuals who have come through a war that is considered over. They have moved through death and survived. I explore silence and secrecy as survival techniques of those still in the throes of war. For many African Americans who practice silence as a part of Black folk culture, their "secret order" and its demand for silence is a means of surviving everyday battles and struggles with death and the threat of death.

2. I concede the impossibility of contemplating every battle of America's race war in one volume, much less in one chapter. Therefore, I focus on four historical events primarily because they have been recreated in either popular literary or cinematic form. These are the Rosewood massacre, the story of the Civil War's first all-black fighting military regiment (the Massachusetts 54th), the alleged slaughter of black soldiers at Mississippi's Camp Van Dorn, and the solitary struggle of Carl Brashear to earn the rank of Master Chief in the U.S. Navy.

3. In *The Color Complex* (1993), Kathy Russell, Midge Wilson, and Ronald Hall claim "colorism" is a source of psychological bias and caste-building that "creates systems of privilege as well as oppression" (4). Singleton highlights this subset of prejudice and intraracial preference during *Rosewood* by depicting light-skinned, sharp-featured black women as the "protected" bodies of racial inheritance who escape the massacre accompanied by the town's children. The dark-skinned (or black, black) women are either murdered or raped *and* murdered. Such wounding serves as a sign of their utter exclusion from protection against the harms of America's race war.

4. Claudia Tate's critique of desire and power describes this type of surplus as textual representations that "do not fit the Western hierarchical paradigm of race as exclusion, vulnerability, and deficiency" (*Desire and the Protocols of Race,* 7). Although Tate does not use the term *surplus* to identify a field or site for the exchange of power, she does present it ideologically as a "characteristic not generally associated with African American personality and culture" (7).

5. Three dollars were deducted from the salaries of the black soldiers for the cost of uniforms, while white soldiers were compensated for this charge with a three-dollar increase in salary.

6. Corporal James Henry Gooding's letter is located in the National Archives, Record Group No. 94, Colored Troops Division, Letters Received, H133, CT 1863. The following is a brief extract: "Now the main question is, Are we Soldiers, or are we Labourers? We are fully armed, and equipped, have done all the various duties pertaining to a Soldier's life, have conducted ourselves to the complete satisfaction of General Officers, who were, if any[thing], prejudiced against us, but who now accord us all the encouragement and honour due us; have shared the perils and [l]abour of [r]educing the first stronghold that flaunted a Traitor Flag; and more, Mr. President. Today the Anglo-Saxon Mother, Wife, or Sister are not alone in tears for departed Sons, Husbands and Brothers. The patient, trusting Descendants of Afric's Clime have dyed the ground with blood, in defense of the Union, and Democracy. Men, too, your Excellency, who know in a measure the cruelties of the Iron heel of oppression, which in years gone by, the very Power their blood is now being spilled to maintain, ever ground them to the dust."

7. This ending is misleading. Of the six hundred men in the regiment, fewer than 281 were killed that day. Many others fought and survived this nation's Civil War until its end.

8. For oral testimony, documentation, and a full review of the story, see the television documentary of the story titled *History Undercover: The Mystery of the 364th*. This program was researched, recorded, and prepared to air when the History Channel dropped it from the programming schedule shortly before the airdate. It is available for purchase, although there are no plans to air it.

9. Carl Maxie Brashear, Master Chief Boatswain's Mate Petty Officer USN (Retired)—the first African American U.S. Navy Master Diver and the first amputee to be certified as a diver—died July 25, 2006, of respiratory and heart failure at the Portsmouth Naval Medical Center, Portsmouth, Virginia. He was seventy-five years old. He retired from the U.S. Navy in April of 1979 after thirty years of service.

10. Another area of vulnerability on this field of struggle is the men's relationship with their wives. When Brashear's wife opposes his decision to amputate his damaged leg, she becomes a deterrent to the transfer of power from Chief Sunday to her husband. At this point in the nar-

rative, she disappears—as if divorced—until the film's last scene. She returns then only as a mother of a son (Brashear's) who will reject her (we assume) in order to receive the patriarchal power his father secures.

11. In "National Brands/National Body," Berlant observes that, in the United States, corporeality and citizenship (and its consequent rights) are incompatible. "White male privilege," she writes, "has been veiled by the rhetoric of the bodiless citizen, the generic 'person' whose political identity is *a priori* precisely because it is, in theory, non-corporeal. . . . setting up a peculiar dialectic between embodiment and abstraction in the post-Enlightenment body politic" (112). Karen Sánchez-Eppler supports this reading of citizenship. According to her, the constitutionally derived U.S. subject, or "juridical person," has always been white and male. More important, however, is that the successful masking of this fact legitimizes that body's right to power. Furthermore, she contends, "authority derives from simulating the impossible position of the universal and hence bodiless subject" (3). Robyn Wiegman argues similarly in *American Anatomies* (1995) that "the figure of the American citizen" emanates from a system of repression that denies the body. "In this constitution of the citizen as a disembodied entity, bound not to physical delineations but to national ones, the white male was (and continues to be) 'freed' from the corporeality that might otherwise impede his insertion into the larger body of national identity" (94). The extreme corporeality associated with African American male and female subjects distances them from consideration as citizens and power brokers.

12. In reality, Carl Brashear experienced similar pain and, like the character portrayed in the film, he had to hide his body—suppress it. He tells his story in an interview with Paul Stillwell of the History Division of the U.S. Naval Institute (Brashear, "Oral History"). Brashear reports: "I had to spend a week at the deep-sea diving school diving with a captain and a commander. . . . They watched me dive for a week as an amputee and run around the building, do physical fitness every morning, lead the calisthenics. . . . [They sent me] back to the diving school. . . . [Chief Warrant Officer Raymond K.] Duell [the officer in charge of the diving school] dove me every day [for a year], every cotton-picking day. I did it every day—weekends and all. At the end of that year he wrote the most beautiful letter. Boy, that was something. I was returned to full duty and full diving—the first time in naval history for an amputee. . . . That was an accomplishment. Sometimes I would come back from a run, and my artificial leg would have a puddle of blood from my stump. I wouldn't go to sick bay. In that year, if I had gone to sick bay, they would have written me up. I didn't go to sick bay. I'd go somewhere and hide and soak my leg in a bucket of hot water with salt in it—an old remedy. Then I'd get up the next morning and run."

4. Silent Mobility

1. Bourdieu defines bodily hexis as a "political mythology realized, embodied, turned into a permanent disposition, a durable manner of standing, speaking, and thereby of feeling and thinking" (*Outline* 93–94).

2. There are three sensory syndromes associated with the inability to feel pain: "(a) progressive sensory radicular neuropathy, a hereditary disease which begins with degeneration of the sensory neurons in the extremities; (b) nonprogressive sensory neuropathy, of unknown etiology, which may involve cranial and thoracic nerves as well as the limbs, and which differs from congenital insensitivity to pain in that deep tendon and axon reflexes are absent in the involved areas, there are other sensory deficits than pain, and demyelination is apparent in sen-

sory nerve biopsies; (c) congenital insensitivity to pain, in which sensory nerve biopsies appear normal and the presumed 'lesion,' if any is central to peripheral receptors and fibers" (Sternbach, "Congenital Insensitivity to Pain" 253).

3. It is important to note the impact of extreme trauma on the affective state of victims like Warner. Henry Krystal comments that, having surrendered to the inevitable danger of a traumatic and painful experience, people will surrender to it. They move from anxiety, which is the signal for avoiding pain and danger, to a pattern of surrender, which can be identified as "freezing," "playing possum," or "panic inaction." Krystal claims such acts of surrender can initiate a "'numbing' process by which all affective and pain responses are blocked" (80). Perhaps a certain amount of "numbing" accounts for the remarkable reports of silent victims of lynching. Regardless of its source, such silence has played a major role in a black cultural mandate for silent suffering and "bearing through" the pain of traumatic experiences.

4. Civil disobedience as advocated by Martin Luther King and Gandhi, or passive resistance, is not referred to here. The silence this chapter explores lacks the appearance and the instructive action of the bodily hexis expressed through passive resistance and the accompanying admission of disobedience. In fact, it often has the appearance, both in gesture and articulation, of submission, not resistance or defiance.

5. According to Wiegman, white lynch mobs operate in a "panoptic mode of surveillance" and performance that "communalizes white power" (*Anatomies* 13). Through this communal "power," the threat of lynching multiplies until it is as much a disciplinary action as the specular scene.

5. Writing in Red Ink

1. In this essay, Cixous demands a radical revision of how and by whom the female body should be written and interpreted. Her ideas are respected and taught in women's studies classes and feminist discussion groups today, with her primary arguments examined at great length. Yet, few of these discussions offer a thorough investigation of what writing in white ink, that good mother's milk, means for women of color. Cixous' version of feminine writing reclaims a darkness tainted with peril by offering a pen of illumination that writes the body in "white ink." Unfortunately, the racialized fictions and wounding of black women's bodies remain unchallenged by her metaphors of discursive reconfiguration and subversion. Writing in white ink allows women who are white to celebrate what Cixous identifies as their "cosmic" libido by inscribing their stories of decensored sexuality and "native strength" onto the pages of an already symbolically charged and racialized space of blackness (Cixous 345). While effectively destroying the idea that women's bodies are unexplorable centers of lack, Cixous' choice of metaphor evades (if not supports) white masculine discourses that define blackness as an icon of extravagant eroticism and licentious desire. Through Cixous' use of metaphors, Medusa recovers her head and control of both the gaze and the interpolating call, while black women's bodies remain captive within the dark continent of male-inscribed body politics.

2. I contend these writers seek wholeness for their characters by realizing that the journey toward wholeness is painful, but, more than this, that the achievement of survival is also a pain that must be faced. Cathy Caruth comments similarly as she speaks of a "deeply disturbing" insight: "the fact that, for those who undergo trauma, it is not only the moment of the event, but of the passing out of it that is traumatic; that survival itself, in other words, can be a cri-

sis" (*Trauma* 9). The texts I discuss in this chapter deal with survival as a crisis from which characters can be delivered once they are able to find and examine the truth of racial and gendered hurt.

3. During the last quarter of the twentieth century, African American women opened a public discussion concerning the psychological and spiritual effects of pain and racial hurt in the lives of individuals and their communities. Writers exposed pain's effects in self-help books (such as *In the Company of My Sisters* [1993] by Julia Boyd and *Yesterday, I Cried* [1998] by Iyanla Vanzant) and in a plethora of novels (like Alice Walker's *Possessing the Secret of Joy* and Toni Morrison's *The Bluest Eye*). Television programs about how one survives the life-"crippling" effects of gender hurt (the black best-selling author and Yoruba priestess Iyanla Vanzant's now defunct talk show, for instance) gained great popularity among black and white women. Black men, however, have not engaged the issue of pain in the same public manner.

6. Expressing, Sharing, and Healing Black Pain

1. Today there are therapeutic centers practicing Primal Integration. The International Primal Association, for instance, claims their brand of psychotherapy results from the work of Arthur Janov, author of *The Primal Scream* (1970).

2. In *Slave Religion*, Albert Raboteau explains that the "ecstatic behavior" of slaves was "not due to any innate emotionalism; nor was it totally due to the need of an oppressed class to release pent-up tension. Rather, the slaves tended to express religious emotion in certain patterned types of bodily movement influenced by the African heritage of dance" (61). These movements, including the "holy dance," are not referred to in this chapter, although they often accompany shouting. I am concerned with the vocalizations—the shrieks, screams, and cries—that allow pain's expression. Although I acknowledge that the shout is also a way to express great joy, I focus here on the extraction of pain.

3. As an event, the church shout is well within the range of what Derrida calls "a differential typology of forms of iteration. . . . In such a typology," he writes, "the category of intention will not disappear; it will have its place, but from that place it will no longer be able to govern the entire scene and system of utterance. . . . [G]iven that structure of iteration, the intention animating the utterance will never be through and through present to itself and to its content. The iteration structuring it *a priori* introduces into it a dehiscence and a cleft . . . which are essential" (*Limited* 18).

4. Racial injustices encourage, if not cause, physical illnesses such as high blood pressure, ulcers, obesity, and diabetes that occur with high frequency in black communities. For a discussion of racism and African American health, see "Getting Political" by Hillel W. Cohen and Mary E. Northridge. Also, see Denise Foley's essay "Being Black Is Dangerous to Your Health."

5. Such tensions link the soulful music of a grandmother's hum to a similar pain found in the down-home blues B. B. King speaks through "Lucille" (his famous guitar). They can even link the poignant melodies of John Coltrane's saxophone to the "frenzy" W. E. B. Du Bois found in a southern black church.

6. Being as envisioned here is not mere existence but is the ontological character of *Dasein*, which translates as "Being there" or "Being-in-the-World." According to Martin Heidegger, Dasein is the human being as an entity engaged in the specifics of daily living and the struggles

of mass culture and socialization. When Dasein is cloaked or unacknowledged, we see only body, a temporal form with weight and presence, but no "life."

7. Maslin's second assessment of the film supports this observation. She writes, "What the estimable 'Amistad' does not have is an Oskar Schindler. It has no three-dimensional major character through whose flawed human nature an unimaginable atrocity can be understood. . . . 'Amistad' divides its energies among many concerns: the pain and strangeness of the captives' experience, the Presidential election in which they become a factor, the stirring of civil war, and the great many bewhiskered abolitionists and legal representatives who argue about their fate. The specific, as in Cinque's being torn from his family, is overwhelmed by generality" ("Pain of Captivity").

8. Scarry offers an explanation of the shift from "real pain" to "fictional power" in her discussion of torture. She writes: "What assists the conversion of absolute pain into the fiction of absolute power is an obsessive, self-conscious display of agency. On the simplest level, the agent displayed is the weapon. Testimony given by torture victims from many different countries almost inevitably included descriptions of being made to stare at the weapon with which they were about to be hurt: prisoners of the Greek Junta (1967–71), for example, . . . were compelled to look at a bull's pizzle coated with the dried blood of a fellow prisoner. . . . It is not accidental that in the torturers' idiom the room in which the brutality occurs was called the 'production room' in the Philippines, the 'cinema room' in South Vietnam, and the 'blue lit stage' in Chile: built on these repeated acts of display and having as its purpose the production of a fantastic illusion of power, torture is a grotesque piece of compensatory drama" (*The Body in Pain*, 27–28). In Buenos Aires, the torture room is called the "Athletic Club," which brings to mind images of pleasure, play, competition, and, possibly, fight. Thanks to Cathie Brettschneider for making me aware of this name.

9. Specular pain, defined by Michel Foucault as the display of a "tortured, dismembered, amputated body, symbolically branded on face or shoulder, exposed alive or dead to public view," is the most devastating weapon the white nation uses to control and contain those it fears (*Discipline*, 8). Through lynching, savage beatings, torture, and rape, advocates of white-nation sociodicy have for three centuries blatantly stood between black people and what Toni Morrison calls "home:" "a-world-in-which-race-does-not-matter" ("Home," 3).

10. Michael F. Basch, a leading expert in the study of empathy, defines it as the ability to know the other's pain without relating to it or attempting to interact with it in a positive way. The distinction he makes concerning empathy is misrecognized often as altruism. He writes, "[M]uch of the time we are empathically attuned to the affective state of others primarily to fulfill our needs and to spare ourselves pain. This is part and parcel of healthy adaptation, but we do not ordinarily call it empathy because it is selfish, though in the non-pejorative sense of that term" ("Empathic Understanding," 119–20).

11. The quote continues, and as it does she begins to relate more to the body of her son through empathy: "I knew the knees . . . and then I began to come on up . . . until I got to the chin and mouth . . . those were Emmett's teeth, and I was looking for his ear. You notice how mine sort of curls up . . . Emmett had the same ears. . . . [T]he one eye that was left, that was definitely his eye, the hazel color confirmed that, and I had to admit that that was indeed Emmett and I said this is my son, this is Bobo" (qtd. in Holloway, *Passed On*, 138).

12. Emotional contagion is sympathy without conscious exertion or reaction—it is involuntary and extreme. Empathy is voluntary but lacks the behavioral components of sympathy. In fact, it is unlike sympathy in its affective associations also. Instead of encouraging feeling "with" someone, it accomplishes an imitation of pain that provides interpersonal understanding.

13. The same herbs slaves used for healing are used today by both black and white American herbalists, but for different purposes. Charles Joyner reports that conjurers treated rheumatism by using oak bark or pokeberry tea (148). *Back to Eden,* considered the herbalist's instruction book, lists white oak bark tea as a treatment for womb troubles, hemorrhoids, varicose veins, and pinworms. The book instructs the herbalist to "[s]immer a tablespoonful in a pint of water for ten minutes. Drink up to three cups a day" (Kloss, 253–54).

14. David Morris explains, "Medieval doctors openly prescribed laughter and comic tales as an effective medicine against plague. . . . Like tragedy, comedy seems to be an enduring response to the dehumanizing powers of pain and suffering" ("About Suffering" 32).

15. Judith Butler's consideration of misrecognition and interpellation of names as social categories is pertinent here. Butler points out that there is always a pause or a sense of pause when certain categorizing names are used. She writes, "[T]here is more often than not some hesitation about whether or how to respond, for what is at stake is whether the temporary totalization performed by the name is politically enabling or paralyzing" (*Psychic Life of Power* 96). Also, see Stephanie A. Smith, "Nigger."

16. In the "Declaration of the Rights of Negro People of the World," black people attending a convention held in New York in 1920 rejected the word formally. Marcus Garvey wrote: "We deprecate the use of the term 'nigger' as applied to Negroes, and demand that the word 'Negro' be written with a capital 'N'" (see UNIA-ACL, "Declaration of Rights of the Negro People of the World." See also Debra Walker King, "The Not-So-Harmless Social Function of a Word That Wounds."

17. Sammy Davis Jr. faced similar complaints and paradoxes. As a child, the performer wore blackface during vaudeville shows. Symbolic violence is also present in many of the television sitcoms so popular today. It is rare when audiences get the opportunity to witness the courage of a black hero like Carl Brashear in *Men of Honor.* The standard is to depict black life in comedy, as magical and strange, or, in dramas, as tragic and hopeless—if at all. *The Green Mile,* for instance, is dramatic in tone, but it is neither a drama nor a serious consideration of the relationship of pain to black people's lives. Because of its magical content and its mysterious (almost nonhuman, but certainly alien) protagonist, it is, at best, a thriller.

18. To my delight, my mostly white female students convinced him of the racial, ethnic, and gendered hurt his suggestion might cause those who are not white and male.

Bibliography

Primary Sources

Baldwin, James. "Going to Meet the Man." *Going to Meet the Man: Stories.* New York: Random House, Vintage Books, 1948. 229–49.

———. "On Being 'White' and Other Lies." *Essence* April 1984: 90–92.

Bambara, Toni Cade. *The Salt Eaters.* New York: Random House, 1980.

Butler, Octavia. *Kindred.* New York: Beacon Press, 1979.

Case, Carroll. *The Slaughter: An American Atrocity.* Ashville, NC?: FBC, 1998.

Douglass, Frederick. *The Narrative of the Life of Frederick Douglass, an American Slave.* 1845. *The Classic Slave Narratives.* Ed. Henry Louis Gates. New York: New American Library, Penguin, 1987. 243–331.

Du Bois, W. E. B. *Dusk of Dawn: An Essay toward an Autobiography of a Race Concept.* New York: Harcourt, Brace and World, 1940.

———. *The Quest of the Silver Fleece.* 1911. Boston: Northeastern University Press, 1989.

———. *The Souls of Black Folk.* 1903. New York: Vintage Books, 1990.

Ellison, Ralph. *Invisible Man.* 1952. New York: Vintage, 1972.

———. *Shadow and Act.* 1953. New York: Vintage, 1972.

Equiano, Olaudah. *The Interesting Narrative of the Life of Olaudah Equiano or Gustavus Vassa, the African.* 1789. Boston: Bedford, St. Martin's, 1995.

Gaines, Ernest J. *A Gathering of Old Men.* New York: Vintage Books, 1983.

———. *A Lesson before Dying.* New York: Knopf, 1993.

Graczy, Michael. "Murder Defendant Talked in Prison of Racial Killing as Gang Initiation." Associated Press, February 19, 1999. http://pqdsb.pqarchiver.com (accessed July 26, 2006).

Griffiths, Paul. "Captives Who Confront Presidents and Gods." Rev. of the opera *Amistad,* dir. George C. Wolfe. *New York Times* December 1, 1997, late ed., E1.

Himes, Chester. *The Quality of Hurt.* New York: Paragon House, 1971.

Holiday, Billie, and William Dufty. *Lady Sings the Blues: The Searing Autobiography of an American Musical Legend.* New York: Penguin Books, 1956.

Hurston, Zora Neale. "How It Feels to Be Colored Me." *I Love Myself When I Am Laughing.* Ed. Alice Walker. New York: Feminist Press, 1979. 152–55.

———. *Their Eyes Were Watching God.* 1937. Urbana: University of Illinois Press, 1978.

Jones, Gayl. *Corregidora.* New York: Random House, 1975.

———. *Eva's Man.* Boston: Beacon Press, 1976.

———. *The Healing.* Boston: Beacon Press, 1998.

King, Joyce. *Hate Crime.* New York: Pantheon Books, 2002.

Mattison, H. *Louisa Picquet, the Octoroon: or Inside Views of Southern Domestic Life.* 1861. *Collected Black Women's Narratives.* New York: Oxford University Press, 1988.

Morrison, Toni. *Beloved.* New York: Knopf, 1987.

———. *The Bluest Eye.* New York: Knopf, 1970.

———. *Sula.* New York: Plume, 1973.

Naylor, Gloria. *Linden Hills.* 1985. New York: Penguin Books, 1987.

———. *Mama Day.* New York: Ticknor and Fields, 1988.

———. *The Women of Brewster Place.* 1982. New York: Penguin Books, 1983.

Walker, Alice. *The Color Purple.* G. K. Hall Large Print Book Series. New York: Harcourt Brace Jovanovich, 1982.

———. *In Search of Our Mothers' Gardens: Womanist Prose.* New York: Harcourt, Brace, Jovanovich, 1983.

———. *The Third Life of Grange Copeland.* New York: Harcourt Brace Jovanovich, 1970.

Williams, Bert. "Bert Williams Joke Books, Book I." Manuscripts, Archives, and Rare Books Division. Schomburg Center for Research in Black Culture. File MG190. New York: The New York Public Library, Astor, Lenox, and Tilden Foundations.

Wright, Richard. *Black Boy.* New York: Harper and Row, 1945.

———. "Fire and Cloud." *Richard Wright: Early Works.* New York: Library of America, Viking Press, 1984. 355–406.

———. *The Long Dream.* 1958. Boston: Northeastern University Press, 2000.

———. *Native Son.* New York: Grosset and Dunlap, 1940.

Secondary Sources

Als, Hilton. "GWTW." *Without Sanctuary: Lynching Photography in America.* Santa Fe, New Mexico: Twin Palms, 2000. 38–44.

Amgelo, Bonnie. "The Pain of Being Black." *Time* May 22, 1989: 120–23.

"A Murder in Jasper." Narrated by Ted Koppel. *Nightline.* ABC. February 23, 1999. Transcript.

Aquinas, St. Thomas. "Whether Pain Is a Passion of the Soul?" *The Summa Theologica of St. Thomas Aquinas. First Part of the Second Part.* Second and Revised Edition. 1920. Translated by the Fathers of the English Dominican Province. *New Advent.* Online edition ed. Kevin Knight. http://www.newadvent.org/summa/203601.htm (accessed July 2, 2003).

Augustine of Hippo. "Of the Justice of the Punishment with Which Our First Parents Were Visited for their Disobedience." *The City of God. Book XIV.* 1997. *New Advent.* http://www.newadvent.org/fathers/120114.htm (accessed June 19, 2004).

Baker, Houston A., Jr. *Blues, Ideology, and Afro-American Literature: A Vernacular Theory.* Chicago: University of Chicago Press. 1984.

Basch, Michael. F. "Empathic Understanding: A Review of the Concept and Some Theoretical Considerations." *Journal of the American Psychoanalytic Association* 31.1 (1983): 101–26.

Berlant, Lauren. "National Brands/National Body: Imitation of Life." *Comparative American*

Identities: Race, Sex, and Nationality in the Modern Text. Ed. Hortense J. Spillers. New York: Routledge, 1991. 110–40.

Beyer, Christian. "Edmund Husserl." *The Stanford Encyclopedia of Philosophy*, Fall 2004 edition. Ed. Edward N. Zalta. http://80-plato.stanford.edu.lp.hscl.ufl.edu/archives/spr2003/entries/husserl/ (accessed October 8, 2004).

Bloom, Harold. "Freud: Frontier Concepts, Jewishness, and Interpretation." *Trauma: Explorations in Memory*. Ed. Cathy Caruth. Baltimore: Johns Hopkins University Press, 1995. 113–27.

Boudreau, Kristin. "Pain and the Unmaking of Self in Toni Morrison's *Beloved*." *Contemporary Literature* 36 (Fall 1995): 447–65.

Bourdieu, Pierre. *The Logic of Practice*. Translated by Richard Nice. Cambridge, UK: Polity Press, 1990.

———. *Outline of a Theory of Practice*. Translated by Richard Nice. Cambridge, UK: Cambridge University Press, 1977.

———. *Pascalian Meditations*. Translated by Richard Nice. Stanford: Stanford University Press, 2000.

Bourdieu, Pierre, and Loïc J. D. Wacquant. *An Invitation to Reflexive Sociology*. Chicago: University of Chicago Press, 1992.

Brashear, Carl. "U.S. Naval Institute's Oral History of Master Chief Boatswain's Mate Carl M. Brashear, USN (Ret.)" Interview by Paul Stillwell. U.S. Naval Station, Norfork, VA, November 17, 1989. http://www.usni.org/oralhistory/B/brashear_excerpt.htm#top (accessed August 1, 2006).

Braxton, Greg. "Is the Pain Too Much to Watch?" *Los Angeles Times* October 18, 1998, calendar section, 8.

Brundage, W. Fitzhugh. *Lynching in the New South: Georgia and Virginia, 1880–1930*. Urbana: University of Illinois Press, 1993.

Brunner, Borgna. "The Tuskegee Syphilis Experiment." Tuskegee University National Center for Bioethics in Research and Healthcare. http://tubioethics.org/connections/Tuskegee/generalbackground.htm (accessed May 2, 2003).

Burke, Edmund. *A Philosophical Inquiry into the Origin of Our Ideas of the Sublime and Beautiful, with Several Other Additions*. New York: P. F. Collier and Son, 1909–14. Vol. 24, part 2 of *The Harvard Classics*. http://www.bartleby.com/24/2/ (accessed May 16, 2004).

Butler, Judith. *The Psychic Life of Power*. Stanford: Stanford University Press, 1997.

Caruth, Cathy. "An Interview with Robert Jay Lifton." Caruth, *Trauma* 128–47.

———, ed. *Trauma: Explorations in Memory*. Baltimore: Johns Hopkins University Press, 1995.

———. "Trauma and Experience: Introduction." Caruth, *Trauma* 3–12.

Cary, Lorene. *Black Ice*. New York: Random House, 1991.

Cixous, Hélène. "The Laugh of the Medusa." *Feminisms: An Anthology of Literary Theory and Criticism*. Ed. Robyn R. Warhol and Diane Price Herndl. New Jersey: Rutgers University Press, 1993. 334–49.

Clark, Elizabeth B. "The Sacred Rights of the Weak: Pain, Sympathy, and the Culture of Individual Rights in Antebellum America." *Journal of American History* 82 (September 1995): 463–93.

Clinton, Bill. "Remarks by the President in Apology for the Study Done in Tuskegee." National Archives. http://clinton4.nara.gov/ textonly/New/Remarks/Fri/19970516-898.html (accessed May 16, 2003).

"Closing Arguments Today in Texas Dragging Death Trial." *CNN*. February 22, 1999. http:// www.cnn.com/US/9902/22/ dragging.death.03/.

Cohen, Hillel W., and Mary E. Northridge. "Getting Political: Racism and Urban Health." *American Journal of Public Health* 90.6 (June 2000): 841–42.

Collins, Patricia Hill. *Black Feminist Thought: Knowledge, Consciousness, and the Politics of Empowerment*. New York: Harper Collins, 1990.

Cosby, Camille. "America Taught My Son's Killer to Hate Blacks." *USA Today* July 8, 1998, NEWS section, 15a.

Cripps, Thomas. "Film." *Split Image: African Americans in the Mass Media*. Ed. Jannett L. Dates and William Barlow. Washington, DC: Howard University Press, 1990. 131–86.

Culler, Jonathan. *On Deconstruction: Theory and Criticism after Structuralism*. New York: Cornell University Press, 1982.

Davis, Cynthia J. "Speaking the Body's Pain: Harriet Wilson's *Our Nig*." *African American Review* 27 (Fall 1993): 391–404.

Delgado, Richard. *The Coming Race War? and Other Apocalyptic Tales of America after Affirmative Action and Welfare*. New York: New York University Press, 1996.

Delgado, Richard, and Jean Stefancic. *Understanding Words That Wound*. Colorado: West-view Press, 2004.

DeLombard, Jeannine. "'Eye Witness to the Cruelty': Southern Violence and Northern Testimony in Frederick Douglass's 1845 Narrative." *American Literature* 73.2 (2001): 245–75.

Derrida, Jacques. *Limited Inc*. Evanston, IL: Northwestern University Press, 1988.

———. *Of Grammatology*. Trans. Gayatri Chakravorty Spivak. Baltimore: Johns Hopkins University Press, 1974.

Dimsdale, J. E. "Stalked by the Past: The Influence of Ethnicity on Health." *Psychosomatic Medicine* 62.2 (March/April 2000): 161–70.

Doyle, Laura. *Bordering on the Body: The Racial Matrix of Modern Fiction and Culture*. New York: Oxford University Press, 1994.

Dray, Phillip. *At the Hands of Persons Unknown: The Lynching of Black America*. New York: Random House, 2002.

Dyer, Richard. *White*. New York: Routledge, 1997.

Dyson, Michael Eric. *Reflecting Black: African-American Cultural Criticism*. Minneapolis: University of Minnesota Press, 1993.

Early, Gerald. *The Culture of Bruising*. Hopewell, New Jersey: Ecco Press, 1994.

"Evelyn Hernandez and Laci Peterson." *Remember Evelyn Hernandez*. http://www.indybay.org/ newsitems/2004/11/13/17050911.php (accessed June 14, 2006).

Farley, Christopher John. "That Old Black Magic." *Time* November 27, 2000, 14.

Foley, Denise. "Being Black Is Dangerous to Your Health." *Racism and Sexism: An Integrated Study*. Ed. P. S. Rothenberg. New York: St. Martin's Press, 1988. 124–30.

Foucault, Michel. *Discipline and Punish: The Birth of the Prison*. Trans. Alan Sheridan. 2nd ed. New York: Random House, 1995.

———. *The History of Sexuality: An Introduction.* Trans. Robert Hurley. Vol. 1. New York: Random House, 1978.

Freeman, H., and R. Payne. "Racial Injustice in Health Care." *New England Journal of Medicine* 342 (2000): 1045–47.

Freud, Sigmund. "Formulations on the Two Principles of Mental Functioning." *The Freud Reader.* Ed. Peter Gay. New York: W. W. Norton, 1989. 301–6.

———. "Three Essays on the Theory of Sexuality." *The Freud Reader.* Ed. Peter Gay. New York: W. W. Norton, 1989. 238–93.

Gabbin, Joanne V. "A Laying On of Hands: Black Women Writers Exploring the Roots of Their Folk and Cultural Tradition." *Wild Women in the Whirlwind: Afra-American Culture and the Contemporary Literary Renaissance.* Ed. Joanne M. Braxton and Andrée Nicola McLaughlin. New Brunswick: Rutgers University Press, 1990. 246–63.

Gates, Henry Louis. "Writing Race and the Difference It Makes." *"Race," Writing, and Difference* Ed. Henry Louis Gates. Chicago: University of Chicago Press, 1986. 1–20.

Geiger, Jeffrey. "Unmaking the Male Body: The Politics of Masculinity in *The Long Dream.*" *African American Review* 33.2 (Summer 1999): 197–207.

Gilroy, Paul. *The Black Atlantic: Modernity and Double Consciousness.* Cambridge: Harvard University Press, 1993.

———. *"There Ain't No Black in the Union Jack": The Cultural Politics of Race and Nation.* Chicago: University of Chicago Press, 1991.

Ginzburg, Ralph. *100 Years of Lynchings.* Baltimore: Black Classic Press, 1962.

Glucklich, Ariel. "Sacred Pain and the Phenomenal Self." *Harvard Theological Review* 91.4 (1998): 389–402.

Gonzalez, David. "Where Police Are Eroding Self-Respect." *New York Times* February 10, 1999, About New York. http://www.nytimes.com (accessed June 24, 2003).

Gonzalez, Susan. "Director Spike Lee Slams 'Same Old' Black Stereotypes in Today's Films." *Yale Bulletin and Calendar* 29.21 (2001). http://www.yale.edu/opa/v29.n21/story3.html (accessed April 19, 2007).

Graham, Maryemma. "Living the Legacy: Pain, Desire, and Narrative Time in Gayl Jones's *Corregidora.*" *Callaloo* 26.2 (2003): 446–72.

Grier, William H., and Price M. Cobbs. *Black Rage.* New York: Bantam, 1968.

Grosz, Elizabeth. *Volatile Bodies: Toward a Corporeal Feminism.* Bloomington: Indiana University Press. 1994.

Gunning, Sandra. *Race, Rape, and Lynching: The Red Record of American Literature 1890–1912.* New York: Oxford University Press, 1996.

Hall, Stuart. "Encoding and Decoding in Television Discourse." *Culture, Media, Language: Working Papers in Cultural Studies 1972-79.* Eds. Stuart Hall et al. London: Hutchinson, 1980. 128–38.

Hall, Stuart, and Paddy Whannel. *The Popular Arts.* New York: Random House, 1964.

Halttunen, Karen. "Humanitarianism and the Pornography of Pain in Anglo-American Culture." *American Historical Review* 100 (April 1995): 303–34.

Harris, Trudier. *Exorcising Blackness: Historical and Literary Lynching and Burning Rituals.* Bloomington: Indiana University Press, 1984.

———. "Pain and the Unmaking of Self in Toni Morrison's *Beloved.*" *Contemporary Literature* 36.3 (1995): 447–65.

———. *Saints, Sinners, Saviors: Strong Black Women in African American Literature.* New York: Saint Martin's Press, 2001.

———. *South of Tradition: Essays on African American Literature.* Athens: University of Georgia Press, 2002.

———. "This Disease Called Strength: Some Observations on the Compensating Construction of Black Female Character." *Literature and Medicine* 14.1 (1995): 109–26.

———. "Violence in *The Third Life of Grange Copeland.*" *CLA* 19 (1975): 238–47.

Hartman, Saidiya V. *Scenes of Subjection: Terror, Slavery, and Self-Making in Nineteenth-Century America.* New York: Oxford University Press, 1997.

"Health Care's Racial Divide: African-Americans Get Less Aggressive Treatment." *ABC News.* February 25, 1999. http://www.abcnews.go.com/Sections/living/DailyNews/racial_healthcare990224.html.

Hedrick, Tace, and Debra Walker King. "Women of Color and Feminist Criticism." *Introducing Criticism at the 21st Century.* Ed. Julian Wolfreys. Edinburgh: Edinburgh University Press, 2001. 57–85.

Henderson, Mae Gwendolyn. "Toni Morrison's *Beloved:* Re-Membering the Body as Historical Text." *Comparative American Identities: Race Sex, and Nationality in the Modern Text.* Ed. Hortense J. Spillers. New York: Routledge, 1991. 62–86.

Hicks, Heather J. "Hoodoo Economics: White Men's Work and Black Men's Magic in Contemporary American Film." *Camera Obscura* 53.18 (2003): 27–55.

History Undercover: The Mystery of the 364th. Prod. Greg Dehart. VHS. History Channel (unaired), 2000.

Ho, Karen, and Wende Elizabeth Marshall. "Criminality and Citizenship: Implicating the White Nation." In *Race Consciousness: African American Studies for the New Century.* Eds. Judith Jackson Fossett and Jeffrey A. Tucker. New York: New York University Press, 1997. 208–27.

Holloway, Karla F. C. *Codes of Conduct: Race, Ethics, and the Color of Our Character.* New Brunswick, NJ: Rutgers University Press, 1995.

———. *Moorings and Metaphors: Figures of Culture and Gender in Black Women's Literature.* New Brunswick, NJ: Rutgers University Press, 1992.

———. *Passed On: African American Mourning Stories.* Durham: Duke University Press, 2002.

Holt, Thomas C. "Marking: Race, Race-making, and the Writing of History." *American Historical Review* 100.1 (February 1995): 1–20.

hooks, bell. *Killing Rage: Ending Racism.* New York: Henry Holt, 1995.

Hudson-Weems, C. *Emmett Till: The Sacrificial Lamb of the Civil Rights Movement.* Troy, MI: Bedford, 1994.

Hull, Gloria T., Patricia Bell Scott, and Barbara Smith, eds. *All the Women Are White, All the Blacks Are Men, but Some of Us Are Brave.* New York: Feminist Press, 1982.

Hunter-Gault, Charlayne. "An Apology 65 Years Late." *Online NewsHour.* Transcript. May 16, 1997. http://www.pbs.org/newshour/bb/health/may97/tuskegee_5-16.html (accessed May 1, 2004).

Jakobson, Roman. "The Metaphoric and Metonymic Poles." *Critical Theory since Plato*. Ed. Hazard Adams. Irvine: University of California Press, 1971. 1113–16.

Jamieson, Kathleen Hall. "The Subversive Effects of a Focus on Strategy in News Coverage of Presidential Campaigns." *1-800-President: The Report of the Twentieth Century Fund Task Force on Television and the Campaign of 1992*. New York: Twentieth Century Fund Press, 1993. 35–61.

Janov, Arthur. *The Primal Scream: Primal Therapy, the Cure for Neurosis*. New York: Putnam, 1970.

Jeffords, Susan. "Masculinity as Excess in Vietnam Films: The Father/Son Dynamic of American Culture." *Feminisms: An Anthology of Literary Theory and Criticism*. Ed. Robyn Warhol and Dianne Price Herndl. New Jersey: Rutgers University Press, 1991. 987–1010.

Jordan, June. *Civil Wars*. Boston: Beacon Press, 1981.

Joyner, Charles. *Down by the Riverside: A South Carolina Slave Community*. Urbana: University of Illinois Press, 1984.

Kennedy, Randall. *Nigger*. New York: Pantheon, 2002.

King, Debra Walker. "The Not-So-Harmless Social Function of a Word that Wounds." *Handbook of the Sociology of Racial and Ethnic Relations*. Eds. Hernan Vera and Joseph Feagin. New York: Springer Science and Business Media, 2007. 104–14.

Kloss, Jethro. *Back to Eden*. 1939. Loma Linda, CA: Back to Eden Books, 1972.

Krystal, Henry. "Trauma and Aging: A Thirty-Year Follow-Up." Caruth, *Trauma* 76–99.

Laub, Dori. "Truth and Testimony." Caruth, *Trauma* 61–75.

Lewis, Monica. "Pregnant Black Woman Missing: Where's the Laci Peterson-Like Coverage?" *BlackAmericaWeb.com*. July 31, 2005. http://www.blackamericaweb.com/site.aspx/bawnews/figueroa801 (accessed June 18, 2006).

Lifton, Robert Jay. *Death in Life: Survivors of Hiroshima*. New York: Random House, 1967.

Litwack, Leon F. "Hellhounds." *Without Sanctuary: Lynching Photography in America*. Ed. James Allen. Santa Fe, NM: Twin Palms, 2000. 8–37.

Lorde, Audre. *Sister Outsider: Essays and Speeches*. Freedom, CA: Crossing Press, 1984.

Mama, Amina. *Beyond the Masks: Race, Gender and Subjectivity*. London: Routledge, 1995.

"Man Guilty in Texas Dragging Death." Associated Press. February 23, 1999. http://www.aol.com/mynews/news/story.adp/cat=0180%id=1999022307224647.

Margolick, David. *Strange Fruit: Billie Holiday, Café Society, and an Early Cry for Civil Rights*. Philadelphia: Running Press, 2000.

———. *Strange Fruit: The Biography of a Song*. New York: Harper Collins, 2001.

Maslin, Janet. "Pain of Captivity Made Starkly Real." Rev. of *Amistad*, dir. Steven Spielberg. *New York Times* December 10, 1997, late ed., sec. E: C2. *New York Times Online*. Nexis. http://NYTimes.com (accessed September 6, 2002).

McKenzie, Edna Chappel. Interview. "Treason?" *The Black Press: Soldiers without Swords*. Produced and directed by Stanley Nelson. PBS. February 8, 1999.

Moody, JoAnne. "Extra Disadvantages for Colonized Minorities." *Faculty Diversity: Problems and Solutions*. New York: RoutledgeFalmer, 2004. 65–86.

Morris, David B. "About Suffering: Voice, Genre, and Moral Community." *Daedalus* 125 (Winter 1996): 25–45.

———. *The Culture of Pain*. Berkeley: University of California Press, 1991.

Morrison, Sean R., et al. "'We Don't Carry That': Failure of Pharmacies in Predominantly Nonwhite Neighborhoods to Stock Opioid Analgesics." *New England Journal of Medicine* 342.14 (April 6, 2000): 1023–26.

Morrison, Toni. "Home." *The House That Race Built*. Ed. Wahneema Lubiano. New York: Vintage, Random House, 1997. 3–12.

———. *Playing in the Dark: Whiteness and the Literary Imagination*. Cambridge: Harvard University Press, 1992.

———, ed. *Race-ing Justice, En-gendering Power*. New York: Pantheon, 1992.

Mulvey, Laura. *Visual and Other Pleasures*. Bloomington: Indiana University Press, 1989.

O'Connell, Geoffrey F. X. "The Mysterious 364th, Parts 1 and 2." *Philadelphia City Paper*, May 17–24, 2001. http://www.cpcn.com/articles/051701/ cs.coverstory1.shtml and http://www.cpcn.com/articles/051701/cs.coverstory2.shtml (accessed October 9, 2002).

"Pain Is Undertreated in African Americans." *AORN Journal Online* October 1, 2002. http://www.findarticles.com/cf_0/m0FSL/4_76/93069842/p1/article.jhtml (accessed May 19, 2003).

Painter, Nell Irvin. "Hill, Thomas, and the Use of Racial Stereotype." Morrison, *Race-ing* 204–14.

———. "Soul Murder and Slavery." *Southern History across the Color Line*, by Painter. Durham: University of North Carolina Press, 2002. 15–39.

Parvin, Paige P. "Strange Fruit." *Emory Magazine* (Summer 2002). http://www.emory.edu/ EMORY_ MAGAZINE/summer 2002 (accessed June 27, 2003).

Patterson, Orlando. *Slavery and Social Death: A Comparative Study*. Cambridge: Harvard University Press, 1982.

Pernick, Martin S. *A Calculus of Suffering: Pain, Professionalism, and Anesthesia in Nineteenth-Century America*. New York: Columbia University Press, 1985.

Plaines, Milford F. *African American Holocaust*. April 30, 1996. http://www.maafa.org/ till.html (accessed June 18, 2005).

"Police: Remains of LaToyia Figueroa Found." Associated Press. http://www.msnbc.msn.com/ id/9016541 (accessed June 18, 2006).

Pryor, Richard, and Todd Gold. *Pryor Convictions and Other Life Sentences*. New York: Pantheon Books, 1995.

Raboteau, Albert J. *Slave Religion: The "Invisible Institution" in the Antebellum South*. New York: Oxford University Press, 1980.

"Recent Shootings at U.S. Schools." *Miami Herald* March 6, 2001, 19A.

Roberts, Dorothy. *Killing the Black Body: Race, Reproduction, and the Meaning of Liberty*. New York: McKay, 1997.

———. "Punishing Drug Addicts Who Have Babies: Women of Color, Equality, and the Right of Privacy." *Critical Race Theory*. Ed. Kimberlé Crenshaw. New York: New York Press, 1996. 384–426.

Rogin, Michael. *Blackface, White Noise: Jewish Immigrants in the Hollywood Melting Pot*. Berkeley: University of California Press, 1996.

Romney, Patricia, Beverly Tatum, and JoAnne Jones. "Feminist Strategies for Teaching about Oppression: The Importance of Process." *Women's Studies Quarterly* 20.1–2 (1992). http:// www.romneyassociates.com/pdf/Feminist_ Approaches.pdf (accessed July 2, 2005).

Russell, Kathy, Midge Wilson, and Ronald Hall, eds. *The Color Complex: The Politics of Skin Color among African Americans.* New York: Anchor Books, 1993.

Sánchez-Eppler, Karen. *Touching Liberty: Abolition, Feminism, and the Politics of the Body.* Los Angeles: University of California Press, 1993.

Scarry, Elaine. *The Body in Pain: Making and Unmaking the World.* New York: Oxford University Press, 1985.

Schulman, Kevin A., et al. "The Effect of Race and Sex on Physicians' Recommendations for Cardiac Catheterization." *New England Journal of Medicine* 340.8 (February 25, 1999): 618–26.

Seymour, Gene. "Racial Myth and Pop Culture." *The Nation* 263 (August 1996): 34–36.

"Showtime Offers Portrait of a Texas Town Divided." *Jefferson City News Tribune, Online Edition* June 6, 2003. http://www.newstribune.com/stories/060603/ent_0606030941.asp (accessed July 30, 2003).

Smith, Stephanie A. "Bombshell." *Body Politics and the Fictional Double.* Ed. Debra Walker King. Bloomington: Indiana University Press, 2000. 152–77.

———. "Nigger." *Household Words.* Minneapolis: University of Minnesota Press, 2006. 123–48.

Smith, Theophus H. *Conjuring Culture: Biblical Formations of Black America.* Oxford University Press, 1994.

Society of Professional Journalists. "Code of Ethics." http://www.spj.org/ethicscode.asp? (accessed July 22, 2006).

Sontag, Susan. Illness as Metaphor *and* AIDS and Its Metaphors. New York: Picador USA—Farrar, Straus and Giroux, 2001.

"Speaking for Laci." Narrated by Katie Couric. *Dateline.* NBC. June 9, 2003. Transcript. MSNBC News. http://www.msnbc.com/news/924408.asp?cp1=1 (accessed June 10, 2003).

Spillers, Hortense J. "Mama's Baby, Papa's Maybe: An American Grammar Book." *Black, White and in Color: Essays on American Literature and Culture,* by Spillers. Chicago: University of Chicago Press, 2003. 203–29.

Steele, Shelby. *The Content of Our Character: A New Vision of Race in America.* New York: Harper Perennial, 1990.

Stern, Max M. "Anxiety, Trauma, and Shock." *Psychoanalytic Quarterly* (1951) 20: 179–203.

Sternbach, Richard A. "Congenital Insensitivity to Pain: A Critique." *Psychological Bulletin* 60 (1963): 252–64.

Tate, Claudia. *Desire and the Protocols of Race: Black Novels and Psychoanalysis.* New York: Oxford University Press, 1997.

"Texas Man Was Alive during Dragging—Witness." ABC News. February 22, 1999. http://abcnews.go.com/wire/World/Reuters.html (accessed February 25, 1999).

Thomas, Jerry. "Emmett's Legacy." *Chicago Tribune* September 5, 1995, 5.

Thomas, Kendal. "Strange Fruit." Morrison, *Race-ing* 364–87.

Thomas-Lester, Avis. "A Senate Apology for History on Lynching: Vote Condemns Past Failure to Act." *Washingtonpost.com* June 14, 2005, A12. http://www.washingtonpost.com/wp-dyn/content/article /2005/06/13/AR2005061301720_pf.html (accessed June 19, 2005).

Tuhkanen, Mikko Juhani. "A (B)igger's Place: Lynching and Specularity in Richard Wright's 'Fire and Cloud' and *Native Son.*" *African American Review* 33.1 (Spring 1999): 125–33.

Turton, Sam. "What Is Primal Integration?" May 2001. *Primalworks.com*. http://www
.primalworks.com/whatisprimal.html (accessed June 18, 2005).

UNIA-ACL. "Declaration of Rights of the Negro People of the World." 1920. http://www
.unia-acl.org/archive/declare.htm (accessed July 7, 2005).

Wailoo, Keith. *Dying in the City of the Blues: Sickle Cell Anemia and the Politics of Race and
Health*. North Carolina: University of North Carolina Press, 2001.

Wallace, Michele. *Black Macho and the Myth of the Superwoman*. 1978. New York: Verso,
1990.

Washington, Harriet A. *Medical Apartheid: The Dark History of Medical Experimentation
on Black Americans from Colonial Times to the Present*. New York: Doubleday, 2006.

West, Cornel. *Race Matters*. New York: Random House, 1993.

West, Malcolm R. "Mamie Till-Mobley, Civil Rights Heroine, Eulogized in Chicago." *Jet Magazine* January 27, 2003: 12–18, 52.

White, Walter Francis. *Rope and Faggot: A Biography of Judge Lynch*. New York: Knopf,
1929.

Wiegman, Robyn. *American Anatomies: Theorizing Race and Gender*. Durham: Duke University Press, 1995.

———. "Black Bodies/American Commodities: Gender, Race and the Bourgeois Ideal in Contemporary Film." In *Unspeakable Images: Ethnicity and the American Cinema*, edited by
Lester Friedman. Urbana: University of Illinois Press, 1991. 308–28.

Williams, David R., and Toni D. Rucker. "Understanding and Addressing Racial Disparities
in Health Care." *Health Care Financing Review* 21.4 (Summer 2000): 75–90.

Williams, Linda. "Melodrama in Black and White: Uncle Tom and *The Green Mile*." *Film
Quarterly* 55.2 (Winter 2001–2): 14–21.

———. *Playing the Race Card: Melodramas of Black and White from Uncle Tom to O. J.
Simpson*. New Jersey: Princeton University Press, 2001.

Williams, Patricia J. "Without Sanctuary." Diary of a Mad Law Professor. *The Nation* 270
(February 14, 2000): 9.

Wispe, Lauren. "The Distinction between Sympathy and Empathy: To Call Forth a Concept a
Word Is Needed." *Journal of Personality and Social Psychology* 50.2 (February 1986):
314–21.

———. *The Psychology of Sympathy*. New York: Plenum Press, 1991.

Woll, Allen. *Black Musical Theatre: From* Coontown *to* Dreamgirls. Baton Rouge, LA:
Louisiana State University Press, 1989.

Woods, Marcus. *Blind Memory: Visual Representations of Slavery in England and America,
1780–1865*. New York: Routledge, 2000.

Wypijewski, JoAnn. "Executioners' Songs." *The Nation* 270 (March 27, 2000): 28–34.

Film- and Discography

Amistad. Dir. Steven Spielberg. Perf. Morgan Freeman, Anthony Hopkins, Djimon Hounsou, and Matthew McConaughey. 1997. DVD. Dreamwork Video, 1999.

Bamboozled. Dir. Spike Lee. Perf. Damon Wayans, Savion Glover, Tommy Davidson, Michael Rapaport, and Jada Pinkett Smith. 2000. DVD. New Line Cinema, 2000.

The Color Purple. Dir. Steven Spielberg. Perf. Danny Glover, Whoopi Goldberg, Margaret Avery, and Oprah Winfrey. 1985. DVD. Warner Home Video, 1997.

Devil's Advocate. Dir. Taylor Hackford. Perf. Keanu Reeves, Al Pacino, and Charlize Theron. 1997. DVD. Warner Home Video, 1998.

Glory. Dir. Edward Zwick. Perf. Matthew Broderick, Denzel Washington, and Morgan Freeman. Based on a book by Lincoln Kristein and letters by Robert Gould Shaw. 1989. DVD. Sony Pictures, 1998.

The Green Mile. Dir. Frank Darabont. Perf. Tom Hanks, Michael Clarke Duncan, David Morse, and James Cromwell. Based on the story by Steven King. 1999. DVD. Warner Home Video, 2000.

Jasper, Texas. Dir. Jeff Byrd. Perf. Louis Gossett, Jon Voight, and Roy T. Anderson. Showtime, 2003. DVD. Showtime Entertainment, 2004.

Living Out Loud. Dir. Richard LaGravenese. Perf. Holly Hunter, Danny DeVito, Queen Latifah, and Martin Donovan. 1998. DVD. New Line, 1999.

Men of Honor. Dir. George Tillman Jr. Perf. Robert DeNiro, Cuba Gooding Jr., Charlize Theron, Michael Rapaport, David Keith, and Joshua Leonard. 2000. DVD. CBS/Fox Home Video, 2001.

Miss Evers' Boys. Dir. Joseph Sargent. Perf. Alfre Woodard, Laurence Fishburne, Craig Sheffer, and Joe Sheffer. HBO Pictures. 1997. DVD. HBO Home Video, 2002.

Mississippi Burning. Dir. Alan Parker. Perf. Gene Hackman, William Dafoe, Frances McDormand, and Brad Dourif. 1988. DVD. MGM, 2001.

The Perfect Husband: The Laci Peterson Story. Dir. Roger Young. Perf. G. W. Bailey, Sarah Brown, Dean Cain, and Dan Cashman. USA Network, 2004. DVD. Sony Pictures, 2004.

Rosewood. Dir. John Singleton. Perf. Jon Voight, Ving Rhames, Esther Rolle, and Elise Neal. Warner Brothers, 1997. DVD. Warner Home Video, 1997.

"Strange Fruit." Rec. Billie Holiday, June 7, 1956. *Lady Sings the Blues.* Verve, 1995.

Index

abreaction, 126

Abu-Jamal, Mumia, 164n21

acting colored, 160

Allen, James, 95, 170n8

Allen, Lewis, 60

Als, Hilton, 49

Alton Telegraph, 92–93

American Dream, the, 11, 63–64

"Americanness," 3–4, 14–15, 17, 32–33; in *Invisible Man*, 63–64; pain-free nature of, 49, 159; in *The Slaughter*, 80–81

Amistad (film), 29, 131–34, 136–37

Amistad (opera), 166n6

Augustine, Saint, 39

Baker, Houston A., Jr., 44

Baldwin, James, 14, 19; "Going to Meet the Man," 18, 65–69, 97–99, 109

Bambara, Toni Cade, *The Salt Eaters*, 142

Bamboozled (film), 35

Basch, Michael F., 175n10

Beloved (Morrison), 113, 115–19

Berlant, Lauren, 88

Berry, Shawn, 166n5

"Between the World and Me" (Wright), 103

Bible, the, 138

black actors, roles for, 34

Black Being, 17, 164n18

black bodies, 5; as abstract symbols, 2–3, 15–16, 32–34, 81, 133–34, 155, 159–60; as memorial time, 6–7, 9–10, 33, 82, 159, 169n1. *See also* racial marking

Black Boy (Wright), 107, 147

black men: as magical heroes, 50–51; as moral Uncle Tom figures, 10, 50; silence and, 19, 96–98, 104, 109, 174n3 (chap. 5)

blackness, 29–30, 115, 173n1

black pain, 8–9, 11–15, 156

blackpain: concept of, 16–17; diminution of, 18–19, 156; legacy of, 15–18, 47–53, 144–45; as memorial time, 47, 154–55, 169n1; oppositional readings and, 21, 109, 155–56, 159–60; recognition of, 132; survival/expulsion of, 20–21, 156, 158–60

Black Panthers, 31

Black Press, The (documentary), 76

black rage, 94–95, 104–9, 124, 150, 158

Black Sheep (Himes), 48–49

black women: gender socialization and, 72; gynecological practices on, 8, 163n12; silence and, 19; survival and, 20, 113–24

black writing, 48–49, 154–55, 158

blood metaphors, 113–21, 124

Bloom, Harold, 19

blues music, 44–46

Bluest Eye, The (Morrison), 113, 121–22, 142–43, 174n3 (chap. 5)

bodily abstraction. *See* black bodies: as abstract symbols

bodily hexis, 92, 94, 96–97

Cultural Frames, Framing Culture

Books in this series examine both the way our culture frames our narratives and the way our narratives produce the culture that frames them. Attempting to bridge the gap between previously disparate disciplines, and combining theoretical issues with practical applications, this series invites a broad audience to read contemporary culture in a fresh and provocative way.

Nancy Martha West
Kodak and the Lens of Nostalgia

Raphael Sassower and Louis Cicotello
The Golden Avant-Garde: Idolatry, Commercialism, and Art

Margot Norris
Writing War in the Twentieth Century

Robin Blaetz
Visions of the Maid: Joan of Arc in American Film and Culture

Ellen Tremper
I'm No Angel: The Blonde in Fiction and Film

Naomi Mandel
Against the Unspeakable: Complicity, the Holocaust, and Slavery in America

Debra Walker King
African Americans and the Culture of Pain